Political Tolerance in America

Political Tolerance in America

Freedom and Equality in Public Attitudes

Michael Corbett
Ball State University

Longman
New York & London

POLITICAL TOLERANCE IN AMERICA
Freedom and Equality in Public Attitudes

Longman Inc., 19 West 44th Street, New York, N.Y. 10036
Associated companies, branches, and representatives
throughout the world.

Developmental Editor: Irving R. Rockwood
Editorial and Design Supervisor: Frances Althaus
Manufacturing and Production Supervisor: Anne Musso

Library of Congress Cataloging in Publication Data

Corbett, Michael, 1943–
  Political tolerance in America.

  Includes bibliographical references and index.
  1. Dissenters—United States—Public opinion. 2. Liberty of
speech—United States—Public opinion. 3. Equality—United
States—Public opinion. 4. Public opinion—United States.
I. Title. JC599.U5C65   323.4'0973   81-11799
ISBN 0-582-28262-4 (pbk.)   AACR2

Manufactured in the United States of America
9 8 7 6 5 4 3 2 1

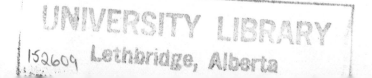

To Sherry Young Corbett

Contents

List of Tables

Preface

I spent the first fifteen years of my life in a poor, rural southern farm community, the ideal training ground for learning bigotry and intolerance. The area in which I grew up was embued with just about any form of intolerance that can be imagined. At the same time that I was being thoroughly trained to be a bigot, I was also being indoctrinated into the slogans of American democracy. I was taught that the United States was the best, most powerful, and richest nation on earth because it stood for such virtues as democracy, freedom, equality, and justice.

In an area in which racial, religious, and sexual discrimination were thoroughly ingrained in the cultural norms, is it possible that we students who attended the local elementary school could also accept such ideas as minority rights, the right to dissent, and equality? Of course we did. We accepted, but did not recognize, the contradiction between principle and practice without so much as the blink of an eyelid. In high school, I did begin to feel some discomfort about certain aspects of the fit between practice and principle, but it has taken much longer to come to a full recognition of that conflict. In the meantime, of course, the gap between practice and principle has narrowed somewhat.

The problem that has disturbed me, and constitutes the reason for writing this book, is that I see among my students and colleagues so little discomfort in their acceptance of both the sloganistic principles of democracy on the one hand and the intolerance in practice on the other hand. It is hoped that this book will help to bring attitudes about tolerance in practice more in line with attitudes about general, abstract principles of tolerance.

This book is written primarily for undergraduates in courses dealing with public opinion, political behavior, women in politics, or minority groups. Because of this audience, esoteric statistical techniques and terminology have been avoided; all material is presented in straightforward language and tables that require no technical knowledge. At the same time, this material has not been incorporated into one source before; therefore, this book should be useful to graduate students and professional colleagues as well as to undergraduates.

This book considers the degree of tolerance among Americans for various types of situations. Tolerance is defined in terms of both support for freedom of dissent and support for equality. Using public opinion survey data, the attitudes of Americans are examined with regard to both general principles and specific applications of tolerance. With regard to freedom of dissent, the focus is on support for First Amendment rights concerning freedom of expression for those whose views are unpopular. With regard to equality, the focus is primarily, but not exclusively, on support for equality for women and blacks. Where available, information concerning such groups as atheists and homosexuals is also discussed. The central questions are: (1) To what extent are the American people politically tolerant or intolerant? (2) What kinds of people are more politically tolerant than others and what helps or hinders the development of tolerance in people? (3) Given answers to the first two questions, what are the future prospects for political tolerance in American society?

Chapter 1 examines the roots and meaning of tolerance in America. The liberal tradition and the exclusions from this tradition are briefly discussed. Arguments in favor of tolerance and arguments against tolerance are considered. In order to set the basis for the focus on tolerance among the people—rather than focusing on the institutional policies and practices—the argument is made that political institutions cannot be counted upon to protect principles of tolerance. Therefore, an examination of levels of tolerance among the general public must be made; the people, in their day-to-day attitudes and behaviors, ultimately determine how tolerant the society will be.

Chapter 2 discusses tolerance in terms of the level of support among Americans for First Amendment rights. Tolerance is shown to be very high for abstract, general statements of principles of tolerance. Tolerance varies greatly, however, when the context is more specific either in terms of the particular political act (e.g., speech making) or the particular political actor (e.g., atheists).

Chapter 3 discusses a number of general observations concerning tolerance among Americans in terms of support for equality. These general observations are intended to cover a wide range of minority and disadvantaged groups, including blacks and women.

Chapter 4 discusses support for equality for black Americans. Trends indicate increasing support for equality for blacks, but there are some substantial problems reflected in public opinion which stand in the way of complete equality for blacks.

Chapter 5 discusses support for equality for women. As with blacks, progress has been made in the level of support for equality for women, but there are some great problems which will make progress toward complete equality slow and difficult for women. Similarities and differences between the movement for equality for blacks and the movement for equality for women are discussed.

Chapter 6 discusses tolerance in context. The gaps between attitudes and behavior and between attitudes and other attitudes are discussed. Tolerance of a group is shown to be dependent to a great extent on attitudes held toward the group rather than on general principles of tolerance. Tolerance in one situation is related somewhat to tolerance in another situation, but the contextual nature of tolerance is more impressive.

Chapter 7 examines the distribution of tolerance in American society. Tolerance is not evenly distributed among all types of people. What kinds of people tend to be more tolerant or less tolerant? An examination is made of the relationships of tolerance to such characteristics of people as education, age, sex, income, race, political party preference, and so on.

Chapter 8 concerns the learning of tolerance. First, a more extensive examination is made of the connection between tolerance and education; this includes a discussion of the nature of the schooling process itself and how it affects tolerance. Second, other learning focal points are examined in terms of their implications for tolerance. This includes discussions of personality, social learning theory, cognitive development, and direct experiences related to tolerance.

Chapter 9 attempts to assess prospects for tolerance in the American future. There are both good and bad signs. Some suggestions are made concerning what might be done, if a willingness to do anything exists, to increase the levels of tolerance in the United States.

This book draws upon public opinion surveys from a variety of published sources, data from the codebooks of the Center for Political Studies at the University of Michigan, and data supplied by the

National Opinion Research Center at the University of Chicago. Extensive use is made of NORC's 1977 General Social Survey, which is further described in the appendix.

A great deal of gratitude needs to be expressed to several persons whose efforts contributed in different ways to the completion of this book. First, I am very grateful to Irving Rockwood, executive editor of the College Division of Longman, whose graciousness and guidance helped to make writing and revising the manuscript much less of an ordeal than it might otherwise have been. Second, the book was greatly improved by comments and suggestions from Prof. Richard D. Shingles (Virginia Polytechnic Institute and State University) and Prof. Paul Abramson (Michigan State University), and I greatly appreciate the help of these two people. I would also like to express my appreciation to two anonymous readers for their comments and suggestions on parts of the manuscript. Finally, and most important, I must acknowledge that I would never have written such a book without the influence on my life of Sherry Young Corbett. It was her influence which led me to recognize and question my own acceptance of the contradiction between tolerance in principle and intolerance in practice.

Michael Corbett

Acknowledgments

For the material in Table 2.1: From Herbert McClosky, "Consensus and Ideology in American Politics." *American Political Science Review*, 58 (June, 1964): 361–382. Copyright © by the American Political Science Association. Reprinted by permission of the publisher.

For part of the material as indicated in Tables 2.2 and 4.5 and all of the material in Tables 4.7, 5.3, and 5.6: From Robert Chandler, *Public Opinion: Changing Attitudes on Contemporary Political and Social Issues*. New York: R. R. Bowker. Copyright © 1972 by Columbia Broadcasting Systems, Inc. All rights reserved. Reprinted by permission of Columbia Broadcasting Systems, Inc.

For part of the material in Table 2.2 as indicated and all the material in Tables 2.4 and 6.1: From David G. Lawrence, "Procedural Norms and Tolerance: A Reassessment." *American Political Science Review*, 70 (March, 1976): 80–100. Copyright © by the American Political Science Association. Reprinted by permission of the publisher.

For part of the material as indicated in Tables 2.2, 4.3, and 4.4: From George H. Gallup, *The Gallup Poll, Volume Three*. New York: Random House. Copyright © 1972 by the American Institute of Public Opinion. Reprinted by permission of the American Institute of Public Opinion.

For part of the material in Table 2.3 as indicated and some of the questions in the Appendix as indicated: From Samuel Stouffer, *Communism, Conformity, and Civil Liberties*. New York: Doubleday. Copyright © 1955 by Samuel Stouffer.

For part of the material and data in Tables 2.3, 4.2 and 4.5 as indicated, for the questions as indicated in the Appendix, and for the material and data utilized in Tables 5.4 and 6.3 through 7.12: National Opinion Research Center (NORC) General Social Surveys, 1972–1980. Chicago, Illinois. Principal investigator: James A. Davis.

For the material used in Table 2.5: From John L. Sullivan, James Piereson, and George Marcus, "An Alternative Conceptualization of Political Tolerance: Illusory Increases 1950s–1970s." *American Political Science Review*, 73 (September, 1979): 781–794. Copyright © by the American Political Science Association. Reprinted by permission of the publisher.

For part of the material as indicated in Table 3.1: From Myra Marx Ferree, "A Woman for President? Changing Responses: 1958–1972." *Public Opinion Quarterly*, 38 (Fall, 1974): 390–399. Copyright © by Columbia University. Reprinted by permission of Columbia University.

For part of the material as indicated in Tables 3.1, 3.5, 4.4, 4.5, and 5.1 and for all the material in Tables 3.3 and 5.5: *Gallup Opinion Index* (April, 1969; November, 1978; October, 1977; August, 1967; July, 1968; March, 1976; June, 1977; and June, 1980). Copyright © by The Gallup Poll Inc. Reprinted by permission of The Gallup Poll Inc.

For the material used in Table 3.2: From a Harris survey reported in Connie de Boer, "The Polls: Attitudes Toward Homosexuality." *Public Opinion Quarterly*, 42 (Summer, 1978): 265–276. Copyright © by Columbia University. Reprinted by permission of Columbia University and by permission of Louis Harris and Associates, Inc.

For part of the material used in Table 4.3 as indicated and all of the material used in Tables 3.4, 4.1, 4.6, and 5.2: 1964–1976 American National Election Studies conducted by the Survey Research Center/Center for Political Studies of the Institute for Social Research, The University of Michigan. The material was made available through the Inter-University Consortium for Political and Social Research.

For part of the material used in Table 3.5 as indicated: From Eugene E. Levitt and Albert D. Klassen, Jr., "Public Attitudes Toward Homosexuality: Part of the 1970 National Survey by the Institute for Sex Research." *Journal of Homosexuality*, 1 (Fall, 1974): 29–43. Copyright © 1974 by The Haworth Press, Inc. All rights reserved. Reprinted by permission of The Haworth Press, Inc.

For part of the material as indicated in Table 4.2: Adapted with permission from Andrew M. Greeley and Paul B. Sheatsley, "Attitudes Toward Racial Integration," in Lee Rainwater (ed.), *Social Problems and Public Policy: Inequality and Justice*. (New York: Aldine Publishing Company.) Copyright © 1974 by Aldine Publishing Company.

For the material used in Table 5.1: From the Institute for Social Research 1973 Fall Omnibus Survey, The University of Michigan. The data were collected by Elizabeth Douvan, Graham Staines, and Toby Jayaratne and the material was made available through the Social Science Archive of the Institute for Social Research.

1

Tolerance in America: Roots and Stems

I know of no country in which,
speaking generally, there is less
independence of mind and true
freedom of discussion than in America.

ALEXIS DE TOCQUEVILLE

INTRODUCTION

Alexis de Tocqueville, a French observer of politics and society, visited the United States in 1835 and voiced concerns which continue to be relevant today. Tocqueville's "highest passion" was liberty, and he held some views which at first might seem strange. He felt that (1) liberty is better protected by a monarchy or aristocracy than by a democracy; (2) equality is a threat to liberty; and (3) repression by the people in a democracy is a more difficult problem than repression by the government. In a monarchy or an aristocracy, the power of the rulers is purely physical; while many of the actions of the individual might be controlled by the rulers, the individual is left free to *think* as he or she pleases. In a democracy, however, the power of the majority is both physical and moral; people are not only compelled to obey the majority but are also pushed by social pressures toward conformity in thinking. The emphasis on equality leads to conformity with public opinion and suppresses differences in views. Tyranny by the government can be prevented in a democracy by certain institutional devices (e.g., separation of powers, checks and balances, a Bill of Rights, and other safeguards), but the tyranny of public opinion, the press of majority social norms on the individual, is a much more difficult problem to handle.

As much as we would like to believe that "democratic virtue" resides in the ordinary American citizen, this is unfortunately not always the case. There is a mostly admirable tendency among Americans to root for the underdog on many occasions; on the dark-

1

er side is another tendency to kick the underdog. Throughout American history there are many cases in which individuals who committed the "crime" of holding or expressing an unpopular minority opinion have been shot, lynched, mutilated, bombed, beaten, tarred-and-feathered, fired, vandalized, or otherwise persecuted by intolerant members of a majority. Alternately, people have simply watched approvingly while the powers of the government were used in repressive acts against unpopular minorities. In 1968 at the national convention of the Democratic Party, the police engaged in what the Walker Commission later termed a "police riot" against Vietnam war protestors in the streets of Chicago. There is no doubt that some of the protestors were committing acts of violence; however, the police response was obviously excessive and indiscriminate in its violence. Television coverage clearly demonstrated many instances in which the police held and beat protestors with clubs. Further, the police violence was not limited to the protestors; more than sixty reporters and many bystanders were also beaten or otherwise mistreated. Protestors began to chant: "The whole world's watching." Millions of people were watching, but evidently the majority saw what it wanted to see. Instead of condemning the extreme police action, the public gave its approval. A survey by the Survey Research Center at the University of Michigan (1968 National Election Study) indicated that, of those who expressed an opinion, only 25% of Americans felt that the police had used too much force; 43% felt that the police had used about the right amount of force; and a third (33%) of Americans responded that the police had not used enough force. Thus, we cannot rest assured that a majority of Americans will always support the rights of a minority—especially if the minority is unpopular.

The purpose of this book is to examine political tolerance in American society. As will be discussed further, political tolerance is conceived here in terms of both support for political freedom and support for equality. The focus of this book is not so much concerned with threats to liberty or equality from the government as from the people. The possibility of repression by the government always exists, but this book concerns the human milieu within which the government exists. The basic questions for examination are: (1) To what extent are the American people politically tolerant or intolerant? (2) What kinds of people are more politically tolerant than others, and what helps or hinders the development of tolerance in people? (3) Given answers to the first two questions, what are the future prospects for political tolerance in American society?

Before getting into these questions, however, we need to examine the conceptual nature of political tolerance and its theoretical basis in the United States.

THE MEANING OF POLITICAL TOLERANCE

Political tolerance is ordinarily defined in terms of support for freedom of expression (e.g., freedom of speech). However, for the purposes of this book, we will also use the term *political tolerance* in a less usual sense to refer to support for political and legal equality (e.g., racial equality). Both concepts of political tolerance will be further defined and described later, but first we need to compare the two.

Support for freedom of expression and support for equality are obviously different conceptually. Freedom of expression entails limitations on the power of the government over individuals and thus falls within the general heading of civil liberties. On the other hand, equality falls within the realm of civil rights. While civil liberties require *inaction* on the part of the government (e.g., the government must not prevent people from criticizing governmental policies), civil rights usually require *action* by the government to prevent discrimination against individuals by other individuals or groups in society or by other parts of the government. For example, with the passage of the 1964 Civil Rights Act, blacks were able to invoke the use of the power of the federal government in order to end certain segregationist practices, some of which were based on custom and some of which were incorporated directly or indirectly into state or local laws. Thus, the two concepts of political tolerance—support for freedom of expression and support for equality—are distinct in meaning.

Not only are the two usages of the term *political tolerance* conceptually different, but they might also imply different attitudinal patterns within individuals. Those who are tolerant in the sense of supporting freedom of expression are not necessarily tolerant in the sense of supporting equality and vice versa. For example, suppose a group planned to hold a demonstration in favor of racial equality. A person who believes in racial equality might nevertheless oppose such a demonstration. Conversely, a person who opposes racial equality might nevertheless support the right of a group to express views favoring racial equality. Thus, there is no *necessary* attitudinal connection between these two different concepts of political tolerance.

Despite the lack of a necessary attitudinal connection between these two concepts of political tolerance and despite their differences in meaning, both concepts will be employed in this book. In the first place, both concepts of tolerance imply a willingness to accept differences among people and to treat individuals as equal units within society. Second, the two concepts do become strongly intertwined in the attitudes of people in certain situations. For example, as will be demonstrated later, people's level of support for freedom of expression is often dependent on who is expressing the ideas or the nature of the ideas themselves; thus Americans do not give equal support to freedom of expression for all groups and ideas. Third, as will be demonstrated, there is a tendency for those who are intolerant in one sense of the term to also be intolerant in the other sense. Finally, the two concepts have been historically intertwined inasmuch as denial of freedom of expression for a group (e.g., blacks) has gone hand in hand with a denial of equality for the group. For these reasons, then, political tolerance will be treated as both support for freedom of expression and as support for equality.

Support for Freedom of Expression

Sullivan et al. (1979: 784) define political tolerance as "a willingness to permit the expression of those ideas or interests that one opposes." Along these same lines, Nunn et al. (1978: 12) indicate that tolerance is "a straightforward attitude that allows people to have freedom of expression even though one may feel that their ideas are incorrect or even immoral." Both of these definitions focus on support for freedom of expression for people even when the ideas are considered wrong or when the people are disliked. Sullivan et al. (1979: 784) argue that tolerance only has meaning in a situation of opposition or disagreement.

Political intolerance, then, refers to opposition to freedom of expression. Intolerance in particular situations might be based on one or more of three attitudes: (1) opposition to certain forms of expression, such as demonstrations; (2) disagreement with the idea being expressed; or (3) dislike of the persons who wish to express their ideas. As we shall see, some Americans simply do not believe in freedom of expression in any meaningful sense. For others, tolerance depends heavily on the particular ideas being expressed or on their attitude toward the person or group expressing the ideas.

For the purposes of this book, support for freedom of expression will be examined in terms of support for the civil liberties contained within the First Amendment to the U.S. Constitution. The rights included within the First Amendment concern freedom of religion, freedom of speech, freedom of the press, the right to peaceable assembly, and the right to petition the government.

Support for Equality

Tolerance in terms of support for equality refers to a willingness to reject unjustifiable discrimination against people. In chapter 3 we will further discuss the difference between justifiable discrimination and unjustifiable discrimination. For present purposes, let us simply say that unjustifiable discrimination is discrimination against a person on the basis of characteristics of the person which are not fundamentally relevant to the situation. For example, it is not justifiable to refuse to hire someone simply because of the person's race or political beliefs. It is justifiable to discriminate in hiring practices against those who are incapable of performing the tasks required of the job.

A tolerant person is willing to support equality for people in a very wide range of political, social, and economic situations regardless of their beliefs, biological/physical characteristics (such as sex or race), or other characteristics (such as ethnic background). Tolerance in this sense requires equality in such legal-political matters as treatment by the law enforcement system, voting, and running for public office. It also requires nondiscrimination in such matters as jobs, housing, and education.

Intolerance, in this sense, supports discrimination against people on the basis of their biological/physical, social, or attitudinal characteristics. An intolerant person might feel that blacks should not be allowed to live in certain neighborhoods, that Jews should not be allowed to run for public office, that women should not be allowed to hold certain jobs, that people who hold unorthodox political or religious beliefs should not be allowed to teach in college, and so on.

Bases of Intolerance

An intolerant person might wish to deny freedom of expression or equality to certain people on the basis of one or more of three general categories of characteristics of people. First, intolerance might be based on biological/physical characteristics. For the purposes of this book, we are concerned with two such characteristics:

race and sex. These are involuntary, "ascribed" characteristics—characteristics with which people are born and over which they have no control ordinarily. These biological characteristics of people take on relevance for the question of tolerance because they are given social significance; the norms of society have prescribed different social roles on the basis of race and sex. Although this book's concern with intolerance based on biological characteristics is limited to race and sex, it needs to be noted that there are other biological or physical characteristics (e.g., age, obesity, height, physical deformities or handicaps) which can lead to a person becoming a target of intolerance.

Second, intolerance can be based on social characteristics. This category is used very broadly here to include a variety of background characteristics of people such as ethnic background, education, income, occupation, region of residence, and so on. Some of these characteristics are ascribed (e.g., ethnic background) and some are not ascribed (e.g., occupation). It is obvious, however, that the nonascribed, voluntary social characteristics of people are not totally under the control of individuals. Children have little control over the type of social environment in which they are born and raised, and the ascribed circumstances of their beginning can greatly influence their later "voluntary" social characteristics.

Third, intolerance can be based on the beliefs and attitudes which people hold. Political, social, economic, religious, and other types of beliefs constitute voluntary characteristics of people which might make them targets of intolerance—or lead them to take an intolerant position toward others. People whose beliefs are not in accord with prevailing cultural norms (e.g., atheists, socialists, homosexuals, members of a Nazi or Communist party) can meet with a great deal of intolerance.

It needs to be noted that these three categories of characteristics of people on which intolerance might be based are by no means completely independent of one another. For example, the political or religious beliefs one holds are very probably due at least in part to one's social background. Further, some characteristics overlap the categories. For example, some people regard Jews as a race in the biological sense; some view Jews as an ethnic group, thus emphasizing social background; and some view Jews primarily in terms of religious beliefs. In short, the formulation of the three categories of people is not airtight; some characteristics overlap categories and characteristics in one category might have a very strong influence on characteristics in another category.

What Tolerance Is Not

Following Nunn *et al.* (1978: 9–12), we need to make two points concerning what tolerance is *not*. First, tolerance is not the same as acceptance. Tolerance requires, with regard to freedom of expression, that we respect the right of people to express their views; it does not require that we uncritically accept those views. It would, in fact, be a very foolish form of tolerance which accepted all viewpoints as being equally valid.

Second, tolerance of a group is also not the same as a lack of prejudice toward that group. As Nunn *et al.* (1978: 9) point out, a person might be prejudiced toward a certain group, yet respect the civil liberties of that group. For example, a person might feel that members of the American Nazi Party are the vilest scum on the face of the Earth, yet defend their right to express their opinions. Tolerance requires that we respect the civil rights and civil liberties of people we dislike, but it does not require that we like them.

We have defined tolerance in terms of support for freedom of expression and in terms of support for equality. We now turn to a brief examination of the theoretical background of tolerance in the United States.

THE LIBERAL TRADITION

Lockean Liberalism

Political tolerance in the United States has its theoretical roots in political liberalism, which was borrowed primarily from British political theorists, especially the seventeenth-century writings of John Locke. This form of liberalism is not the same as twentieth-century liberalism; a distinction will be made later. From the Declaration of Independence to the present, American political thought has been overwhelmingly liberal in its thrust. Let us begin with a nutshell abridgment of the basic political theory of John Locke:

We hold these truths to be self-evident, that all men are created equal, that they are endowed by their Creator with certain unalienable rights, that among these are life, liberty, and the pursuit of happiness. That to secure these rights, governments were instituted among men, deriving their just powers from the consent of the governed, that whenever any form of government becomes destructive of those ends, it is the right of the people to alter or abolish it.

The above is, of course, part of the American Declaration of Independence. Thomas Jefferson borrowed these ideas from Locke, although it is very doubtful that anyone had ever expressed these ideas before with such elegance.

Locke began his theory with the idea of a "state of nature," the human condition prior to the creation of governments. This is simply a way of getting into certain types of questions, such as: What is human nature? What rights did people have before governments were established? Why were governments established? What is the proper role for the government? Locke's answers to such questions provide the core for his form of liberalism.

The cornerstone of any political theory is the political theorist's view of human nature. One cannot prescribe what kind of political system is desirable for humans without taking into account the nature of the building blocks, the humans themselves. Locke began with a view of human nature as being fundamentally good (or at least malleable and capable of being made good) and rational (capable of deciding on courses of action which would lead to desired goals). Thus, humans can be expected to pursue moral ends in a rational manner.

In the state of nature, people have natural rights, rights which they possess simply by virtue of being human beings. These basic, natural rights are life, liberty, and property. Further, these rights are inalienable; they cannot be taken away from people either in a state of nature or by any government.

People in a state of nature are also free in the sense that they are not subject to the control of other people. When there are violations of the rights of an individual, the individual is also free to punish the transgressor.

Given all this, life in a state of nature is pretty good. Good, rational individuals are pursuing their own goals in their own ways, provided that they do not violate the rights of other individuals. Why, then, do people form governments? The basic problem in the state of nature concerns the equitable protection of basic rights; problems of fairness occur when individuals punish transgressions against their own rights. Thus, governments are formed in order to make these rights secure. People form a "social contract" whereby they voluntarily give up their right to punish violations against their own rights to a government whose fundamental purpose for existence is the protection of these rights in an equitable and orderly fashion. However, the government still must base its rule of an individual—each and every individual—on the voluntary consent of that individual. Without getting into the complications involved in Locke's notion of consent, let us just note the ultimate importance of this idea: if a government doesn't do what it is supposed to do—protect the rights of its citizens—then consent can be withdrawn and the government can be abolished or altered.

Individual freedom—liberty—forms the core of liberalism. Liberty and liberalism both have their root in the Latin word *liber* which means free. Further, Locke placed the emphasis on the value of individualism rather than on the needs of the society as a whole. What role, then, is there for a government in a society composed of good, rational human beings whose individual goals are of paramount importance? Aside from protecting individual rights and conducting relations with other nations, the role of the government is minimal.

Three additional observations need to be made concerning Lockean liberalism. First, the individual goals which Locke wished to free the individual to pursue were to a very great extent economic goals. Recall that the fundamental natural rights are life, liberty, and *property*. Locke's work provided the *political* rationale for a laissez-faire, capitalist economic system; the *economic* rationale was provided by Adam Smith.

Second, Locke did not believe in equality—neither political, nor social, nor economic. Economic equality and economic individualism are obviously contradictory concepts. Social classes existed in England and Locke retained an aristocratic bent of mind, thus rejecting social equality. Locke spoke of the natural equality of men, but he did not favor political equality as we ordinarily think of it. Rather, his concept of political equality is similar to Aristotle's concept of "distributive justice" in which citizens receive justice from the government in proportion to their merits as individuals. In Locke's system, individuals *within* classes were to be treated equally, but equality was not to exist *between* classes.

The third observation is that Locke's theoretical system did not require a democratic political system; any system would do just so long as it was based on the consent of individuals and protected the fundamental rights of those individuals. Locke appears to have favored an aristocracy; it is not necessary to have a democracy in order to have freedom in the Lockean sense.

Many of Locke's ideas, especially those concerning natural rights and the consent of the governed, were incorporated into the American Declaration of Independence. As we shall see, however, the stance toward the government's role changed somewhat when the U.S. Constitution was written.

Madisonian Democracy

Following Dahl (1956), we can refer to the type of liberalism which formed the basis of the U.S. Constitution as "Madisonian democracy." Note that the group of people who wrote the Constitution (the Federalists) was different from the group of people led by Jefferson in writing the Declaration of Independence. The basic differences between the Jeffersonians and the Federalists concerned the type of economy that was to be built and the role of the government in this process. The Jeffersonians wanted an agrarian society with—in line with Locke's ideas—a minimal central government. The Federalists wanted to develop industry, business, transportation, and trade, and they saw a need for a stronger central government to provide the right kind of environment for this development. The weak central government under the Articles of Confederation— which was more in line with Lockean liberalism—was not adequate for provision of protection, currency stability, and assistance for the growth of commercial interests. The liberal writers of the Constitution, having rejected a strict laissez-faire concept of government, set out to use the powers of the government for purposes other than the protection of natural rights.

If a stronger central government was to be created, then how was liberty to be protected? As Dahl (1956: 10) notes, the goal of Madisonian theory was to create a nontyrannical republic. A republic is a government of representatives elected by the citizens and responsible to the citizens. A tyranny exists when citizens are deprived of their natural rights. There were two basic problems: majority tyranny and minority tyranny. Tyranny by a minority was not considered to be much of a possibility; it could be prevented by operation of the republican principle (majority rule). Madison was much more concerned that the operation of majority rule would endanger the rights of "certain minorities whose advantages of status, power, and wealth would, he thought, probably not be tolerated indefinitely by a constitutionally untrammeled majority" (Dahl, 1956: 31).

Madison's chief problem was to create a political system in which a relatively disadvantaged majority "faction" would not be able to infringe on the rights (especially property rights) of the relatively advantaged minority. His basic solution to this problem was to disperse political power. The federal system of government with power shared between the states and the central government was well suited to the dispersion of power. The separation-of-powers idea also dispersed power among the three branches of government. Further, it was expected that the Senate, the President, and the Supreme Court—none of which was to be elected by the general citizenry—would be attuned to establishment interests. The power of the masses would be confined to the House of Representatives. And just to hedge this bet, checks and balances were also added; the power of one branch of government could be checked to a certain degree by each of the other two branches.

These institutional devices were expected to provide a certain level of protection for the rights of the elite minority. However, Madison also relied on the sheer size and diversity of the new republic to prevent the formation of a tyrannical majority faction. Most of those responsible for the Constitution did *not* place any reliance on a national bill of rights as a protection against tyranny; the Bill of Rights in the U.S. Constitution was added as a series of amendments after the original Constitution was ratified, although their adoption became politically a condition for ratification. Many of those involved in the formulation of the Constitution initially viewed the inclusion of natural rights in the Constitution as both unnecessary and potentially dangerous—unnecessary because many states already had such rights in their individual constitutions and potentially dangerous because the inclusion of certain rights might imply that people had no other basic rights outside of those that had been explicitly included.

Thus, the adoption of the U.S. Constitution embodied some basic concepts of John Locke's liberalism, but it also represented a shift away from the idea of a government whose basic function was simply to protect the rights of citizens. We now examine liberalism as it exists in the United States today.

Liberalism Today

The United States began as a liberal nation and has continued, with modifications, to be a liberal nation. Political debate today is primarily—but not exclusively—between one strand of liberalism and another strand of liberalism. Most of the people we term "conservative" today (e.g., Ronald Reagan, Gerald Ford, Barry Goldwater) are actually "classical liberals," people who still accept without fundamental change liberalism as it was originally formulated by John Locke or Thomas Jefferson. The people we term "liberals" today (e.g., Ted Kennedy, George McGovern, Walter Mondale) are also liberals, but they have modified the original Lockean liberalism along the lines of the "positive liberalism" of the nineteenth-century British political theorist T. H. Green.

Basically all liberals have certain beliefs in common: (1) a belief in the basic goodness and rationality of human nature; (2) a strong belief in individual freedom; and (3) a strong emphasis on the value of the individual. The basic questions which separate liberals into different camps concern the nature of liberty and the role of government. Classical liberals view liberty in terms of the absence of governmental restraints on individual freedom; therefore, the welfare of the individual is best served by a minimal government which interferes as little as possible with the workings of the free enterprise system. Positive liberals view liberty in terms of opportunity for individual development, and they do not view a strong government as necessarily dangerous to individual freedom. On the contrary, the power of the government is to be used in order to enhance individual freedom and development. Further, the power of the government is needed in order to protect the individual from other groups—primarily economic groups—in society. Classical liberalism, the positive liberals say, freed the individual from the government only to become enslaved to other groups in society. Thus, positive liberals have supported the notion that the government must make sure that the economy runs smoothly and that jobs must be provided for the unemployed; they have also supported unemployment compensation, minimum wage laws, social security, medicare, industrial safety standards, and welfare programs. Such programs and others constitute what is termed the "welfare state" in the broader sense of the term. The freedom of the individual is to be enhanced by using the powers of the government rather than simply freeing the individual from governmental power. The view of freedom held by positive liberals also leads to a greater degree of concern with equality than is contained in classical liberalism; thus, there is greater support in positive liberalism for the idea of equality of opportunity, especially for disadvantaged groups. Overall, then, classical liberals and positive liberals are in agreement about certain fundamental values concerning human nature and worth, but they diverge on the nature of freedom and the proper role of the government.

The concept of tolerance as support for freedom of expression is strongly endorsed in both positive liberalism and classical liberalism. As we shall see, however, the concept of equality has had a rough road in American history.

WHO GOT LEFT OUT IN THE COLD?

We hold these truths to be self-evident, that all white, property-owning, male adults are created equal.

The above restatement of Jefferson's famous line is more in accord with what Jefferson, Locke, and many other liberals actually meant. The liberal philosophy was not intended to encompass *all* humans; it did not even extend fully to all white men. Full political freedom and equality were the property of a minority of the population. Plamenatz (1963: 249) notes that Locke regarded property as a means to freedom, yet he accepted the established social order wholeheartedly even though most men in that social order lacked the property which Locke regarded as an essential condition for the achievement of any meaningful freedom. "In practice, therefore, he was concerned only for the freedom of a small part of the community" (Plamenatz, 1963: 249).

Because of historical developments in the United States, exclusion from the tenets of liberalism due to a lack of property has become a relatively minor problem. Property, for example, is not often used as a qualification for any sort of political participation. This is not, of course, to deny that—all other things being equal—the person with the greater amount of material resources has a greater opportunity to be effective in the political process.

Slaves were an obvious exclusion from liberalism. Slaves were freed by the Thirteenth Amendment (1865) to the U.S. Constitution. The first sentence of Section 1 of the Fourteenth Amendment (1868) reads:

All persons born or naturalized in the United States, and subject to the jurisdiction thereof, are citizens of the United States and of the State wherein they reside.

This important sentence defined citizenship so that black Americans are citizens, thus overturning the ruling of the Supreme Court in the infamous Dred Scott Decision of 1857 that blacks could not be citizens.

The purpose of the second sentence in Section 1 of the Fourteenth Amendment was to secure equal rights, due process, and equal protection of the laws for all citizens, including blacks (except —as we shall see—they didn't really mean *all* citizens):

No state shall make or enforce any law which shall abridge the privileges or immunities of citizens of the United States; nor shall any State deprive any person of life, liberty, or property, without due process of law; nor deny to any person within its jurisdiction the equal protection of the laws.

Section 1 of the Fourteenth Amendment has been a tremendously important part of the U.S. Constitution for civil rights and civil liberties. Section 2 of the Fourteenth Amendment stipulates that the number of U.S. representatives from a state would be reduced if the state abridged or denied the vote to any adult *male* citizen. The Fifteenth Amendment guaranteed the right to vote regardless of "race, color, or previous condition of servitude." Thus, the Fourteenth and Fifteenth Amendments together established on paper the citizenship and equality of black *males*.

After the Civil War, all black males were legally free and equal citizens under the Constitution. It is obvious, however, that racial equality was not actually established in practice by these constitutional amendments. Even today, American liberalism still has not fully encompassed racial minorities; racial discrimination still exists.

Women constitute another obvious exclusion from liberalism. When Jefferson or Locke referred to the equality of men, they meant men literally. It was more than a hundred years after Locke's death before a major liberal theorist, John Stuart Mill, even entertained on a theoretical level the idea that women should have equal rights. A *literal* interpretation of Section 1 of the Fourteenth Amendment would give women equal rights. However, the men who wrote the Fourteenth Amendment actually meant that all *male* citizens (note their reference to male citizens in Section 2) should have equal rights, due process, and equal protection of the laws. The Supreme Court has generally interpreted this aspect of the Fourteenth Amendment the way the writers meant it rather than the way they wrote it. Women did not even get the right to vote (except in some states) until the Nineteenth Amendment was ratified in 1920. A tremendous amount of discrimination on the basis of sex has occurred in this country throughout its history. At present, the following proposed amendment (known as the Equal Rights Amendment, or ERA) is being debated:

Equality of rights under the law shall not be denied or abridged by the United States or by any State on account of sex.

This amendment might not be ratified. American liberalism has not yet expanded to include women on an equal basis with men.

During U.S. history there has been discrimination against a number of groups. This discrimination has sometimes been legal or constitutional (e.g., women could not vote until 1920) and sometimes it has been—in the broader sense of the term—social (e.g., no one would sell houses to Jews in certain areas). Women and blacks have already been discussed as victims of discrimination. Additionally, Jews, Catholics, and atheists have at various times been the targets of intolerance. In an earlier time, some "help wanted" ads ended with the clause: "No Irish need apply." In addition to the discrimination against the Irish, there has been discrimination against immigrants from many other countries, especially non-English-speaking countries. American Indians have, of course, faced serious discrimination in their native land.

Lastly, American liberalism has not been fully extended to those whose opinions or life-styles are grossly out of harmony with prevailing social and political norms. In 1859 John Stuart Mill (1951: 104) wrote:

If all mankind minus one, were of one opinion, and only one person were of the contrary opinion, mankind would be no more justified in silencing that one person, than he, if he had the power, would be in silencing mankind.

This is a very liberal sentiment, more liberal than Lockean liberalism. Despite the great emphasis on freedom of expression in Locke's theory and in the American version of liberalism, there are vague limitations on this commitment to freedom of expression. Locke himself made exceptions concerning the right to freedom of expression. While it is not completely clear just what some of these exceptions entailed, Locke definitely did not favor toleration of either Catholics or atheists. In the American context, there are a number of groups (e.g., atheists, homosexuals, socialists, members of the American Nazi Party, members of the American Communist Party) whose views or life-styles are so out of accord with prevailing norms that their claims to full liberty and equality are not met with much tolerance in American society today.

THE USES OF TOLERANCE

In this section we will briefly consider arguments for and against tolerance. The primary focus here is on tolerance as support for freedom of expression; however, the issue of equality is also involved in that the conflict can be interpreted in terms of whether all people have an equal right to express their views.

Opposition to Tolerance

Throughout the history of the world, there have been some who have argued against freedom of expression or, at least, freedom of expression in any meaningful sense. People who oppose freedom of expression in specific circumstances might not be doing it on the basis of any particular theoretical rationale other than that they oppose the particular ideas being expressed. They might even be unaware of any broader principles involved; in principle they might be very supportive of general ideas concerning freedom of expression. However, there are some people who have argued against the principle of freedom of expression itself. A basic argument along these lines is that true freedom for the individual involves the freedom to hear and speak *only* the truth. People who take this kind of position usually think of "the Truth" as something objective—not a matter of personal opinions and values— and absolute, and naturally they consider themselves to be possessors of such "Truth." Given this position, it is argued that people should not be allowed to spread nor allowed to hear that which is false.

Many arguments concerning tolerance have centered around religious matters. Some Catholic and some Protestant theologians have taken the position that only the truth deserves to be heard. On the other hand, Locke's opposition to toleration of Catholics was based on his perception that Catholics themselves were intolerant. In the past, religious intolerance has led to the torture and aeath of thousands of people. Obviously, there is much greater tolerance among Catholics, Protestants, and Jews in the world today than in the distant past, but the situation in Northern Ireland reminds us that intolerance on the basis of religious identification can still be extreme.

Although religious intolerance has declined, the same general type of argument concerning the expression of "the Truth" persists here and there. Some people hold that false political, social, or economic views do not deserve a hearing. If one really believes certain ideas, then why would one favor freedom of expression for those who would spread false ideas?

Most arguments against freedom of expression come from the right wing of the political spectrum, which places less emphasis on human freedom and greater emphasis on social controls over the individual. This low value on human freedom is due partly to the right wing's view of human nature as basically bad (or sinful) and irrational. Thus, it is not unusual for the right wing—especially the extreme right—to oppose freedom of expression. However, there have also been arguments against tolerance from some on the left wing, most notably the neo-Marxist Herbert Marcuse. Marcuse (1969) argued, like many of those on the right who rejected tolerance, that there is an objective, absolute truth. However, the prevailing American ideology, liberalism, is so entrenched that people automatically reject the truth (as Marcuse saw it) even when it was expressed to them. The presentation of many different viewpoints actually reinforces the status quo of liberalism because it gives the appearance that all views have received a hearing. Thus, the truth is unable to penetrate the mind-set of Americans who are so thoroughly indoctrinated. In order to counteract this entrenched way of thinking, Marcuse argued that tolerance of the liberal establishment must be withdrawn; only the left (his perception of the left) should be tolerated. This would include

...the withdrawal of toleration of speech and assembly from groups and movements which promote aggressive policies, armaments, chauvinism, discrimination on the grounds of race and religion, or which oppose the extension of public services, social security, medical care, etc. [Marcuse, 1969: 100].

Thus, on both the left wing and the right wing, those who believe in an absolute, objective truth sometimes take an intolerant view toward the presentation of views which run counter to the truth as they see it.

Support for Tolerance

Arguments in favor of tolerance, at least with regard to freedom of expression, center around three fundamental benefits: (1) it is good for the society or political system; (2) it is beneficial in the search for truth; and (3) it is intrinsically good for the individual.

The first argument, that tolerance is good for the political/social system, usually has stability or conflict resolution as its central value. Freedom of expression is good because it maintains the stability of the system; it keeps pressures from building up which could destroy the system. This is somewhat similar to Marcuse's proposition that freedom for the expression of many different viewpoints actually strengthens the existing system. Sullivan *et al.* (1979: 781) express the stability value of tolerance as follows:

Although a democratic regime may be divided by fierce conflicts, it can remain stable if citizens remain attached to democratic or constitutional procedures and maintain a willingness to apply such procedures...on an equal basis for all, even to those who challenge its way of life. In this instrumental sense, tolerance is understood as valuable because it helps to maintain a stable democratic regime.

Another possible benefit to the political system revolves around the value of citizen participation. Emerson (1966: 3) proposes that freedom of expression can serve as a stimulus for participation by citizens in political decision making; the free expression of ideas presumably will lead to more active involvement in the democratic process.

The second argument is that the free expression of ideas is beneficial in the search for truth. Ebenstein (1969: 543) summarizes three arguments formulated by John Stuart Mill in defense of freedom of expression. First, any silenced opinion may be true, and if we silence an opinion we must assume that we are incapable of being wrong. Thus, the truth might be lost when we silence an opinion, and we could only silence the opinion if we were absolutely sure that we could not possibly be wrong. Second, a silenced opinion might be partly true, and we need the competition of different opinions in order to arrive at the complete truth. Opinions might be partly right and partly wrong; when they are expressed freely, we presumably have a better chance at correcting mistakes in the opinions we hold. Third, even if the silenced opinion is completely wrong and the prevailing opinion is completely correct, we run the risk that the prevailing truth will become dogma and prejudice unless it is exposed to the challenge of open discussion.

The third argument in favor of freedom of expression of ideas is that such expression is intrinsically good for individuals; it is a benefit in and of itself without regard to any usefulness it might have for society or in the search for truth. Sometimes it is said, in line with the second argument presented above, that in a democracy a minority must be free in order to attempt to persuade the majority to accept its point of view. However, sometimes a minority has no realistic chance of converting a majority to its point of view; it seems extremely unlikely, for example, that the Prohibition Party of today will be successful in persuading a majority to prohibit alcoholic beverages. While the expression of views by such a minority can—in line with the first argument—add to the legitimacy and stability of the political system, this expression can also fulfill a human need regardless of whether it has any effects on the views of others. The expression of views may be intrinsically rewarding to the individual. Further, this type of intrinsic reward need not be limited to minorities. Those who are in the majority on an issue might also enjoy expressing—or listening to others express—the majority sentiments. Thus, even when the expression of views is unnecessary or futile, people may nevertheless derive satisfaction from such expression.

Having considered the meaning of tolerance, the philosophical background of tolerance, and the basic arguments for and against tolerance as freedom of expression, we turn now to an examination of tolerance in relation to American political institutions.

POLITICAL INSTITUTIONS AND TOLERANCE

A Tolerant Political System

A tolerant political system is one in which people can, within tightly justified limits, hold and express their own views without fear of reprisal, no matter what those views are. Further, people must be treated as equals under the law regardless of any views they hold and regardless of any irrelevant biological/physical characteristics (e.g., race or sex) or social characteristics (e.g., ethnic background). We do not wish to go very far here into what constitutes justifiable limits on freedom of expression; this is a very complicated question. On certain types of ideas concerning limitations, there is nearly a consensus. For example, just about everyone would agree that it is not intolerant to hold someone responsible for falsely yelling "fire" in a crowded theater; nor is it considered to be intolerant to hold responsible someone who knowingly and maliciously slanders or libels another person with falsehoods. Much trickier questions arise when we get into such matters as the publication of materials which are regarded as obscene or speeches which advocate the overthrow of the government. In a tolerant society, however, those who wish to impose any limitations on freedom of expression must have a very tightly defined and well-justified basis for such limitations; such limitations are not justifiable solely on the basis of the unpopularity or extremism of the views to be expressed.

Constitutionally, the two concepts of tolerance we are presenting here receive their primary expression in two amendments to the U.S. Constitution. With regard to tolerance in terms of freedom of expression, the First Amendment reads:

Congress shall make no law respecting an establishment of religion, or prohibiting the free exercise thereof; or abridging the freedom of speech, or of the press; or the right of the people peaceably to assemble and to petition the Government for a redress of grievances.

The First Amendment specifically prohibits Congress—not the states—from abridging certain freedoms. However, the interpretations of the Fourteenth Amendment have gradually "incorporated" such freedoms with regard to the states as well as the national government. With regard to tolerance as support for freedom of expression, then, we will be focusing primarily on support for the civil liberties contained within the First Amendment (which does not include all civil liberties).

With regard to tolerance in terms of equality, the second sentence in the Fourteenth Amendment is very relevant:

No State shall make or enforce any law which shall abridge the privileges or immunities of citizens of the United States; nor shall any State deprive any person of life, liberty, or property, without due process of law; nor deny to any person within its jurisdiction the equal protection of the laws.

The most relevant concern here is the "equal protection of the laws" clause. While this sentence in the Fourteenth Amendment prohibits the government from doing certain things, equality—as noted before—often requires positive action on the part of the government; this is the realm of civil rights.

The question here is this: Can we depend on American political institutions for the protection of freedom of expression and equality? The answer is that we can not. We cannot rely on governmental institutions to protect the basic rights of individuals, nor can we expect that such institutions will guarantee equality before the law. The reasons for this will be discussed below.

Governmental Repression

In the first place, political institutions themselves sometimes engage in repressive activities. The revelations resulting from the Watergate scandal provide recent and ample proof that government power is sometimes used to override the rights of individuals. The FBI, CIA, and IRS were used as weapons against the "enemies" of the Nixon administration. Further, this was not the first time such activities had been carried out; one "defense" which was offered for the Nixon administration was that it wasn't doing anything that hadn't been done before.

It has often been alleged that J. Edgar Hoover maintained his position of power because he had damaging information on many political figures in Washington. Since his death, it has been publicized that he used the FBI's power in an illegal manner to harass and spy upon groups or individuals whose political views he considered to be wrong. For example, files were kept on people who attended some meetings of women's liberation groups. Another example is Hoover's attempt to discredit Martin Luther King.

Earlier reference was made to the massive police action at the 1968 Democratic National Convention in which some police officers clearly engaged in illegal repressive actions. Other massive police actions involving illegal methods have also occurred. For example, during May 3–5, 1971, in Washington, D.C., war protestors threatened to tie up traffic. The police response was mass arrest; anyone at an intersection who even looked suspicious was arrested. Altogether, approximately 13,000 people were arrested, regardless of whether they had committed any crime.

Dye and Zeigler (1978) maintain that political leaders often respond in a repressive fashion when they feel threatened. Mass activism (such as riots, demonstrations, extremism, or violence) leads to fear and insecurity among political elites (leaders), who respond repressively:

Dissent is no longer tolerated, the news media are censored, free speech curtailed, potential counterelites jailed, and police and security forces strengthened—usually in the name of "national security" or "law and order." Elites convince themselves that these steps are necessary to preserve liberal democratic values [Dye and Zeigler, 1978: 17].

Thus, one reason why we cannot count on political institutions to protect freedom of expression and equality is that the leaders of such institutions themselves sometimes engage in repressive actions, especially if they feel that a crisis exists.

Foot-Dragging

A political institution which takes no action to repress individual rights might still be a threat to tolerance by closing its eyes to repression of individuals by other groups in society or by other levels and branches of government. For example, for most of U.S. history, American political institutions have simply ignored discrimination against black people. Even after official recognition was given to the concept of equality for blacks—let's use the passage of the 1964 Civil Rights Act as a turning point—changes have occurred very slowly because many of those charged with the enforcement of such policy have dragged their feet in order to avoid offending powerful political interests (e.g., Southern senators and representatives).

The Supreme Court

The Supreme Court is supposedly insulated enough from outside political pressure that it can protect individual rights even when it is unpopular to do so. Most unpopular groups will have little success in getting legislative or executive branches of government to buck public opinion; hence, "their appeal to the judicial branch has frequently been their sole hope for the attainment of justice under the law" (Abraham, 1977: 31).

The Supreme Court, however, does not get too far ahead of public opinion. If we set aside the question of property rights, the Court's record in protecting individual rights prior to the Warren Court (1954–1969) is not very impressive. Edgerton's (1938) study of cases handled by the Supreme Court up until 1933 indicated that it had made no substantial contribution to the protection of freedom of expression. A later examination by Dahl (1957) came to essentially the same conclusion, while indicating that the Warren Court might be an exception.

Presidents select nominees for the Supreme Court on the basis of their political views. This usually means that the nominee will not be too far out of accord with the current political mood of the country. Further, the Senate must confirm the nominee, thus adding to the tendency to recruit Supreme Court justices who do not seem to conflict dramatically with current majoritarian preferences.

Aside from the selection process, other factors can contribute to the Court's typical unwillingness to go out on a limb to protect unpopular causes. If the Court makes a decision that is extremely unpopular, the power and prestige of the Court may be reduced, the decision might simply be ignored for the most part, or other branches or levels of government might devise methods to circumvent the decision. The Supreme Court cannot simply make a decision and expect that the decision will be self-enforcing; other people will enforce—or fail to enforce—the decision.

The Supreme Court under Chief Justice Earl Warren broke new ground in the protection of individual rights and the promotion of equality. Many of the decisions of the Warren Court were very unpopular at the time, and the impact of some of these decisions demonstrates what can happen when the Court makes a decision in defense of minority rights which runs counter to popular sentiment. In the famous 1954 *Brown* v. *Board of Education* case, the Court ruled that "separate but equal" school facilities for white and black children were unconstitutional and that desegregation should proceed "with all deliberate speed." Many public officials have responded to this directive with foot-dragging, outright defiance, encouragement of violence, and various devices to circumvent the decision. Desegregation of schools has proceeded at an extremely slow pace and has not yet been completely accomplished.

To take another example, in a series of cases beginning most dramatically with *Engel* v. *Vitale* in 1962, the Warren Court ruled that religious observances in public schools were unconstitutional violations of the principles of separation of church and state and religious freedom. This decision raised intense opposition. In the South, it was sometimes said that the Supreme Court had "taken God out of the schools and put the niggers in." "Impeach Earl Warren" signs sprouted in places. Senator Dirksen of Illinois proposed a constitutional amendment, the "prayer amendment," to allow prayers in the public schools. Support for this amendment waned when it became apparent that many organized religious groups (e.g., the National Council of Churches) opposed it. On the other hand, while the decisions of the Warren Court have presumably resolved the legal issue, they have not entirely resolved the question in practice; many public schools continue to have religious observances.

In sum, the Supreme Court is not an automatic safeguard for either freedom of expression or equality. It will seldom set itself up against strongly held majority sentiments to protect a powerless minority. When it does, its decisions might be resisted or circumvented, at least initially. Krislov (1968: 220) *approvingly* notes the role of the Court:

It is well that Court action has proven to be more a matter of providing mitigating restraints than steering courses and setting policy. Even in the field of defining the modes and content of free expression, ultimate reliance must be on the political system and populace as a whole rather than "a bevy of platonic guardians."

In its bare essentials, this means that the "rights" of minorities ultimately depend on the will of majorities. Krislov evidently feels that this is an accurate description of the situation and that it is a desirable state of affairs.

WE THE PEOPLE

Governmental institutions in a republic are not capable by themselves of fully protecting the freedom of expression and the equality of individuals, especially individuals whose views are greatly out of accord with current social norms. This should not be surprising. By comparison, the purpose of the police is to protect individuals from crime; yet crimes do occur, and some of them are committed by the police themselves.

Tolerance in a society requires tolerant political institutions and political leaders whose behavior is tolerant. But tolerant political institutions and leaders cannot guarantee a tolerant society; a tolerant society requires a tolerant people. Tolerance in American society depends to a great extent on the attitudes and behavior of people in their day-to-day lives. The people, if they so choose, have a wide range of legal, extralegal, and illegal sanctions which they can impose on individuals who do not conform. Laws and courts, even when they are willing, cannot afford complete protection to the nonconformist. The level of tolerance in a society can, of course, be affected by the behavior of leaders and by the nature of political institutions. Likewise, the types of people who become leaders and the nature of political institutions can be affected by the level of tolerance in the general public.

The purpose of this book, then, is to examine tolerance—as support for freedom of expression and as support for equality—in the American public. In order to do this, the results from a number of studies of public opinion will be utilized.

SUMMARY

Political tolerance is defined in terms of two different concepts: support for freedom of expression and support for equality. Support for freedom of expression is a willingness to allow the expression of views by people we dislike or whose views we oppose. Support for equality entails opposition to unjustifiable discrimination against people. Both concepts have in common a willingness to accept differences among people and treat individuals as equal units within society. Intolerance toward individuals can be based on three general categories of characteristics of people: biological/physical characteristics, social characteristics, and belief for attitudinal characteristics.

Political tolerance in the United States has its theoretical roots in political liberalism which places a great deal of emphasis on human freedom and worth. Lockean, or classical, liberalism defined freedom primarily in terms of the absence of governmental restraints on the individual. In adapting liberalism, the writers of the U.S. Constitution attempted to set up a system in which neither majority nor minority repression would occur. At the same time, they went beyond the minimal role for the government envisioned originally by Lockean liberalism. The United States has continued to be a liberal political system; political debate today is primarily between those who advocate the original, classical liberalism (now called conservatism) and positive liberalism which views governmental power as a means of enhancing the freedom and growth of the individual.

Although both positive and classical liberals give strong support to the principle of freedom of expression, the tenets of liberalism have not historically been held to apply to all Americans. Instead, full citizenship originally applied only to white, property-owning men. The property requirement gradually faded into insignificance in most situations, but it has been much more difficult to remove the race and sex qualifications. Aside from blacks and females, there has also been discrimination against a number of other groups throughout American history on the basis of social characteristics or beliefs.

The primary argument of those who have opposed tolerance— at least with regard to freedom of expression—is that there is an objective truth which is not just a matter of opinion or values, and the true freedom of the individual is served by hearing and speaking only the truth. On the other side, it is argued that freedom of expression is beneficial for the political system, it is beneficial in the search for truth, and it provides intrinsic value for the individual.

A tolerant political system is one in which people can, within tightly justified limits, hold and express their views without fear of reprisal, and it is a system in which people are treated as equals before the law. However, we cannot depend on political institutions to protect freedom of expression and equality. Political institutions themselves sometimes engage in repressive acts. Further, in response to political pressures, political institutions might drag their feet in the enforcement of laws or policies designed to protect freedom of expression or promote equality. The Supreme Court, supposedly the institution which can politically afford to protect the rights of minorities, does not have a good record in this regard for most of its history. Because of the process by which a Supreme Court justice is selected and because unpopular decisions can lead to a reduction in its power and prestige, the Supreme Court does not often go against strongly held majoritarian preferences in order to protect individual rights. The decisions of the Warren Court which went against public opinion (e.g., cases dealing with school integration and religious observances in the schools) led to a great deal of hostility toward the Court and efforts to circumvent or delay enforcement of the rulings.

Thus, political institutions and leaders cannot guarantee a tolerant society. A tolerant society requires a tolerant people. The question of the level of tolerance among American citizens forms the basis for the following examination.

2

Tolerance and
the First Amendment

INTRODUCTION

Purpose of Chapter

This chapter concerns the degree of support among Americans for the basic rights included within the First Amendment of the U.S. Constitution: freedom of speech, freedom of the press, freedom of religion, and the rights to peaceable assembly and to petition the government. Tolerance here is conceived of in terms of the extent to which people will allow the exercise of such freedoms by other people. In the next chapter, we will examine the degree of tolerance in the United States in terms of support for equality; the topic of equality must, however, be examined to some extent in this chapter. We will see, for example, that many of those who support freedom of speech do not support it *equally* for all viewpoints.

A Note of Caution

The information presented in the tables in this chapter and in almost all the tables in the rest of the book is based on various national surveys conducted by various organizations. Three points need to be made concerning the interpretation of these results. First, all these surveys contain some error. These surveys are based on probability samples of the adult U.S. population, unless otherwise indicated. A probability sample is a sample in which each member of the population has a known probability of being sampled. At least at the initial stage of such a sampling procedure, each adult in the United States should have the same chance of being selected as any other adult. Such scientifically selected samples, typically including about 1000 to 1600 people, are very accurate in their representation of the views of the whole nation. However, there will almost always be some error in the results. Without getting into the complexities of sampling theory, let us just say that it is reasonably safe to interpret most of the national survey results discussed in this book as being accurate within about 3 percentage points. Suppose, for example, a national survey (Wilson, 1975: 71) asks: "Should people be allowed to make a speech against God?" A "yes" answer is given by 32% of the sample. Given a possible error of 3%, this means that if everyone in the adult U.S. population had answered the question, the percentage saying "yes" might be as low as 29% (32% minus 3% error) or as high as 35% (32% plus 3% error). The actual percentages could be even lower or even higher, but most of the time they will be within this range. Some of the surveys discussed in this book are more accurate than this (e.g., the Stouffer study) and some are less accurate. It also needs to be noted that this range of error applies to the results for the total sample; when subgroups of the sample are discussed, the range of error is usually greater.

The second problem is that questions concerning a particular topic might be worded differently in different surveys and such variations in question wording can have a substantial effect on the results. In the preceding paragraph, Wilson's (1975) results were given for the question: "Should people be allowed to make speeches against God?" From these results, we might conclude that only 32% of the population would allow atheists to give speeches on their views. However, a 1974 National Opinion Research Center (NORC) survey reports that 62% would allow "somebody who is against all churches and religion" to "make a speech in your city against all churches and religion." This is quite a difference in results. These two questions, however, are not really the same. In one case, the "cue" is speeches "against God," and in the other case, the "cue" is speeches "against churches and religion." Evidently it is much more acceptable to make speeches against the institutions of churches and religion than it is to make speeches against God. Note also that the term *atheist* was not used in either question. If this term had been used, the results might have been altered even further. The labels that are attached to viewpoints can have an effect on how people react to those viewpoints. The point is that we need to be somewhat cautious in interpreting the results of a single survey question.

A third problem is that the opinion expressed by a person in a survey situation might not accurately reflect the person's actual attitude. An attitude is a fundamental, stable predisposition to react in a certain way in a certain situation. We use the opinions expressed by people in survey situations as *indicators* of these underlying attitudes, but the expressed opinions might be influenced by the survey situation itself. Two types of problems have particular relevance to research on tolerance. First, the problem of *response set* occurs when a person tends to automatically answer questions in a particular direction, regardless of the content of the question. On questions with a "yes-no" or "agree-disagree" format, some people have a tendency to respond positively (the "yea-sayers") and some people tend to respond negatively (the "nay-sayers"). More will be said on this problem in a later chapter. The problem of *social desirability* occurs when people recognize that there is a socially accepted answer to a question and they give this socially accepted answer—regardless of whether it reflects their actual attitude—rather than taking a position counter to the norms of society. This particular problem might greatly affect responses to questions which concern the very general norms of tolerance in American society; for example, almost everyone will answer affirmatively to the question: "Do you believe in freedom of speech?" Thus, the results of the surveys might be due in part to the nature of the survey itself; more will be said on this type of problem later.

GENERAL PRINCIPLES

Tolerance in the Abstract

When asked about general, abstract statements concerning First Amendment rights, Americans seem to be almost completely tolerant. Prothro and Grigg's (1960) study of the citizens of Ann Arbor and Tallahassee found that at least 94% of the respondents agreed with each of the following general statements related to principles of democracy:

- Democracy is the best form of government.
- Public officials should be chosen by majority vote.
- The minority should be free to criticize majority decisions.
- Every citizen should have an equal chance to influence government policy.
- People in the minority should be free to try to win majority support for their opinions.

Thus, there is a strong consensus favoring general, abstract principles of democracy, including the ideas of majority rule and minority rights. Since the beginning of survey research relevant to these types of questions in this country, results have repeatedly shown this almost unanimous support for general principles of American democracy, and this support extends to the freedoms contained in the First Amendment. For example, an early poll indicated that in 1938, 95% answered "yes" to the question: "Do you believe in freedom of speech?" (Cantril, 1951: 244). Responses to five of the questions used by McClosky (1964) are presented in Table 2.1. These five statements embody some very important ideas contained in the popular theory of democracy in the United States: equality before the law, freedom of speech, freedom of dissent generally, freedom from censorship of the press, and freedom of conscience with regard to religion. More than three-fourths of the respondents agreed with each of these five general statements. The more general the statement is, the higher is the level of agreement. Almost everyone (94%) agreed with the concept of equality before the law implied in the statement: "No matter what a person's political beliefs are, he is entitled to the same

TABLE 2.1
Percentages Giving Tolerant Responses to General
Democratic Principles: 1957–58 McClosky Survey[a]

	Percent Agree
No matter what a person's political beliefs are, he is entitled to the same legal rights and protections as anyone else.	94
I believe in free speech for all no matter what their views might be.	89
People who hate our way of life should still have a chance to talk and be heard.	82
Nobody has a right to tell another person what he should and should not read.	81
Freedom of conscience should mean freedom to be an atheist as well as freedom to worship in the church of one's choice.	77

SOURCE: Herbert McClosky, "Consensus and Ideology in American Politics," *American Political Science Review*, 58 (June, 1964), p. 366.

[a] The sampling procedures involved in this national survey did not include a strict probability sample; this and other unusual features of this survey probably make it somewhat less accurate than most national probability surveys.

legal rights and protections as anyone else." More than three out of four of the respondents even supported the idea that freedom of conscience means not only the right to hold whatever religious beliefs one wants to but also the right not to hold any religious beliefs at all.

In sum, when Americans are asked whether they agree with broad, abstract principles associated with our popular conceptions of democracy, they overwhelmingly support such principles. Very few people oppose the general principles of majority rule, minority rights, freedom of speech, freedom of the press, freedom of religion, and equality before the law.

Now for the catch. As McClosky (1964), Prothro and Grigg (1960), and other studies have demonstrated, when general principles concerning tolerance are translated into *specific applications* of such principles, the level of tolerance drops dramatically. Zellman and Sears (1971: 110) aptly note this finding with regard to freedom of speech:

The most striking feature of adult Americans' attitudes toward free speech is their acceptance of the general principle coupled with their unwillingness to extend it to concrete situations involving political dissenters and other nonconformists.

We need, then, to make some distinctions concerning the degree of specificity involved in questions concerning tolerance.

Tolerance and Levels of Specificity

So far we have been concerned with general statements of democratic principles. Before going further, we need to distinguish between such general statements regarding tolerance and—at the other end of the continuum—very specific statements concerning tolerance. This general-specific continuum is based on how specific a tolerance statement is with regard to the *political actor* and the *political act* involved. The political actor is the person or group who is to express a viewpoint. Distinctions might be made among political actors on the basis of either the viewpoint to be expressed (e.g., socialism, racism, opposition to busing, support for abortion, and so on) or on the basis of the group characteristics of the political actors themselves (e.g., blacks, women). A political act is any attempt to influence public policy or practices; here we are mostly concerned with the political acts implied in the First Amendment (speech making, demonstrating, petitioning, and political writing) which involve freedom of expression.

General statements of tolerance contain an abstract principle of tolerance without reference to any particular political actor or any reference to an intention for a particular political act to be carried out. Consider the general statement of tolerance: "I believe in freedom of speech for everyone regardless of what their political views are." This statement says nothing about belief in freedom of speech for a particular group or viewpoint. Logically, a person who believes in freedom of speech for everyone would believe in freedom of speech for a particular group (e.g., socialists); in reality, however, agreement with the general statement does not necessarily predict a person's attitude toward tolerance for a particular group or viewpoint. The general statement of tolerance of speech above also says nothing about the exercise (actual or hypothetical) of the political freedom; it does not ask about a specific political act of speech making. Responses to such a question might be quite different if the emphasis were placed more on the actual exercise of the freedom (e.g., "Do you believe that groups who are not satisfied with a public policy should be allowed to present their views in public speeches in your community?").

At the other end of the continuum are very *specific statements* regarding tolerance. Such statements specify the group which is to present its viewpoint, the viewpoint to be presented, and the political act by which the viewpoint is to be presented. For example: "Should a group of socialists be allowed to hold a demonstration in your community in order to argue in favor of government ownership of certain industries?"

When Americans are asked questions concerning tolerance, their level of tolerance depends to a great extent on the level of specificity involved in the question. The general-specific continuum is helpful in organizing the information concerning tolerance, but it will be necessary to use it rather loosely in places. Statements or questions concerning tolerance may be very general or very specific in specifying the context: Who is to present a viewpoint? What viewpoint is to be presented? How is the viewpoint to be presented? Further, the context might be specified with regard to one or two of these questions while being general with regard to the rest of the situation; this type of situation is intermediate on the general-specific continuum. An example of an intermediate question concerning tolerance is: "Do you believe people should be allowed to hold demonstrations in your city to protest government policies?" This question implies a particular political act (demonstrations) but specifies neither the group nor the viewpoint involved. The statement "Socialists are entitled to the same political freedoms as anyone else" implies a group and viewpoint, but no particular political act is suggested. In short, we can consider questions or statements concerning tolerance as falling somewhere on a continuum running from very general statements in which little or no context is specified, through intermediate statements in which part of the context is specified, to specific statements in which a great deal of the context is specified.

We have seen that tolerance among Americans is very high when the statement of principle is very general. We will now examine the results in situations in which the context is made more specific—either intermediate or very specific.

SPECIFIC APPLICATIONS

The Drop in Tolerance

The results from McClosky's (1964) study presented earlier indicated a strong consensus in favor of general principles concerning tolerance. McClosky also included a series of questions to indicate specific applications of these general principles. The results for these specific application questions, which are basically intermediate in their level of specificity, indicate a sharp drop in tolerance. For example, recall that 89% had supported the idea of free speech for all regardless of what their views are. However, when the context is more specific, the proportion of the respondents in opposition to freedom of speech grows. More than a third of the respondents (37%) agreed with the idea that a man "oughtn't to be allowed to speak if he doesn't know what he's talking about" (McClosky, 1964: 367). To take another example, 50% of the respondents agreed that: "A book that contains wrong political views cannot be a good book and does not deserve to be published" (McClosky, 1964: 367). In short, McClosky's study demonstrated a very strong, consensual support for general principles of tolerance; when the context was made somewhat more specific, the level of tolerance dropped greatly.

This type of finding with regard to specific applications of principles of tolerance is crucial in understanding American attitudes toward freedom of expression, and we need to demonstrate it further. In order to make several points, tolerance in situations of intermediate specificity will be discussed first and then tolerance in more specific situations will be discussed.

Intermediate Situations

Table 2.2 presents questions from several different studies concerning political acts associated with the First Amendment. Note that none of these items specifies the nature of the viewpoint to be presented or the particular group which is to present the viewpoint. Thus, the political act is specified (or implied) but the political actor is not specified. The results (the percentages supporting freedom of expression) demonstrate quite clearly that many Americans are very willing to back away from support of principles of tolerance once they are no longer talking about vague, abstract ideals. In fact, on only two of the eight questions is there even majority support for freedom of expression.

Of the political freedoms involved in Table 2.2, freedom of the press and the right to petition the government appear to have the most support. However, only a little over half (55%) of the respondents reject the idea of greater control over what the newspapers can print. Less than a majority (42%) support the right of the media to report a story which the government feels is harmful to our national interest. The support for government censorship of the press when the "national interest" issue is involved means that the press cannot rest secure in its First Amendment rights.

The right to petition the government draws majority support, but note that only 59% give unqualified support to this political act. This is a long way from the consensus on democratic principles in the abstract. There is a similar erosion of support for freedom of speech. Less than a majority (48%) would always allow a minority to criticize a government decision which is liked by a majority. When the concept of national interest is raised, the minority fully supporting the right to criticize the government when the criticism is "damaging to our national interest" drops to 42%. People appear to be willing to violate individual rights in the name of the "national interest," perhaps without considering whether such violations are themselves damaging to the national interest.

The least supported First Amendment right is the right to demonstrate. Setting aside those who said it depends on the circumstances, only 18% gave unqualified approval for "protest meetings or marches that are permitted by the local authorities." Note, however, that this particular question asks whether the respondent *approves* of such protests, not whether such protests should be *allowed* or not. Further, the possibility of violence no doubt has some effect on attitudes toward demonstrations. When the question specifies a *peaceful* demonstration, 47% gave unqualified sup-

TABLE 2.2
Percentages Supporting Freedom of Expression[a]

Freedom of Speech	Percent Tolerant
1. Do you think everyone should have the right to criticize the government, even if the criticism is damaging to our national interest? (*Yes*) 1970	42
2. If the government makes a decision that most people think is a good one, do you think other people should be allowed to criticize it? (*Always*) 1971	48

Demonstrations

3. As long as there appears to be no clear danger of violence, do you think any group, no matter how extreme, should be allowed to organize protests against the government? (*Yes*) 1970	21
4. How about taking part in protest meetings or marches that are permitted by the local authorities? Would you approve of doing that, disapprove, or would it depend on the circumstances? (*Approve*) 1968	18
5. Do you think people should be allowed to hold a peaceful demonstration to ask the government to act on some issue? (*Always*) 1971	47

Petitions

6. Do you think people should be allowed to circulate petitions to ask the government to act on an issue? (*Always*) 1971	59

Freedom of the Press

7. Except in time of war, do you think newspapers, radio, and television should have the right to report any story, even if the government feels it's harmful to our national interest? (*Yes*) 1970	42
8. Would you approve or disapprove of placing greater curbs, or controls, on what newspapers print? (*Disapprove*) 1961	55

SOURCES: Questions 1, 3, and 7 are from a 1970 CBS survey reported in Robert Chandler, *Public Opinion: Changing Attitudes on Contemporary Political and Social Issues* (New York: R. R. Bowker, 1972), pp. 6–8. Questions 2, 5, and 6 are from a 1971 National Opinion Research Center survey reported in David G. Lawrence, "Procedural Norms and Tolerance: A Reassessment," *American Political Science Review*, 70 (March, 1976), p. 92. Question 4 is from the Survey Research Center's 1968 American National Election Study. Question 8 is from a 1961 Gallup survey reported in George H. Gallup, *The Gallup Poll, Volume Three* (New York: Random House, 1972), p. 1722.

[a] The responses indicating support for freedom of expression are given in parentheses after each question, followed by the date of the survey.

port—still less than majority support and a long way from a tolerant consensus. In the other question concerning demonstrations, it is specified that there is no clear danger of violence—which leaves open the possibility that there is some danger of violence—but it also implies that the group involved in the demonstration might be an extremist group. Under these circumstances, only a fifth (21%) support the right to demonstrate. Thus, Americans' low support for the right to demonstrate appears to be partly due to fears of violence or disturbances. There is a conflict of different values here; many Americans apparently feel that it is more important to minimize the possibility of violence or disturbance than it is to protect the right to demonstrate.

In these intermediate situations in which part of the context is specified, the level of support for freedom of expression is much lower than for principles of tolerance contained in very general statements. We now examine support for freedom of expression in contexts which are more specific.

Specific Situations

How supportive of First Amendment rights are Americans in very specific situations in which the political actor and the political act are both specified? The answer is: it depends. It depends to a large extent on what the political act is and who is going to present a viewpoint. In some specific situations, support for freedom of expression is very high; in other situations, it is very low.

Support for freedom of expression for unpopular groups is low in the United States. Americans do not strongly support First Amendment rights for groups whose viewpoints are outside the mainstream of prevailing American norms. This finding has been substantiated by many studies (e.g., Stouffer, 1955; Prothro and Grigg, 1960; Wilson, 1975; Davis, 1975; Lawrence, 1976; Nunn *et al.*, 1978; Sullivan *et al.*, 1979).

In 1954, during the height of the McCarthy era and the Cold War, an important study was carried out by Samuel Stouffer (1955). Stouffer asked a series of questions concerning: (1) an admitted Communist; (2) a person who favored government ownership of railroads and big industries; and (3) a person who was against all churches and religion. Note that the terms *socialist* and *atheist* were not explicitly used. Respondents were asked three questions about each of these three persons: (1) Should the man be allowed to give a speech in the respondent's community presenting his views? (2)

Should the man be allowed to teach in a college or university? (3) Should a book written by the man presenting his views (Communism, socialism, or atheism) be removed from the public library? The 1954 results are presented in Table 2.3 along with 1977 results from the National Opinion Research Center's (NORC) follow-up of American attitudes on these questions. NORC also asked the same series of questions about a person "who believes that blacks are genetically inferior," a person who "advocates doing away with elections and letting the military run the country," and "a man who admits that he is a homosexual."

TABLE 2.3
Percentages Supporting Freedom of Expression in Specific Situations

	Percent Tolerant	
	1954	1977
Allow Speech by:		
Atheist	37	62
Socialist	59	—
Communist	27	56
Racist	—	59
Militarist	—	51
Homosexual	—	62
Oppose Removing from Library Book Written by:		
Atheist	35	59
Socialist	53	—
Communist	27	55
Racist	—	61
Militarist	—	55
Homosexual	—	55
Allow to Teach in College:		
Atheist	12	39
Socialist	33	—
Communist	6	39
Racist	—	41
Militarist	—	34
Homosexual	—	49

SOURCES: 1954 results are from Samuel Stouffer, *Communism, Conformity, and Civil Liberties* (New York: Doubleday, 1955); 1977 results are from the National Opinion Research Center, University of Chicago. See appendix for full wording of the questions.

Several points can be derived from the results in Table 2.3. First, tolerance for unpopular groups is low. In 1954, less than a majority of Americans would allow an atheist or a Communist to give a public speech or teach in college, and only small minorities would oppose the removal from public libraries of books written by such persons. Tolerance of socialists was somewhat higher, but still only a third of Americans in 1954 would allow a socialist to teach in college.

We need to note that teaching in college is obviously not a First Amendment right. To a certain extent, we are getting into the topic of tolerance in terms of support for equality before the law rather than tolerance in terms of support for freedom of expression. However, freedom of expression is also involved here. Freedom of expression requires that people be allowed to express their views without fear of reprisal; opposition to allowing a person to teach in college because of the views held by the person constitutes a reprisal, and therefore it has a "chilling effect" on freedom of expression.

The second point is that tolerance toward atheists and Communists (and probably socialists, too, if they had been included in NORC's follow-up study) increased considerably between 1954 and 1977. For example, in 1954, only 37% would allow a speech by an atheist; by 1977, a majority of 62% would allow such a speech. Thus, tolerance toward certain unpopular minorities has grown quite substantially in recent times. However, this level of tolerance still does not even approach consensus support for the First Amendment rights of unpopular minorities.

The third point is that intolerance of very unpopular groups appears to be about the same regardless of where they fall on the left-right political spectrum. Socialism and Communism are left-wing ideologies and atheism is also usually associated with the left. Militarists and racists are associated with the right wing of the political spectrum. Homosexuals, of course, are not really on the left-right political spectrum. The results in Table 2.3 indicate that tolerance for racists, militarists, and homosexuals is very similar to the other hypothetical groups. All six of these groups are small, unpopular minorities which deviate dramatically from prevailing social norms, and differences in tolerance toward these groups are not great. In general, a majority (generally about 55% to 60%) supports the freedom of these groups to express their views (in speeches or in books), but only a minority (generally about 39%) would allow such persons to teach in college.

Variations in Tolerance

We have demonstrated that tolerance of very unpopular groups is low, but we have not yet demonstrated the extent to which Americans' level of support for First Amendment rights is dependent upon the particular group involved. Table 2.4 shows that support for the right to demonstrate or the right to petition is heavily dependent upon the group or viewpoint involved. Almost everyone (95%) would allow either a group concerned about crime in their community or a group of their neighbors to circulate a petition; 81% would allow each of these groups to demonstrate. Thus, support for freedom of expression for these mainstream, noncontroversial groups is very high. Thereafter, however, intolerance increases. Only 69% would allow a group of black militants to circulate a petition and only 61% would allow them to demonstrate. The least support is provided for the group calling for the legalization of marijuana; only 41% would allow them to demonstrate and only 52% would allow them to circulate a petition. Thus, the nature of the group involved has a great deal to do with the extent to which Americans support freedom of expression.

Table 2.4 also demonstrates that Americans make distinctions on the basis of the political act involved as well as on the political actor. Support for the right to circulate a petition is higher than

TABLE 2.4
Percentages Allowing Demonstrations
and Petitions by Specific Groups (1971)

Group	Percent Allowing Group to:	
	Demonstrate	Petition
A group concerned about crime in their community	81	95
A group of your neighbors	81	95
A group of black militants	61	69
A group calling for the government to make sure that blacks can buy and rent homes in white neighborhoods (asked of whites only)	55	70
A group calling for the legalization of marijuana	41	52

SOURCE: Selected results adapted from Table 1 in David G. Lawrence, "Procedural Norms and Tolerance: A Reassessment," *American Political Science Review*, 70 (March, 1976), p. 88.

support for the right to demonstrate. This again supports the idea that the possible disruption involved in a political act has an effect on the extent to which Americans are willing to allow the political act.

Pluralistic Intolerance

As indicated earlier, the 1977 NORC results indicate that people have become more tolerant in recent times toward such groups as atheists and Communists. Such results have led some writers to the conclusion that Americans are becoming more tolerant in general. Sullivan *et al.* (1979), however, argue that in order to assess the level of tolerance of a person, we must find out how tolerant that person is toward the group which he or she most dislikes. Although intolerance toward certain groups has definitely decreased, it is possible that people have simply changed the targets of their intolerance. If people are highly intolerant toward atheists at one time and much more tolerant toward them at a later time, we can say that intolerance toward atheists has decreased; however, we cannot say that intolerance in general has decreased, because it is possible that people are simply intolerant toward different groups now. The high intolerance toward particular groups (Communists, socialists, and atheists) included within Stouffer's (1955) original study was probably due in part to the Cold War tensions at that time. With the decline of Cold War tensions, intolerance toward such groups has decreased. Different circumstances, however, can produce new targets for intolerance.

Sullivan *et al.* (1979) asked respondents in a 1978 national NORC survey to identify the group which they liked the least. Having chosen their individual "least liked" groups, the respondents were then asked six questions about the group. Some of these questions directly concern freedom of expression, and some get into the question of equal treatment for the disliked group. We again get into the overlap between support for freedom of expression and support for equality; people might not support equality before the law for those groups whose views they dislike, and this constitutes an obstacle to freedom of expression. Results for these six questions are presented in Table 2.5.

Let us briefly examine the question of equality for disliked groups first. It is clear from the results that Americans do not strongly support equality before the law with regard to these questions for their least liked group. While 59% rejected the idea that members of the disliked group should have their phones tapped,

TABLE 2.5
Percentages Tolerant of Their "Least Liked" Group in 1978[a]

	Percent Tolerant
Members of the (group) should be banned from being President of the U.S. (*Disagree*)	16
Members of the (group) should be allowed to teach in public schools. (*Agree*)	19
The (group) should have their phones tapped by our government. (*Disagree*)	59
The (group) should be allowed to hold public rallies in our city. (*Agree*)	34
Members of the (group) should be allowed to make a speech in this city. (*Agree*)	50
The (group) should be outlawed. (*Disagree*)	29

SOURCE: Adapted from Table 2 in John L. Sullivan, James Piereson, and George E. Marcus, "An Alternative Conceptualization of Political Tolerance: Illusory Increases 1950s–1970s," *American Political Science Review*, 73 (September, 1979), p. 787. Only the national results are used here.

[a] The individual respondent's least liked group was inserted in each question. The tolerant response is indicated in parentheses.

only 16% disagreed with the idea of banning a member of the group from being President of the United States and only 19% would allow a member of the group to teach in public schools.

Turning to the questions dealing more directly with freedom of expression, we see that only 29% of the respondents would oppose *outlawing* their least liked group. Thus, intolerance of the least liked group is so high that most Americans would even deny their legal right to exist. Further, only half (50%) would allow members of the group to give a speech, and only a third (34%) would allow members of the group to hold public rallies. Thus, if we consider the degree of tolerance Americans have for their individual least liked groups, such tolerance is very low.

Given such low levels of tolerance, what can prevent the massive violation of the civil liberties of a particular group? Laws and political institutions soften the effects of such intolerance; further, political leaders are generally more tolerant than the general public, a finding that will be discussed in a later chapter, and this helps to reduce the chances that a particular group will be persecuted. Another factor, however, is the fact that different people are intolerant toward different groups. Sullivan et al. (1979: 793) argue that the sheer diversity of targets means that intolerance does not become focused on a few select groups whose civil liberties are then violated on a massive basis. Referring to this situation as "pluralistic intolerance," Sullivan *et al.* (1979: 793) conclude that, even though levels of intolerance are quite high, the diversity of the targets prevents any substantial threat to civil liberties.

The conclusion that the condition of pluralistic intolerance does not lead to a substantial threat to civil liberties is a matter of judgment; it assumes that no problem presently exists. Given the results we have discussed, this assumption seems questionable. As an absolute minimum, we would expect that such low levels of tolerance in the American public would have a "chilling effect" on the expression of views by those groups whose beliefs are out of accord with the prevailing norms.

In the previous section we saw that support for tolerance in general statements of principles is very high. In this section we have seen that support for freedom of expression can be very low in some specific situations and very high in others. If the political actor is disliked, political tolerance toward the political actor is very low. Thus, there is a big gap between general principles and specific applications of tolerance.

POSSIBLE REASONS FOR THE GAP

Why is there such a contrast between the amount of support given to freedom of expression in the abstract and the amount of support given to such freedom when the context is made more specific? More will be said on this in a later chapter, but we can briefly speculate here on several possible reasons. First, some people might simply be unaware of the logical connection between general principles and applications of the principles. Some people might be incapable—either intellectually or psychologically—of carrying the general principles of tolerance to their logical conclusions. People are generally *taught* general principles concerning freedom of expression, but (as will be discussed in chapter 8) they are not usually taught specific applications. Thus, people might be unaware that there is any conflict between their support of the "slogans" of American democracy on the one hand and their rejection of applications of such ideals on the other hand.

Second, people might feel that there are logical, justifiable, reasonable exceptions or qualifications which must be made concerning the application of the general principles. A person could believe in freedom of speech for everyone but feel that it is obvious that such freedom applies only in certain circumstances. Some, for example, feel that it is not inconsistent with their belief in freedom of speech to deny freedom of speech to those who themselves oppose such freedom. A person might also feel that it is no violation of the right to demonstrate to allow demonstrations only under circumstances in which it can be absolutely guaranteed that this political act will be carried out in a completely orderly and peaceful manner. This view seems to be perfectly reasonable and democratic to some people.

Third, as already indicated, people hold different values which can conflict with one another under certain circumstances; the assignment of higher priority to one of these values can lead to a result which is inconsistent with the other value. Let's use an ordinary everyday example first. Suppose a person places a high value on honesty in dealing with people and also places a high value on kindness to people. In some cases, being honest to people and being kind to them can come into conflict with each other. In such situations, the person will have to choose between the two values in conflict, and the outcome will be inconsistent with one or the other of the two values. In the same way, some people can value freedom of speech and also hold other values which might come into conflict with the freedom of speech value under certain circumstances. For example, a person might assign greater priority to the value of social harmony, or patriotism, or the national interest, or whatever. The person might genuinely believe in freedom of speech, but the priority of this belief is lower in his or her hierarchy of beliefs than certain other values.

There are, then, several reasons for the gap between support for general principles of tolerance and specific applications of such principles. Part of this discussion will be further elaborated later in an examination of how people learn—or fail to learn—tolerance.

RELIGIOUS FREEDOM

The First Amendment begins: "Congress shall make no law respecting an establishment of religion, or prohibiting the free exercise thereof." Most of the discussion of First Amendment rights has concerned the expression of views (through speeches, demonstrations, petitions, and the press) and has not concerned religious freedom in a direct way. The exception to this is the examination of tolerance toward the expression of views by atheists. Other than this, not much has been said about religious freedom for the simple reason that there is not much survey information on people's attitudes concerning religious freedom issues. In the next chapter, we will get further into the question of equal treatment for people who hold certain religious views, but we are still left with little information on attitudes toward the exercise of religious freedom.

One aspect of religious freedom about which some survey information is available is the question of separation of church and state. In terms of the principles, there is not supposed to be an official religion in the United States. In actual practice, however, there is a semiofficial religious heritage based broadly on a Judeo-Christian foundation encompassing Protestants, Catholics, and Jews. On occasion, some people have objected to this church-state overlap. It is offensive, for example, to atheists to have the words *under God* in the Pledge of Allegiance, or to have *In God We Trust* on coins and paper money. Jews and some other religious groups outside the mainstream Protestant-Catholic tradition have sometimes objected to certain aspects of the church-state overlap which institute or honor Protestant-Catholic traditions at the expense of their traditions (e.g., state laws requiring stores to close on Sunday, which is the Sabbath for Protestants and Catholics but not for some other religious groups). For the most part, the objections of minorities to the church-state overlap have simply been ignored or ridiculed.

One area in which objections to the church-state overlap have recently ceased to be ignored is religious observances in the schools. During the 1960s, the Supreme Court handed down a series of decisions which declared that religious observances in the schools were unconstitutional, but these decisions have not been fully implemented. The reason for the failure to fully implement these decisions is that there is not strong public support for them. Various surveys have consistently shown that over 90% of Americans profess a belief in God. Further, approximately 90% of Americans are either Protestant or Catholic, and about 44% attend church at least two or three times a month (NORC 1977 General Social Survey). Within this context, it is not surprising that a majority of Americans are in favor of religious observances in the schools despite the Supreme Court's ruling. In 1963, 70% of Americans disapproved of the Supreme Court ruling that no state or local government could require the reading of the Lord's Prayer or Bible verses in public schools (Gallup, 1972: 1837). The proportion who disapprove of the Supreme Court's decision has declined only slightly over time to 64% in 1977 (NORC General Social Survey). In 1968, 81% of Americans favored starting each school day with a prayer (Survey Research Center 1968 National Election Study). In 1974, only 8% opposed *requiring* that the Lord's Prayer or Bible verses be read in schools; 31% favored requiring such religious observances and 58% would leave the decision to communities to decide (NORC 1974 General Social Survey). This indicates that Americans generally do not see this as a matter of minority rights; they see the question as one which the majority has the right to decide.

In the United States, religious differences among people do not cause much conflict for the vast majority in their day-to-day lives. Protestants and Catholics constitute the bulk of the population, and there are very few differences in *religious* views between these two groups that would ordinarily lead to even minor conflict. The church-state overlap violates the principle of separation of church and state, and it is a violation of the religious freedom of those who are not within the (primarily) Protestant-Catholic consensus. Despite this inconsistency with the First Amendment, however, the overlap has tremendously strong support in the American public. It is likely that minorities who object to the church-state overlap will continue to have most of their objections ignored or rejected.

SUMMARY

This chapter has examined the degree of tolerance among Americans in terms of support for freedom of expression as indicated in First Amendment rights. Let us briefly review some of the most fundamental findings.

First, Americans give overwhelming support to principles of tolerance when such principles are presented in a general, abstract fashion (e.g., "Do you believe in freedom of speech?").

Second, when the principles of tolerance are stated in an intermediate level of specificity, the level of tolerance among Americans decreases quite substantially. When the political act (e.g., speech making) or the political actor (the group or person who is to present a viewpoint) is specified (but not both political actor and political act), Americans are no longer responding to a set of slogans about American democracy, and the level of tolerance decreases.

Third, when Americans are asked about First Amendment rights for situations that are very specific (both the political act and the political actor are specified), the degree of tolerance depends on what the political act is and who the political actor is. Tolerance is very high when the group presenting the viewpoint is relatively noncontroversial and the political act is low in potential for social disruption. For example, almost everyone will allow a group of their neighbors to circulate a petition against crime. Tolerance decreases as the political act increases in its potential for social disruption; tolerance also decreases to the extent that the group is unpopular or its viewpoint is in conflict with prevailing sociopolitical norms. For example, support for the right of a group of atheists (a viewpoint deviating strongly from the norm) to hold a demonstration (a political act with a relatively high potential for social disruption) is very low.

Fourth, with regard to trends in tolerance, it is clear that tolerance among Americans for certain groups (Communists, socialists, and atheists) has increased dramatically since the 1950s. Some also argue that tolerance in general has increased. It is possible, however, that the old targets of intolerance have simply been replaced with new targets. Sullivan et al. (1979) demonstrate a very low level of tolerance among Americans for the groups which they like the least. On the other hand, Abramson (1980) points out that respondents in the Sullivan et al. (1979) study were more tolerant of their least liked groups than people were of Communists or atheists in 1954, thus providing some evidence that perhaps tolerance in general has increased.

Fifth, Americans do not strongly support freedom of religion. The right to religious freedom (including separation of church and state) of those who are not religious or those whose religious views are outside the Protestant-Catholic mainstream tends to be treated rather lightly by Americans. Objections to the church-state overlap are largely ignored.

We have seen that Americans do not give equal support to the rights of different groups to express their views. We turn now to a more extensive discussion of tolerance in the United States in terms of support for equality before the law and equal protection of the laws.

3

Tolerance as Support
for Equality

INTRODUCTION

Purpose of Chapter

In this and the following two chapters, we will examine American tolerance in terms of the level of support for legal equality, including equality before the law and equal protection of the laws. We have already gotten into this subject to a limited extent in the preceding chapter. We found, for example, that Americans hold different levels of support for First Amendment rights for different groups. We also found that many Americans are willing to prohibit members of certain groups from such activities as teaching in a college or holding the office of President. We will now examine support for equality more extensively.

Focus on Blacks and Women

Most of the information to be presented in these three chapters concerns support for equality for two particular groups, blacks and women. As discussed in chapter 1, these two groups were historically excluded from the liberal ideology which expounded freedom and equality for white men. Both groups have faced massive discrimination throughout American history, and both have made relatively recent strides toward the achievement of equality. In their efforts to achieve equality, blacks and women have had certain problems in common, but their situations have also been quite different in certain respects. Further, the efforts of blacks and women to achieve equality are similar in certain respects to such efforts by other minority groups, particularly ethnic or racial minorities such as Hispanics and native Americans. However, blacks and women are readily identifiable on the basis of biological/ physical characteristics, thus distinguishing them from many minority groups whose identifying characteristics center around belief systems (e.g., Jews, Catholics, atheists, socialists) or ethnic background (e.g., Americans of Polish, Italian, or Irish descent).

Although there are good theoretical reasons for focusing on blacks and women in these chapters, the basic reason is that these are the two groups about whom the most survey information on public attitudes is available. Both groups encompass dramatic movements in recent times and survey researchers have attempted to gauge public reactions to these movements. Both groups are also relatively large in comparison with some minority groups. Women are, of course, a slight majority of the population, and there are over 25 million black people in the United States. Many other groups which might be considered have received less attention from survey researchers because they were less dramatic (and therefore less salient to the general public) or extremely small in numbers. The focus of this book is on attitudes of tolerance in the American public; if there is no information available concerning public attitudes toward a particular minority, then there is little we can say about tolerance for that group.

Despite the limitations on the information available, an attempt will be made in this chapter to formulate some generalizations which encompass attitudes toward equality for a wide range of minorities. The situation of certain minority groups (e.g., Jews) will also be briefly discussed. Because of the much greater amount of information available concerning attitudes toward blacks and women, each of these two groups will be discussed more extensively in separate chapters.

Equality and Discrimination

We need to clarify the term *equality before the law* as it is used in this chapter. Without getting into a complex legal or philosophical analysis, we can just say that support for equality before the law will be examined in terms of (1) support for equality in political and legal rights and (2) opposition to unjustified discrimination in such matters as hiring for jobs, job promotions, housing, public transportation, and sales and services in public facilities.

Unjustified discrimination refers here to discrimination against persons on the basis of characteristics (biological/physical, social, or belief characteristics) which are not fundamentally relevant to the situation. Discrimination against people can be justifiable or unjustifiable, depending upon whether the basis on which it is done is truly relevant to the situation. For example, an employer who wishes to hire a bookkeeper is certainly justified in discriminating against people who have an inadequate knowledge of bookkeeping (a relevant characteristic for the situation), but it is not justifiable to discriminate against a person simply because the person is black (an irrelevant characteristic for the situation). What about an employer who refuses to hire women for a particular job because the job requires physical strength? This too is unjustified discrimination. While it is true that the average man has greater physical strength than the average woman, this policy would automatically exclude those women who do have the physical strength for the job. The employer is justified in not hiring people who lack the physical strength for the job (a relevant characteristic) but not in automatically excluding people on the basis of sex (an irrelevant characteristic).

It must be acknowledged that it is not always an easy matter to determine whether a particular characteristic is a relevant or an irrelevant basis for discrimination in a particular situation. One approach to this problem is to define relevance on the basis of legality; thus, discrimination is unjustified in a situation if it is done on the basis of a characteristic which the law prohibits from being taken into consideration in such situations. Since a great deal of what I consider to be unjustifiable discrimination is illegal today, this approach is helpful. However, not all of what I consider to be unjustified discrimination is prohibited by law. For example, sexual discrimination is still legally permitted in some situations (e.g., husband-wife property ownership matters in some states) in which sex is not truly relevant. Although the concept of relevance will continue to be a difficult problem, another distinction can be made which should aid in clarifying the concept. A characteristic is irrelevant as a basis for discrimination if ignorance of that characteristic would cause no problem in the situation (e.g., for the successful completion of a job); conversely a characteristic is a relevant basis for discrimination if ignorance of that characteristic would cause problems. For example, suppose a person applies for a job. No real problem would result if by some magical process no one knew such irrelevant characteristics of this person as race, sex, political beliefs, ethnicity, and so on. However, a problem would develop if *relevant* characteristics (e.g., the physical or mental ability to do the job) were not known. Thus, relevant characteristics for discrimination are characteristics which could directly cause intrinsic problems in a situation; irrelevant characteristics can cause problems only as a result of the personal or social attitudes which have been developed toward these characteristics.

Another distinction concerning the usage of the concept of equality needs to be made. We are dealing here with equality before the law, including the idea of equal protection of the laws; we are not dealing with equality in terms of a more equal distribution of the wealth of the country. There is a great deal of inequality of income and wealth in the United States, and much of this economic inequality is due to unjustified discrimination. This inequality of wealth and income raises very important political and social questions, but an extensive analysis of such questions is outside the scope of this book.

GENERAL OBSERVATIONS

Here an attempt will be made to develop a series of general observations regarding the American public's attitudes toward equality. These observations are intended to apply to a wide range of groups, blacks and women included. In this way, I hope to develop a perspective which transcends the limitations on the information available concerning the public's attitudes toward equality for particular groups.

Increases in Tolerance

In chapter 2, we saw that there had been a dramatic increase in tolerance since the 1950s toward certain groups in terms of support for First Amendment rights. In terms of support for equality, there has been a similar trend of increasing tolerance. One important indicator of tolerance toward members of a particular group is the expressed willingness of the public to vote for a member of that group for public office. Fortunately, survey researchers have been interested in this type of question for some time, at least with regard to hypothetical black, women, Jewish, or Catholic candidates. The results of these polls (Table 3.1) indicate substantial increases in tolerance during the last twenty or thirty years. Although the surveys from the 1930s did not use strict probability samples and are probably less accurate than later surveys, they indicate that during the 1930s only about a third of Americans were willing to vote for a woman for President. This proportion slowly but steadily rose to 76% in 1978. The trend with regard to a hypothetical black candidate followed basically the same pattern. Jews started out at a higher point (46% willing to vote for a Jewish candidate in the 1930s) and ended up at a higher point (82% in 1978) than blacks or women. Catholics were accorded the most equality of these four groups and by 1978, 91% of Americans were willing to vote for a Catholic candidate for U.S. President.

TABLE 3.1
Percentages Willing to Vote for a Woman or
Minority Candidate for President, 1937–1978[a]

Year	Woman	Black	Jew	Catholic
1936–37	31	—	46	64
1958	55	38	62	68
1963	56	47	77	84
1969	55	67	86	88
1972	70	69	—	—
1978	76	77	82	91

SOURCES: Information for a woman, black, or Jewish candidate for 1958–1972 is from Gallup polls and National Opinion Research Center polls reported in Myra Marx Ferree, "A Woman for President? Changing Responses: 1958–1972," *Public Opinion Quarterly*, 38 (Fall, 1974), p. 392. Other information is from *Gallup Opinion Index* (April, 1969 and November, 1978).

[a] The format for the woman-for-President question is, "If your party nominated a woman for President, would you vote for her if she were qualified for the job?" For other candidates, the format is, "If your party nominated a generally well-qualified man for President, and he happened to be a [e.g., black], would you vote for him?"

These trends indicate that intolerance on the basis of sex, race, and religious preference has declined. On the other hand, note that there are still people who would automatically exclude each of these groups from the Presidency. Anti-Catholicism was once rather extensive in the United States, but it now appears to reside chiefly in a rather tiny minority. Intolerance toward the other three groups continues more extensively.

Since attitudes toward these four groups have followed a pattern of increasing tolerance, it is probably safe to say that tolerance toward many other types of minorities has also increased. We might speculate, for example, that if we had similar information concerning attitudes toward a Polish-American for President, it would show that such support is greater than at an earlier time. It is also apparent, however, that the degree of willingness to vote for a member of a particular group for President might not be high enough to make it actually possible for such a candidate to get elected. Further, even with increases in tolerance, there is still not yet a majority willing to vote for members of certain particularly unpopular minority groups. For example, in a 1978 survey, Gallup included questions about a hypothetical atheist candidate and a hypothetical homosexual candidate for President. Only 40% would vote for an atheist and only 26% would vote for a homosexual candidate (*Gallup Opinion Index*, November, 1978: 26).

In sum, there is an apparent trend toward greater support for equality. At the same time, this level of support might not be high enough in some situations to be effective, and in other situations it is still low in absolute terms.

Perception of Discrimination

One problem which complicates the quest for equality for many victims of discrimination in the United States is that many Americans, even when they support discrimination, refuse to acknowledge the existence of discrimination. As we shall see later, sometimes even the victims of discrimination deny its existence. The results in the first column of Table 3.2 indicate that only a minority of Americans perceive that there is discrimination against blacks,

TABLE 3.2
Perception of Discrimination against Specific Groups and Support for Outlawing Job Discrimination

Group	Percent Who Perceive Discrimination against the Group[a]	Percent Who Support Outlawing Job Discrimination against the Group[b]
Homosexuals	55	54
Blacks	41	73
Puerto Ricans	33	73
Mexican-Americans	32	74
Women	31	76
Jews	19	75
Catholics	5	75

SOURCE: 1977 Harris Poll reported in Connie de Boer, "The Polls: Attitudes toward Homosexuality," *Public Opinion Quarterly*, 42 (Summer, 1978), pp. 272–273.

[a] Question: "Do you feel that [group] are discriminated against more than most other people, less, or no more than others." The "more" responses are reported above.

[b] Question: "Would you favor or oppose a law which outlawed discrimination against [group] in any job for which they were qualified?"

Puerto Ricans, Mexican-Americans, women, Jews, or Catholics. The only group against whom a majority perceives that there is discrimination is homosexuals. As we shall see later, when questions concerning blacks or women are worded differently, the proportion who perceive discrimination against these groups is higher. Nevertheless, this tendency on the part of many Americans to deny the existence of discrimination persists. This important pattern of attitudes among many people has important consequences for any group which attempts to overcome discrimination; it is difficult to get support from people to end discrimination when such people will not acknowledge the existence of discrimination.

Support for Laws against Discrimination

Another important point, which will be further documented later, is that Americans don't necessarily support laws or policies to end discrimination. The results in the second column of Table 3.2 show that approximately three-fourths of the respondents would favor outlawing job discrimination against each of the groups except homosexuals. However, three points need to be made. First, there is still a substantial minority which does not support such laws. Second, Americans have generally been much more supportive of equality in job-related issues than in many other areas. Third, the respondents were asked this question in 1977, after job discrimination against most of these groups had already been outlawed.

Blaming the Victim

There is sometimes a tendency among Americans to put the blame for a wrong on the victim who has been wronged. This pattern is demonstrated by the tendency of some people to place the responsibility for an act of rape on the woman who has been raped. During 1938, a survey asked Americans: "Do you think the persecution of the Jews in Europe has been their own fault?" A majority of Americans (58%) responded that the persecution was either partly or entirely the fault of the Jews themselves (Cantril, 1951: 381). When the National Guard killed four students at Kent State University during a demonstration, a majority of Americans (63%) indicated that the students were more to blame for the deaths than the National Guard was (Chandler, 1972: 148).

This pattern of blaming the victim is also found with regard to attitudes toward the victims of discrimination; the victims themselves may be held responsible for their lack of equality. This has been especially true with regard to attitudes toward blacks (as will be demonstrated in the next chapter), but it also applies to attitudes toward disadvantaged minorities generally. This pattern constitutes another obstacle in the path of any group which is attempting to overcome discrimination. It is very difficult to get support for ending discrimination from a person who blames the victims of discrimination for their lack of equality.

Opposition to Compensatory Programs

A history of discrimination against a group in society places obstacles in the path of that group's achievement of equality in terms of income, education, jobs, and other matters. The removal of such obstacles at some point in time does not automatically bring about equality; by that point, the group might be at a virtually permanent disadvantage. In order to counteract the effects of past discrimination and bring the group up to par with the rest of society, compensatory programs might be used. For a period of time or until such time as certain goals are met, "reverse discrimination" in favor of the disadvantaged group might be used. Americans, however, do not support such efforts to correct the effects of past discrimination. Table 3.3 indicates that the overwhelming majority of Americans (83%) reject the idea of giving preferential treatment to women and members of minority groups in getting jobs and college admissions. Further, the breakdown by sex and race indicates

TABLE 3.3
Attitudes toward Compensatory Programs
by Sex and Race, in Percentages

Some people say that to make up for past discrimination, women and members of minority groups should be given preferential treatment in getting jobs and places in college. Others say that ability, as determined by test scores, should be the main consideration. Which point comes closest to how you feel on this matter?

	Give Preference	Ability	No Opinion
Total Sample	10	83	7
Men	10	84	6
Women	11	82	7
Whites	8	86	6
Nonwhites	27	64	9

SOURCE: *Gallup Opinion Index*, June, 1977, p. 23.

that a large majority of both women (82%) and nonwhites (64%) reject such programs. Thus, there is little support for programs to compensate the victims of discrimination.

Individual Action vs. Collective Action

Another important attitude held by many Americans concerning equality for women or minority groups is the feeling that the solution for discrimination must be brought about through individual efforts rather than collective efforts. The victim of discrimination is urged to work hard and be assured that success will be forthcoming; collective action to overcome discrimination is unnecessary. Table 3.4 demonstrates that Americans overwhelmingly (85% in 1976) accept this type of idea with regard to blacks: the best way for blacks to handle discrimination is to act like any other American—work hard, get a good education, and mind their own business. The results also show—although the question is worded differently—that a substantial proportion of Americans accept this type of idea with regard to women. In 1976, 47% gave their approval to the idea that the best way for women to overcome discrimination is to pursue their individual career goals in as feminine a way as possible—as opposed to the idea that women must work together to change laws and customs that are unfair to all women. Note, however, that a shift of opinion occurred between 1972 and 1976; in 1972, a majority (58%) selected the individualistic solution to discrimination against women, but in 1976, a majority (53%) chose the collective solution. Some substantial changes in public attitudes concerning the situation of women occurred during the 1970s. Nevertheless, with regard to women and to members of minority groups, many Americans (perhaps a strong majority, depending on the particular group involved) oppose collective efforts— and public policies—designed to overcome discrimination; instead, they place the responsibility on the victim of discrimination who is to overcome such discrimination through vigorous individual efforts.

Qualifications on Support for Equality

We noted in chapter 2 that Americans give consensual support to general principles related to the popular theory of democracy, including equality and freedom of expression; however, support for specific applications of such principles is much lower. The idea of equality is taught as a "slogan" in the American political system, and a person's agreement with such general, abstract ideas does

TABLE 3.4
Individual Achievement vs. Collective Action to Overcome
Racial and Sexual Discrimination, 1972–1976

Pair Statements[a]	1972, in %	1976, in %
Racial Discrimination "Discrimination affects all black people. The only way to handle it is for all blacks to organize together and demand rights for all."	17	15
OR		
"Discrimination may affect all blacks but the best way to handle it is for each individual to act like any other American—to work hard, get a good education and mind his own business."	83	85
Sexual Discrimination "Women can best overcome discrimination by pursuing their individual career goals in as feminine a way as possible."	58	47
OR		
"It is not enough for a woman to be successful herself; women must work together to change laws and customs that are unfair to all women."	42	53

SOURCE: Center for Political Studies, University of Michigan.
[a] Respondents were asked to indicate with which of the two statements they agreed more.

not necessarily indicate that person's attitude with regard to specific applications of such principles. In terms of specific applications, the person might support inequality for a wide range of groups. Or the person might support equality for groups he or she likes and reject equality for disliked groups. For example, a person might perceive injustice in discrimination against blacks and thus support racial equality while feeling that the inequalities between men and women are perfectly natural and fair. Or, to take another example, a person might feel that it is wrong to discriminate against people on the basis of such biological characteristics as race or sex, but that it is reasonable to discriminate against people who have voluntarily subscribed to beliefs (political, social, economic, religious, or other types of beliefs) which deviate from prevailing norms. Thus, a person's stance on the abstract concept of equality doesn't tell us much about that person's attitude concerning a specific application of the concept. Moreover, this process of qualifying support for equality must be taken one step further. Even those who support equality for a particular group might greatly qualify that support. Some of these qualifications will be briefly discussed here; they will be further illustrated later.

First, those who support equality for a particular group in principle might not support it in practice. It is easy to pay lip service to a principle; it is usually much more difficult to abide by the principle in everyday life, especially if abiding by the principle might entail personal costs of some sort.

Second, those who support equality for a particular group might support it only for certain types of situations. For example, a person might have a genuine belief in racial equality for job-related matters but oppose neighborhood integration. Or, to take another example, a person might support the principle of equal pay for equal work for homosexuals but oppose the employment of homosexuals in many types of occupations. Attitudes toward equality for particular groups in society usually follow a spectrum, with high support for equality in certain types of situations and low support for equality in certain other types of situations. In the next chapter, this pattern will be further demonstrated with regard to equality for blacks, and it will be suggested that the degree of support for equality in particular situations depends to a certain extent on the amount of personal—as opposed to impersonal—contact involved in the situation.

Third, those who support equality might give it such low priority that the support has no practical effect. In chapter 2 it was suggested that some of those who believe in freedom of speech might oppose it in specific circumstances because it conflicted with another, higher priority value which they hold (e.g., fear of social disruption). Similarly, those who support equality might oppose it when it conflicts in specific circumstances with other values they hold. For example, although some of the people who oppose busing for purposes of racial integration of schools are simply racists, it is clear that not everyone who opposes busing is a racist. Many of these nonracists who oppose busing are simply weighing two values: the value of school integration vs. the costs of busing (inconvenience, distance, possible traffic dangers, increased taxes, etc.). In the weighing process, the value of racial integration and equality might lose out to other values. Thus, among many Americans who believe in equality for a particular group, the priority given to this value is so low that it will provide no help toward actual progress in achieving equality. The value on equality might be so low for some people that it has no effect whatsoever on their decisions and behavior.

Summary of Observations

In this section, an attempt has been made to develop a series of observations which related to support for equality for a wide range of groups. First, it appears that there has been an increase in support for equality for a number of groups over the last twenty or thirty years; however, in absolute terms, support for equality is not very high for some groups. Second, there is a tendency among many Americans to deny the existence of discrimination; this constitutes an obstacle for any group which is attempting to achieve equality. Third, Americans don't necessarily support laws or policies to end discrimination. Fourth, there is a tendency among some Americans to blame the victims of discrimination for their situation; this creates another obstacle in the path of those who would achieve equality. Fifth, Americans do not support the idea of compensatory programs to make up for past discrimination against a group. Sixth, many Americans seem to feel that the responsibility for overcoming discrimination must be placed on the individual victim of discrimination; individual efforts, rather than collective efforts, are stressed. Finally, many who support equality for a particular group qualify that support. They might support equality for a group in principle but not in actual practice. They might support equality for the group in some situations but not in others. Or they might give the value of equality such low priority in their hierarchy of values that it has no practical effects.

Having developed a series of generalizations concerning support for equality for a range of groups, we turn our attention in the rest of this chapter to the situation of certain types of groups. Then in the two chapters which follow, the situation of blacks and women will be discussed more extensively.

EQUALITY AND RELIGION

It is probably safe to say that there is very little discrimination against Protestants on the basis of their religious preference and that those who discriminate against Catholics today are a very small minority. Those who would discriminate against Jews are a minority, but not an insignificant minority. Other religious groups in the United States are so small that we have no information concerning how the public feels about them. Lastly, the majority of Americans do support discrimination against atheists. Thus, with regard to discrimination on the basis of religious views, the basic concern needs to be limited to attitudes toward Jews and atheists.

Equality for Jews

Jews constitute only about 3% of the American population. With regard to attitudes toward this minority, we have already seen that the percentage willing to vote for a Jew for President increased from only 46% in the 1930s to 82% in 1978; we have also seen that 75% of Americans expressed support for outlawing job discrimination against Jews. Thus, substantial anti-Semitism appears to be confined to a rather small group. Stember's (1966: 208) examination of a variety of polls taken between the 1930s and the 1960s led him to the conclusion that there was a massive decline in anti-Semitism during this period. Similarly, Solotaroff and Sklare (1966: 3) state that anti-Semitism is no longer a particularly overt phenomenon and that most Jews are not bothered with bigotry or discrimination in their daily lives.

It appears that many Americans are somewhat *prejudiced* against Jews, but the level of support for *discrimination* against Jews is rather low. Selznick and Steinberg (1969: 185) conclude that anti-Semitism of most Americans is limited to acceptance of anti-Semitic beliefs and support for relatively mild forms of discrimination. Quinley and Glock (1979: 186) similarly conclude that anti-Semitism today basically involves holding negative images of Jews (e.g., that Jews are deceitful, dishonest, pushy, clannish, vain, and that they largely control the media, motion picture, and banking industries). Quinley and Glock (1979: 7) suggest that roughly one-third of the American public is anti-Semitic, a third is moderately prejudiced, and the other third is unprejudiced.

Another way to examine tolerance toward Jews is to look at attitudes toward intermarriage. In 1978, 69% of Americans approved of marriage between Jews and non-Jews, which is about the same as the 73% who approved of intermarriage between Protestants and Catholics (*Gallup Opinion Index*, November, 1978: 27). This again demonstrates that anti-Semitism is a minority—but a substantial minority—phenomenon in terms of discrimination.

Although those who have studied anti-Semitism in the United States usually conclude that support for discrimination against Jews has declined to a rather low point, many of them (e.g., Selznick and Steinberg, 1969; Stember, 1966) also express the fear that the trend could be reversed in times of crisis. During 1960, a wave of anti-Semitic vandalism and violence occurred. Public opinion strongly condemned these acts, but such acts continue, and this demonstrates the potential for anti-Semitism should there ever be a reversal of the trend toward the support for equality for Jews. The greater activity of neo-Nazi groups in the United States in recent times is also cause for concern. Selznick and Steinberg (1969) are concerned about the lack of a strong, clearcut commitment among Americans to reject anti-Semitism. They present the results for the question: "If a candidate for Congress should declare himself as being against the Jews, would this influence you to vote for him or against him?" If there was a strong, positive commitment to reject anti-Semitism, we might expect that almost everyone would say they would vote against such a candidate. However, only 58% indicated that they would vote against such a candidate (Selznick and Steinberg, 1969: 54).

In sum, although prejudice against Jews may be fairly widespread in the United States, support for discrimination against Jews is fairly low. However, given the lack of a strong, positive consensus to reject anti-Semitism, the possibility remains that under certain circumstances there could be a revival of support for substantial discrimination against American Jews.

Equality for Atheists

Like Jews, atheists constitute a small minority of less than 5% of the American population. Agnostics constitute another group about the same percentage of the population as atheists. Since the information available concerns atheists and since the general population probably makes little distinction between atheists and agnostics, the remarks here will be limited to attitudes toward atheists.

The available information concerning public attitudes toward equality for atheists has already been presented; here this information will be summarized and an attempt will be made to generalize from this information. Earlier it was indicated that in 1978, only 40% of Americans were willing to vote for an atheist for President. Considering that 75% indicated a willingness to vote for a woman, a Jew, or a black for President, this indicates that support for equality for atheists is at a very low level. Also, only a minority (39% in 1977) would allow an atheist to teach in college. Further, there was not strong support for First Amendment rights for atheists; in 1977, only 62% would allow an atheist to give a public speech and only 59% opposed removing a book written by an atheist from the public library. From these results, we can generalize that there is fairly strong support among Americans for discrimination against atheists in a number of situations. It is clear, for example, that there has actually been discrimination against atheists in hiring for jobs. For example, until relatively recently, applicants for teaching positions in some public school systems had to affirm their belief in God.

As indicated earlier, the church-state overlap in the United States is offensive to atheists and constitutes a form of discrimination against them. However, in terms of many other possible types of discrimination against atheists, there are several factors which serve to minimize actual discrimination. First, atheists as a minority are not readily identifiable—as blacks are—and therefore are not such easy targets for generalized discrimination. Second, religion is a topic which people usually avoid in most types of day-to-day situations, thus reducing the possibility of discrimination against *any* person on the basis of religious views. Third, perhaps because of the two reasons above and also because atheists are such a tiny minority, the support for discrimination against atheists is ordinarily a rather passive belief.

In sum, there is widespread support for discrimination against atheists, but the relative invisibility of atheists prevents much actual discrimination against them under most circumstances, except for the symbolic discrimination arising out of the church-state overlap (e.g., religious observances in the schools). On the other hand, atheists who are known to be atheists or who wish to openly espouse their beliefs will probably face a much greater level of discrimination from the American public.

EQUALITY AND HOMOSEXUALS

Homosexuals are a very unpopular minority and support for discrimination against them is high. Levitt and Klassen (1974: 34) report that 84% of the respondents in their national survey considered homosexuality to be obscene and vulgar, and a 1973 National Opinion Research Center survey found that 69% of Americans said that sexual relations between two adults of the same sex are always wrong. Thus, an overwhelming majority of Americans disapprove of homosexuality; this disapproval no doubt has an effect on the level of support for equality for homosexuals. It also needs to be noted, however, that Americans are split on the question of whether there should be laws against homosexuality: in 1977, 43% said "yes" and 43% said "no" (with 14% undecided) on the question of whether homosexual relations between consenting adults should be legal (*Gallup Opinion Index*, October, 1977: 18).

We saw in chapter 2 that support for First Amendment rights for homosexuals was not high; for example, in 1977, only 62% would allow a speech by a homosexual and only 55% would oppose removing a book by a homosexual from the public library. Also, only 49% would allow a homosexual to teach in college. Earlier in this chapter, we saw that a majority (55%) perceived that there is discrimination against homosexuals and 54% support outlawing job discrimination against them. Although in most of the situations above a majority does oppose discrimination against homosexuals, the majority is not strong; there is certainly no consensus in favor of equal treatment of homosexuals.

In 1977, a majority (56%) said that homosexuals should have equal rights in terms of job opportunities (*Gallup Opinion Index*, October, 1977: 3). This question, however, is rather general. In the same survey, Gallup asked whether homosexuals should or should not be hired for certain occupations. Levitt and Klassen (1974) had asked similar types of questions in 1970. Results from both surveys

TABLE 3.5
Percentages Who Would Not Allow Homosexuals
to Work in Specific Occupations[a]

Occupation	1970	1977
Schoolteacher	77	71
Court judge	77	—
Minister (1970)/clergy (1977)	77	60
Doctor	68	50
Government official	67	—
Armed forces	—	43
Beautician	28	—
Salesperson	—	24
Florist	13	—

SOURCES: 1970 data, Eugene E. Levitt and Albert D. Klassen, Jr., "Public Attitudes toward Homosexuality," *Journal of Homosexuality*, 1 (Fall, 1974), p. 33; 1977 data, *Gallup Opinion Index*, October, 1977, pp. 4–8.

[a] The Gallup question was: "Do you think homosexuals should or should not be hired for the following occupations." Levitt and Klassen asked whether homosexual men should or should not be allowed to work in the following professions. In order to make the two studies more comparable, those with no opinion have been excluded in computing the percentages.

are presented in Table 3.5. There is very strong support for discrimination against homosexuals in certain occupations; for example, over 70% would not allow a homosexual to teach in school. It also appears that some people are opposed to hiring homosexuals in just about any occupation; for example, 13% would not even allow a homosexual to work as a florist.

In recent times, many homosexuals in certain areas of the country have "come out of the closet" to demand equal rights in such matters as jobs and housing. This gay rights movement has been partly successful in some places (e.g., San Francisco), and it has met with failure in other places (e.g., in 1977, the voters in Miami, Florida, overturned a city ordinance which prohibited discrimination against homosexuals in such matters as jobs and housing). The 1970 questions asked by Levitt and Klassen and the 1977 questions asked by Gallup were not exactly the same; thus, we cannot place a great deal of confidence in a comparison of these results to determine the trend in attitudes. With this caution in mind, however, we can speculate on the trends in attitudes toward equal job opportunities for homosexuals by looking at the three occupations which both studies included. In all three cases (schoolteacher, minister or clergy, and doctor), opposition to having a homosexual work in such an occupation appears to have decreased between 1970 and 1977. Again, we cannot be certain that there was an actual change in attitudes because the questions were worded differently in the two surveys. But it does appear that there is a trend toward greater support for equality for homosexuals. On the other hand, the questions concerning freedom of expression for homosexuals discussed in chapter 2 have been asked by the National Opinion Research Center since 1973; an examination of the results for the 1973–1977 time period indicates that the proportion favoring freedom of expression for homosexuals remained almost exactly the same throughout this time period, indicating no trend toward greater support for the rights of homosexuals. Thus, we cannot be sure whether tolerance for homosexuals is increasing or remaining stable.

EQUALITY AND ETHNICITY

There is not much information on national attitudes concerning discrimination against people on the basis of ethnic background. We saw earlier that about a third of the population believes that there is discrimination against Puerto Ricans and Mexican-Americans; that same 1977 Harris survey (reported in De Boer, 1978: 272–273) indicated that only 14% perceived discrimination against either Japanese-Americans or Chinese-Americans, and only 7% perceived discrimination against Italian-Americans. Further, approximately three-fourths of the respondents indicated support for laws to end any job discrimination against each of these groups. There is probably some *prejudice* against almost all ethnic groups (except perhaps Anglo-Americans), and there has been very serious *discrimination* against some ethnic groups. However, if the question were asked, it is highly probable that those who would support in *principle* a policy of discrimination against any group on the basis of ethnic background would be a rather small minority. This generalization is more accurate with regard to some ethnic groups than it is for others. Ethnic groups whose members are not easily identifiable are more easily accepted in American society; support for discrimination against such groups could be expected to be rather low.

On the other hand, support for discrimination based on ethnicity is higher for those ethnic groups which are more easily identifiable. This is especially so when the concepts of ethnicity and race become intertwined. Aside from blacks (Afro-Americans), the best example of this problem is the situation of Mexican-Americans, a population of about 7 to 8 million. In parts of the United States, the Southwest especially, there is a great deal of prejudice and discrimination against Mexican-Americans and others with a Spanish surname (Gomez, 1974; Rivera, 1976). In certain areas, Hispanics have been treated as badly as blacks have. The same is true for native Americans, another group which is viewed in terms of both ethnicity and race. And, of course, there are other groups (e.g., Japanese-Americans or Vietnamese-Americans) who are distinguished on the basis of both ethnicity and race-related concepts. Racial concepts need not, however, form the basis for the high visibility of a particular ethnic group; the group might be easily identifiable on the basis of its retention of traditional language, clothes, or customs. But whatever the basis for the distinction, we could expect support for discrimination on the basis of ethnicity to be much higher for those ethnic groups which are easily identifiable.

As a final note on discrimination and ethnicity, it is clear that the situation of a particular ethnic group within the United States can depend quite heavily on the international situation. In times of crisis or tension in international affairs, intolerance toward a particular ethnic group can grow tremendously. The most recent example of this is the situation of Iranians living in the United States during the hostage crisis; many Iranians (or those who look like they might be Iranians) here have been harassed by Americans who were frustrated and angry over the hostage situation. One of my students reported that he was harassed numerous times during the hostage situation because people thought he was Iranian; ironically, he is an anti-Iranian Libyan.

In sum, prejudice and discrimination against people on the basis of ethnicity still exists. However, it appears that support for discrimination on the basis of ethnicity on *principle* has declined, just as support for discrimination against blacks on principle has declined.

SUMMARY

In this chapter an attempt has been made to formulate some generalizations which encompass attitudes toward equality for a wide range of minorities, despite the lack of information on the public's attitudes toward equality for most minorities in the United States. In the next two chapters many of these generalizations will be demonstrated further. Also, the situations with regard to public support for discrimination on the basis of religious views, homosexuality, and ethnic background have been briefly discussed.

It might be useful to think in terms of a "ladder of equality." At the top of the ladder is a level at which the public supports equality and rejects discrimination. People at this level need not worry about anyone discriminating against them except in very limited circumstances. Near the top of the ladder are those groups for which public support for discrimination has nearly disappeared; Catholics, for example, are just one step from the top. Below that are groups for whom support for discrimination still exists but is not generally very substantial; Jews and many ethnic groups would be at this level. Below that are groups for whom public support for discrimination is somewhat stronger; Mexican-Americans, blacks, and highly visible ethnic groups would be at this level. Below that are groups for whom American public support for discrimination is strong; such particularly unpopular groups as homosexuals, atheists, Communists, and socialists—groups whose *beliefs* are dramatically out of accord with prevailing norms—occupy this level.

Given this concept of a ladder of equality, it appears that in the last twenty or thirty years almost all these groups have moved up the ladder to some extent. In the next two chapters, a more extensive examination will be made of the situations of two groups (blacks and women) who have definitely moved up the ladder in recent years in terms of public support for equality.

4

Support for Equality
for Black Americans

BACKGROUND

A number of general observations have been made concerning American support for minority groups in the previous chapter. In this chapter, a more extensive exploration will be made of the attitudes Americans hold concerning equality for black citizens. Earlier a trend toward greater tolerance of blacks was noted with respect to the public's willingness to vote for a black person for President. This trend also applies to a number of other issues involving equality for blacks. Before getting into recent trends, however, let's take a look at some of the earlier surveys on this topic. It should be noted that these earlier surveys were not based on strict probability samples and therefore probably contain more error than recent surveys.

During the 1940s, racial segregation was the rule—integration was the exception—and this separation of the races was widely supported by the public. In 1944, Gunnar Myrdal's *An American Dilemma* was published, indicating that Americans gave strong support to certain principles of democracy and equality but denied these principles in connection with black people. The pervasiveness of racial separatism is indicated by poll results from the early 1940s (Cantril, 1951: 508, 510, 988):

- 84% favored separate sections of towns and cities for blacks.
- 69% favored separate restaurants for whites and blacks.

- 66% favored school segregation.
- 52% thought whites should have the first chance at jobs.
- 51% favored racial segregation in the armed forces.
- 51% favored racial segregation in street cars and buses.

Some progress was made in desegregation during the 1950s, and by the end of the decade, it was no longer so acceptable to advocate openly racist policies. At that point, people would generally agree with the idea of racial equality as an abstract principle. McClosky's (1964) 1957–58 study, however, indicates that more specific statements of racist sentiments still received substantial support. For example, 49% agreed: "When it comes to the things that count most, all races are certainly not equal" (McClosky, 1964: 370).

A lot that was relevant to the race issue occurred during the 1960s. With Martin Luther King, Jr., as the most prominent leader, black and white civil rights workers in the early 1960s engaged in a series of marches, sit-ins, freedom rides, and other methods to confront the American conscience. The peaceful efforts of civil rights workers were met with violence and harassment, but—largely in reaction to the publicized violence—public opinion in favor of civil rights began to grow. Following President Kennedy's assassination, President Johnson was able to obtain passage of legislation that President Kennedy had wanted in order to outlaw discrimination against blacks in a number of areas; the 1964 Civil Rights Act was a major victory for the elimination of any legal basis for racial discrimination. This victory was followed by others, such as the 1965 Voting Rights Act which would assure that blacks in the South could no longer be prevented from voting. By the end of the 1960s, the legal basis for racial discrimination was almost totally demolished.

During the latter part of the 1960s, however, black protests took a different turn. Many blacks had expected that their lives would be dramatically improved by the victories of the civil rights movement, but immediate changes in their *economic* situation were not forthcoming. Marx (1969: 12) aptly notes that the right to sit next to a white man in a restaurant is irrelevant to those who have no money for restaurants. There was little change in the economic situation of blacks (Dye, 1971; Thurow, 1976). Unemployment among blacks remained high in comparison with whites and the median family income of black families remained at little better than half the median income of white families. For example, in 1947, the median family income of blacks was 51% of the median family income of whites; by 1975, the proportion had only increased to 58% (Dye and Zeigler, 1978: 350). Thus, although black Americans have made progress in desegregation, they have not made much progress in their economic situation.

The contrast between the rising expectations of blacks and the actual results led to a great deal of frustration on the part of many blacks. Although never achieving much support or power, some new organizations developed which rejected the nonviolence of Martin Luther King's approach. The frustration also led to a series of riots by blacks in the ghettos of some cities during the late 1960s. It became popular to say at this point that there was a "white backlash," that many whites who supported equality for blacks were backing away from the commitment in reaction to the violent incidents of the later 1960s. Evidence to be discussed later, however, indicates that there really wasn't any substantial white backlash.

The dramatic changes in the situation of blacks were made during the 1960s; thereafter, changes would be less dramatic and slower. The process of desegregation is not yet complete, however, and the economic disparity between whites and blacks is still very substantial.

TRENDS IN ATTITUDES TOWARD INTEGRATION

General Views of Desegregation

Table 4.1 presents results on attitudes toward desegregation in general from 1964 to 1976. During this time, support for desegrega-

TABLE 4.1
General Attitudes toward Desegregation, 1964–1976, in Percentages

Are you in favor of desegregation, strict segregation, or something in between?

	1964	1968	1976
Desegregation	32	36	39
Something in between	44	47	49
Segregation	23	16	9
Don't know	1	1	3

SOURCE: Survey Research Center/Center for Political Studies, University of Michigan.

tion increased a small amount, from 32% to 39%. Perhaps more important, the support for strict segregation decreased from 23% to only 9%; thus, strict segregationists became a very small minority of the population. On the other hand, the results show that many Americans (primarily whites but some blacks as well) have a mixed attitude toward desegregation; at each point in time, the preference of almost half was for "something in between" segregation and desegregation, a finding that has very important consequences for the progress of racial integration in the United States.

The mixed attitude of Americans toward racial equality is further demonstrated by other findings. For example, in 1972, 44% of Americans (including blacks) agreed with the statement: "In many

TABLE 4.2
Trends in Prointegration Attitudes, 1963–1977[a]

	Percent Giving Prointegration Response		
	1963	1972	1977
Do you think white students and black students should go to the same schools, or to separate schools? (Same)	63	86	85
How strongly would you object if a member of your family wanted to bring a black friend home to dinner? (Not at all)	49	70	71
White people have a right to keep blacks out of their neighborhood if they want to, and blacks should respect that right. (Disagree)	44	56	56
Do you think there should be laws against marriage between blacks and whites? (No)	36	59	71
Blacks shouldn't push themselves where they're not wanted. (Disagree)	27	22	27

SOURCES: 1977 data, National Opinion Research Center, University of Chicago; 1963 and 1972 data, Andrew M. Greeley and Paul B. Sheatsley, "Attitudes toward Racial Integration," in Lee Rainwater (ed.), Social Problems and Public Policy: Inequality and Justice (Chicago: Aldine, 1974), p. 242.
  [a] The responses indicating prointegration are given in parentheses after each question.

respects, equality has gone too far in this country" (Center for Political Studies). In 1970, a majority of both whites (54%) and blacks (67%) indicated that they thought whites in this country did not want complete equality between the races (Chandler, 1972: 23). Further, in 1970, a third of whites thought it would be a good idea for blacks to have "a completely separate country of their own some place away from the United States" (Chandler, 1972: 25).

Specific Aspects of Integration

The 1963–1977 trend information on racial attitudes in Table 4.2 supports two points. First, there is a clear trend of increasingly greater support for racial integration. For example, support for school integration increased from 63% in 1963 to 85% in 1977. The second point is that support for integration varies from one question to another, from one context to another. Greeley and Sheatsley (1974: 242) report that three additional questions used in earlier surveys are no longer even asked because "virtually all Americans now accept without question integration in jobs, public transportation, and public facilities." In addition to these areas, as already indicated, an overwhelming majority accept the principle of school integration. There is a smaller but still strong majority of 71% who oppose laws against interracial marriage and who would not object at all to having a member of the family bring home a black friend for dinner. The majority opposing neighborhood segregation is smaller (56%). Finally, the majority takes an anti-integration stand on the vague idea that blacks shouldn't push themselves where they're not wanted.

Equality and Social Distance

White Americans are highly supportive of racial integration in some issue areas, moderately supportive in some, and not very supportive of racial integration in other issue areas. Rodgers and Bullock (1974: 479) indicate that the average white American is an integrationist in situations in which social distance is high and a segregationist in situations in which social distance is low. *Social distance* basically refers to the extent to which one wants to keep interactions between oneself and members of a particular group on a distant, impersonal basis. Bogardus (1959) designed an attitude scale to measure the social distance a person feels toward members of various groups. On one end of the scale, indicating the greatest social distance, the respondent would not even allow a member of the group to visit the respondent's country. The next step involves somewhat less social distance: the respondent would allow a member of the group to visit the respondent's country. Next, citizenship would be allowed. Next, the respondent would allow the group member to work in the same occupation as the respondent. Next, the respondent would allow the group member as a neighbor. Next, the respondent would accept the group member as a personal friend. Finally, the least social distance is indicated by a willingness to have the group member as kin through marriage.

The general concept of social distance appears to be very helpful in explaining the differences in support for integration in different situations. In situations involving great social distance, situations in which contact can be kept on a relatively impersonal basis, there is high support for racial integration. There is a great deal of social distance involved, for example, in such areas of integration as public transportation; passengers on a bus usually interact—if they interact at all—on an impersonal, distant basis. Neighborhood integration or intermarriage, on the other hand, are much more personal; the social distance is greatly reduced in these types of situations and so is the level of support for racial integration.

Another point needs to be made concerning the high majority of 71% who oppose laws against interracial marriage. This does not mean that 71% *approve* of interracial marriage; it simply means that they oppose laws against it. Since the social distance is very low in this type of situation, it could be expected that this would be one of the last areas in which racial integration was achieved fully. In 1978, Gallup reports that only 32% of whites (compared to 66% of blacks) *approved* of interracial marriage (*Gallup Opinion Index*, November, 1978: 27). Further, white Americans disapprove of interracial marriages much more than the citizens of many other democracies (*Gallup Opinion Index*, November, 1968: 12). On the other hand, the 32% approval in 1978 represents quite a change from only 4% of whites who approved of interracial marriage in 1958 (*Gallup Opinion Index*, November, 1972: 12).

The pattern of greater resistance to racial integration in situations in which social distance is low applies to friendships as well as to interracial marriage. Many whites and many blacks prefer to have friends and neighbors only of the same race as themselves (Campbell, 1971: 8; Marx, 1969: 21).

Neighborhood integration, as already noted, is an area in which there is resistance, although the trend is for greater acceptance. Table 4.2 shows that a majority (56%) oppose the idea that whites have a right to keep blacks out of their neighborhoods. The decreasing opposition to racial integration in the neighborhoods is also indicated by responses of whites to the question: "If blacks came to live next door to you, would you move?" In 1963, almost half (45%) said they would move, but by 1978, only 13% said they would move (*Gallup Opinion Index*, November, 1978: 25). On the other hand, the *preference* of most people still seems to be for a basically racially segregated neighborhood; in 1976, 35% said they preferred a racially segregated neighborhood and another 29% preferred a neighborhood that was mostly the same race as themselves (Center for Political Studies). Further, many people apparently think that it would be acceptable to have neighborhood segregation if there were a law passed to support it; in 1976, a majority (56%) of whites agreed with the idea of a law which would allow a homeowner to refuse to sell to blacks (National Opinion Research Center). Also, whites evidently do not want neighborhood integration to be encouraged; in 1977, 55% opposed voluntary programs by business and religious groups to encourage blacks to buy homes in white suburbs (National Opinion Research Center). In sum, attitudinal support for racial integration in the neighborhoods has increased among Americans, but there appears to be a lot of mixed emotions and qualifications still remaining for this low social distance area.

The resistance of whites to integration in situations in which social distance is low is also demonstrated by the "club" question. In 1977, the National Opinion Research Center asked respondents if they would try to change the rules if they belonged to a club which excluded blacks. Only 39% said they would try to change the rules. Further, of those who said they would try to change the rules, only 42% would resign if they failed to get the rules changed. Thus, of the total number of respondents, only a small minority of 16% would resign from a club which refused to let blacks join.

In sum, there is no doubt that attitudes concerning racial equality and integration have become substantially more tolerant in the last twenty to thirty years; on the other hand, support for racial integration in particular situations depends heavily upon the amount of social distance involved. Support for racial integration in relatively impersonal situations is high; support for integration in more personal situations is lower.

ATTITUDES TOWARD THE PACE OF INTEGRATION

It was during the 1960s that the most dramatic changes in race relations occurred, and it appears that this was the time that white Americans were most upset about the pace of the changes that were taking place. Brink and Harris (1967: 120) state that by the late 1960s, "the Negro revolution was getting under the skin of millions of white people in America." Some of those who were disturbed by the changes didn't want the changes to occur at all; others apparently wanted the changes to take place at a very slow pace over a long period of time; a small proportion of whites wanted immediate integration and equality. Although blacks felt that integration efforts were proceeding at about the right pace or too slowly (Aberbach and Walker, 1973: 165), many whites expressed the sentiment: "The blacks are pushing too fast; they should wait." In 1963, Martin Luther King responded to this sentiment in his famous "Letter from Birmingham City Jail" (reprinted in Dye and Zeigler, 1972: 215):

For years now I have heard the word "Wait!" It rings in the ear of every Negro with a piercing familiarity. This "wait" has almost always meant "never."

The results in Table 4.3 clearly demonstrate that during the 1960s, a majority (63%) felt that the civil rights leaders were

TABLE 4.3
Attitudes toward the Pace of Integration, in Percentages

(A) Some people say that the civil rights people have been trying to push too fast. Others feel they haven't pushed fast enough. How about you? Do you think that civil rights leaders are trying to push too fast, are going too slowly, or are they moving at about the right speed?

	1964	1968[a]	1976
Too fast	63	63	39
About right	25	28	47
Too slowly	5	7	8
No opinion	6	3	5

(B) Do you think integration should be brought about gradually or do you think every means should be used to bring it about in the near future?

	1961
Gradually	61
Near future	23
Never	7
No opinion	9

SOURCES: (A) Survey Research Center/Center for Political Studies, University of Michigan. (B) George Gallup, *The Gallup Poll, Volume Three* (New York: Random House, 1972), p. 1724.
[a]Percentages for 1968 do not total to 100% due to rounding.

pushing too fast. By 1976, after the dramatic changes had taken place, the proportion who thought civil rights leaders were pushing too fast was down to a still substantial 39%. Table 4.3 also indicates that in 1961, during the beginning of the push for civil rights, only a minority (23%) wanted to bring about integration quickly. Some were completely opposed to integration, but the majority (61%) wanted such integration to be gradual. In 1964, after the passage of the Civil Rights Act, Gallup asked people whether the law should be strictly enforced right from the beginning or whether a gradual, persuasive approach should be used. A majority (62%) chose the gradual approach (Gallup, 1972: 1908). This resistance to the rate of change is also indicated by the finding that a majority (52%) of whites in 1970—sixteen years after the Supreme Court ruled that school integration should proceed with all deliberate speed—felt that school integration was going too fast; only 15% of blacks took this position (*Gallup Opinion Index*, April, 1970: 7).

The attitude of resistance to the pace of integration continues, but it is not so strong as it was before. Coupled with this attitude is the belief that substantial changes have taken place in the situation of blacks, that blacks are much better off than they were. While people are correct in thinking that very substantial changes in race relations have occurred, white Americans probably overestimate the extent to which the situation, especially the economic situation, of blacks has improved. It is also possible that whites have overestimated the extent to which the problem of racial equality in general has been resolved.

PERCEPTION OF DISCRIMINATION

In chapter 3, there was a discussion of the tendency among many Americans to deny the existence of discrimination against particular groups. For example, in 1977, only 41% perceived that there was discrimination against blacks. This topic needs to be pursued further because the refusal of many people to admit the existence of discrimination against blacks has influenced past and present policies and attitudes concerning racial equality.

In 1963, when racial discrimination against blacks was still *openly* practiced, a majority (56%) of Americans indicated that they felt that blacks were treated as well as whites (Table 4.4). Only 21% said that blacks were not treated very well and only 3% said they were treated badly. By 1978, some substantial changes had been made, but it is highly doubtful that the extent of these changes justified the views of 71% of Americans that blacks were treated the same as whites. Throughout the time period 1963–1978, less than one-fourth of Americans (even with blacks included) were willing to acknowledge that blacks were not treated as well as whites.

TABLE 4.4
Perception of Discrimination against Blacks, in Percentages

How well do you think blacks are treated in this community—the same as whites are, not very well, or badly? (*White respondents only*)

	1963	1967	1978
Same as whites	56	74	71
Not very well	21	14	13
Badly	3	1	3
Don't know	20	11	13

Do you think most businesses in your area discriminate against Negroes in their hiring practices or not? (*1968*)

	Yes	No	No Opinion
White respondents	21	65	14
Southern respondents	16	69	15

In general, do you think blacks have as good a chance as white people in your community to get any kind of job for which they are qualified, or don't you think they have as good a chance?

	As Good	Not as Good	Don't Know
1963 Total sample	43	48	9
1978 Total sample	67	24	9
1978 Whites	73	18	9
1978 Blacks	38	56	6

SOURCES: *Gallup Opinion Index* (August, 1967, p. 13; July, 1968, pp. 19, 21; November, 1978, pp. 28–29).

In Campbell's (1971) study of white attitudes in 1968, only 22% believed that "many" blacks faced discrimination in jobs and promotions, while another 34% conceded that "some" blacks faced such discrimination. In 1968, almost two-thirds (65%) of whites believed that businesses did not discriminate against blacks in their hiring practices (Table 4.4). It is interesting to note that in the South, where job discrimination was still blatantly obvious, an even higher proportion (69%) of whites denied the existence of such discrimination. By 1978, blacks and whites still held very different views on the existence of job discrimination. A strong majority of whites (73%) believed that blacks have just as good a chance as whites for jobs for which they are qualified; a majority of blacks (56%) did not think so.

Another area in which widespread, blatant discrimination against blacks has been practiced is housing. Yet, in 1968, Campbell's (1971) results indicated that only 38% of whites thought that "many" blacks faced housing discrimination, while another 30% acknowledged that "some" blacks faced such discrimination.

These results indicate clearly that, even during times when discrimination against blacks is open and obvious, a substantial proportion of white Americans simply do not accept the fact of existence of such discrimination. In some cases, the basis of the denial is probably a racist motive; by denying the existence of any problem, the solution to the problem can be attacked or resisted. In some cases, the basis of the denial of the problem might simply be ignorance. American citizens generally have low levels of information concerning political problems (Erikson et al., 1980: 18–19), and the denial of racial discrimination might simply result from a lack of information. In many cases, however, the basis of the denial of racial discrimination is probably a desire to avoid unpleasant, conflict-laden realities.

BLAMING THE VICTIM

In chapter 3, there was a discussion of the tendency among some Americans to place the responsibility for a wrong on the victim who has been wronged. This applies quite well to the attitudes of many people toward the inequality of blacks. It also helps to justify the denial of discrimination. A person can acknowledge that there are differences in such matters as housing, education, and employment between whites and blacks but deny that these differences are due to discrimination by placing the responsibility on blacks themselves. Taking this one step further, one can completely eliminate any perception of any problem of racial equality whatsoever by attributing happiness to the victim; thus, blacks are often stereotyped as being happy and carefree. They live the way they do because they like it that way.

Blaming the victim eliminates the problem of racial discrimination in the minds of many Americans. Campbell's (1971: 42) examination of white attitudes indicates that over half (58%) see the employment, education, and housing problems of blacks as due to the failure of blacks to better themselves; only 19% attributed the conditions of blacks to discrimination. With regard to the attitudes of whites, Campbell (1971: 42) concludes:

They appear to believe that Negroes simply lack the will to succeed as other minorities have done in preceding generations. In relying on this "free will" explanation, white Americans place the whole burden of Negro disadvantage on Negroes themselves and therewith tend to deny the reality of the problems Negroes face.

This tendency to blame the victim has consequences for attitudes concerning policies to be carried out; since whites accept no responsibility for the conditions of blacks, any efforts to compensate blacks for three hundred years of slavery are unacceptable (Rodgers and Bullock, 1974: 479).

Problems of legal and political equality cannot be completely separated from problems of economic and social equality, because racial discrimination has led to the economic inequalities between whites and blacks. Many people seem to feel that equality of opportunity is all that is required and that this is achieved simply by the elimination of discriminatory practices. Since racial discrimination practices have been outlawed, blacks are presumed to have achieved equality of opportunity; thus, if they do not achieve economic equality, it is their own fault. In most cases, it appears reasonable to conclude that the relatively bad economic condition of many blacks is not primarily due to *current* discrimination directed specifically at blacks, although such discrimination still exists. William Julius Wilson (1978), a black sociologist, argues in *The Declining Significance of Race* that the problems of poor blacks are due more to class—their economic and social background and the mental outlook produced by such a background—than to current racial discrimination; therefore, solutions should be sought by improving these conditions rather than blaming the problems on racial discrimination. Nevertheless, these problems do stem from past and present racial discrimination, and it appears that white Americans are unwilling to accept responsibility for such conditions. Instead, they place the responsibility on the blacks themselves.

The tendency to blame blacks—rather than racial discrimination—for their condition is not new. Even in 1942, when strong majorities of white Americans supported racial discrimination in both principle and practice in a very wide range of situations, 45% of those with an opinion believed that blacks themselves were to blame for the fact that they didn't have the same chance as whites in the United States (Cantril, 1951: 989).

Table 4.5 presents further evidence of this tendency. In 1968, a majority (58%) placed the blame for the condition of blacks on blacks themselves; only 23% placed the blame on whites. In 1970, only 15% blamed discrimination for the lack of progress among blacks; 49% said that blacks had not worked hard enough. In 1977, a majority (56%) rejected the idea that the fact that blacks have worse jobs, income, and housing than whites was due primarily to discrimination; 49% agreed with the idea that such differences were attributable to the low motivation and willpower of blacks.

Marx's (1969) study of the attitudes of blacks demonstrates another aspect of the "blame the victim" syndrome: sometimes the victims accept the blame. A majority of blacks in the study agreed

TABLE 4.5
White Attitudes toward the Reason for
the Situation of Blacks, in Percentages[a]

(A) Who do you think is more to blame for the present conditions in which Negroes find themselves—whites or Negroes themselves? (*1968*)

White people	23
Negroes	58
No opinion	19

(B) Which do you think is the main reason that Negroes have not made more progress in this city: discrimination against them because of their race or because Negroes have not worked very hard at the opportunities available to them? (*1970*)

Discrimination	15
Negroes not worked hard enough	49
Both	15
Other or no opinion	21

(C) On the average, blacks have worse jobs, income, and housing than white people. Do you think the differences are: (*1977*)

	Yes	No	Don't Know
Mainly due to discrimination	39	56	5
Because most blacks just don't have the motivation or willpower to pull themselves up out of poverty	49	48	4

SOURCES: (A) *Gallup Opinion Index*, July 1968, p. 20 (B) CBS survey reported in Robert Chandler, *Public Opinion: Changing Attitudes on Contemporary Political and Social Issues* (New York: R. R. Bowker, 1972), p. 19. (C) National Opinion Research Center, University of Chicago.

[a] Percentages for a question may not total to 100% due to rounding.

with the statement: "Negroes who want to work hard can get ahead just as easily as anyone else." More than a third of these blacks also agreed that: "Before Negroes are given equal rights, they have to show that they deserve them" (Marx, 1969: 24). In both these questions, Southern blacks were more likely than non-Southern blacks to accept the self-blame implied in these statements. Shingles' (1979) study of a sample of black students in a Southwestern university in 1975 found a self-debasement attitude among some blacks, an attitude which indicated acceptance by blacks themselves of some stereotypic traits attributed to blacks (e.g., laziness, irresponsibility). Thus, the negative attitudes of many whites toward blacks have been internalized to some extent by many blacks themselves.

ATTITUDES TOWARD TACTICS AND LAWS

While there have been changes in attitudes toward greater support for racial equality, many white Americans are reluctant to support policies or tactics which are needed to bring about actual equality (Rodgers and Bullock, 1974; Kilson, 1976). This has been true with regard to political and legal equality, but it is even more relevant with regard to economic equality. The tendency to place the responsibility for the condition of blacks on blacks themselves leads to a reluctance on the part of whites to do anything to bring about equality. In chapter 3, it was indicated that many Americans look upon the solution to the problems of disadvantaged groups in terms of rigorous individual efforts to overcome obstacles rather than collective action to combat discrimination. This attitude suggests that the way for blacks to get ahead is to get a good education, work hard, and mind their own business. Whites have been disturbed by collective efforts to overcome discrimination, they have been lukewarm at best with regard to laws to prohibit discrimination, and they have been hostile toward certain tactics involved in the quest for equality.

Support for Laws and Government Action

It has already been demonstrated that Americans reject the idea of laws or government programs which, in order to compensate for past discrimination, would discriminate in favor of a disadvantaged group until it was brought up to par with the rest of society. However, Americans have also been lukewarm toward making discrimination against disadvantaged groups illegal. In Campbell's

(1971: 23) study of the attitudes of whites in 1968, 67% favored laws to prevent job discrimination against blacks, but only 40% favored laws to prevent discrimination in renting housing. Thus, there was no consensus at that time—nor at this time—for making discrimination against blacks illegal.

During the 1960s, opposition to federal action to achieve racial integration often rallied around the slogan of "states' rights." The proposition was that federal government activities in integration were an infringement of the rights of states. In many cases, the obvious meaning of support for states' rights was opposition to racial integration. Those who favored racial equality usually supported the power of the federal government; those who opposed integration usually supported the power of the states. Thus, when Gallup (1972: 1851) reported that in 1963, 43% felt that each state should have the right to decide what to do about integration, this can be interpreted as an anti-integration sentiment. Americans seemed to be coming closer to acceptance of integration in principle, but they were reluctant to have the government take steps to bring about actual integration. It appears that Americans wanted integration to come about on a voluntary basis, at a very gradual pace, and with a minimum of disruption. Federal action represented bigger changes on a more immediate basis. Many people could probably best be described as "anti-integrationist" rather than as "prosegregationist." In Campbell's (1971: 129–131) study of whites, only a third felt that the government in Washington should bring about racial equality in jobs or bring about school integration, and less than half felt that the government in Washington should support the right of blacks to go to any hotel or restaurant they could afford. People apparently did not disagree with the principle of racial integration and equality in jobs, schools, and restaurants; they simply did not want the government to do anything to bring about such integration and equality.

Table 4.6 further demonstrates this tendency with regard to federal action to achieve school integration. In 1964, 1968, and 1976, there were large proportions who felt that the federal government should stay out of school integration. Returning to Table 4.2, we see that support for the principle of school integration increased from 63% in 1963 to 85% in 1977; however, Table 4.6 indicates that between 1964 and 1976 opposition to federal action to achieve such integration actually increased from 44% to 55%.

Increased opposition to federal efforts to achieve school integration is probably due in large part to the use of busing to achieve such integration—although only about 7% of students who ride

TABLE 4.6
Attitudes toward Federal Action to Achieve
School Integration, in Percentages[a]

Some people say that the government in Washington should see to it that
white and Negro children are allowed to go to the same schools. Others
claim that this is not the government's business. Do you think that the
government in Washington should:

	1964	1968	1976
See to it that white and Negro children go to the same schools	48	43	34
Stay out of this area as it is none of its business	44	50	55
Mixed or other answer	8	8	12

SOURCE: Survey Research Center/Center for Political Studies, University of
Michigan.
[a] Percentages may not total to 100% due to rounding.

buses are bused for purposes of achieving racial integration (Rist,
1978: 40). In 1978, only 28% of whites—compared with 75% of
nonwhites—favored busing to achieve racial balance in the schools
(*Gallup Opinion Index*, November, 1978: 4). Thus, about three-
fourths of whites oppose busing as a means of achieving school integration, but an even higher proportion claim to support the principle of school integration. This presents a dilemma. In most cases,
due to historical patterns of economic discrimination and to neighborhood segregation, busing is the only means of achieving racial
integration in the schools. While many people might sincerely believe in school integration, they oppose the tactic necessary to
bring it about, apparently because they place a higher priority on
the problems associated with busing than they do on the value of
racial integration.

Protest Demonstrations

In 1963, Martin Luther King was arrested in Birmingham, Alabama,
for taking part in peaceful civil rights demonstrations which had
been received with outbursts of violence by white racists. While in
jail, he received a letter from a group of local clergymen asking him
to stop the demonstrations because of the violent reaction to such
protests and to try to reach his goals through negotiation. In response, King wrote his "Letter from Birmingham City Jail" (reprinted in Dye and Zeigler, 1972: 213–221), an exposition of the

basis for nonviolent direct action to end racial discrimination. King pointed out that the clergymen's reference to negotiation instead of protest demonstrations was meaningless since the holders of power refused to negotiate, and he presented the core idea of the protests (Dye and Zeigler, 1972: 214):

You are exactly right in your call for negotiation. Indeed this is the purpose of direct action. Nonviolent direct action seeks to create such a crisis and establish such creative tension that a community that has constantly refused to negotiate is forced to confront the issue.

King s basic strategy was to confront the American conscience, to force a resolution of the "American dilemma" posed by Gunnar Myrdal (1944). White Americans believed in certain ideals while coexisting with a denial of these ideals for blacks. The contrast between ideal and reality had to be exposed so starkly that whites could not simply ignore the reality.

The strategy of nonviolent protest imposed a terrible cost on civil rights workers. Many were jailed, beaten, attacked by police dogs, battered by water from fire hoses, and otherwise harassed. Some were murdered. Further, other blacks were murdered as extreme racists bombed black schools and churches. But this costly strategy was based on the assumption that the conscience of white Americans would be awakened and that blacks would be "free at last."

As Dye (1971: 113–114) notes, a protest is "a means of acquiring bargaining leverage for those who would otherwise be completely powerless." Although the protest demonstration might be the only tool available to powerless groups, it is not necessarily an effective tool. The protest cannot be used with a high probability of success (Lipsky, 1968). Further, while blacks achieved some success by using protest demonstrations in the early 1960s, Rustin (1965) argues that protests can only deal with certain aspects of racial discrimination, and that other forms of political action are required to eliminate institutional racism in American society. Thus, blacks cannot use protests today as an effective tool against more subtle forms of discrimination; the political tools of blacks today resemble those of more established interest groups. Nevertheless, American attitudes toward black protest demonstrations will be examined because protest demonstrations in the cause of blacks or other groups in society are still used to some extent and because support for a First Amendment right is involved.

Table 4.7 demonstrates a sharp contrast in the attitudes of whites and blacks toward protest activities. In 1970 respondents

TABLE 4.7
Attitudes toward Protest Methods by Race, 1970

Method	Percent Who Do Not See Method as a Good Way to Get Equal Rights for Blacks[a]		Percent Who Would Not Use Method Themselves for a Very Important Cause[b]	
	Blacks	Whites	Blacks	Whites
Going to meetings	4	10	9	21
Peaceful demonstrations	22	64	27	76
Boycotting stores	19	66	27	74
Picketing stores, businesses	30	78	42	89
Demonstrations that might lead to violence	86	97	88	98

SOURCE: CBS survey reported in Robert Chandler, *Public Opinion: Changing Attitudes on Contemporary Political and Social Issues* (New York: R. R. Bowker, 1972), p. 27.

[a] Question: "There have been many types of actions aimed at the problem of equal rights for Negroes—both whites and Negroes have participated in these actions. As I read some of these actions to you, tell me if you think they are good ways for people to use to get what they want."

[b] Question: "This time tell me if you would or would not do each of these things for a cause that you thought was very important."

were asked whether each of a list of protest activities was a good idea or a bad idea in connection with getting equal rights for blacks. Only the mildest form of activity, going to meetings, raised little objection from whites. A majority of whites (64%)—compared to only 22% of blacks—objected to peaceful demonstrations. The same pattern holds with regard to boycotting stores, even though such action requires no confrontation. Picketing stores and businesses does involve confrontation, and 78% of whites (only 30% of blacks) didn't think it was a good idea. There was a consensus among both whites and blacks against demonstrations that might lead to violence. Thus, out of this list of protest activities, strong majorities of whites opposed each activity except going to meetings, whereas a majority of blacks were opposed only to violent demonstrations.

Respondents were also asked if they themselves would take part in each of these protest activities for a cause which they thought was very important. A fifth of whites would not even go to meetings for such a cause. Three-fourths of whites would not take part in a peaceful demonstration nor boycott stores; and very few whites would picket stores or take part in demonstrations that might lead to violence. These results show a very strong predisposition on the part of white Americans to reject activities that are conflictual or disruptive even when such activities are used to achieve a good cause. This puts at a disadvantage any group whose only political tool is the protest demonstration.

Other survey results concerning black protests present a similar picture. In 1961, some civil rights workers engaged in integrated "freedom rides" on buses through the South. In one such ride, the bus was burned by racists; continuing the ride on another bus, the riders were later violently attacked and beaten; at a later point on the ride, the riders were arrested. While a strong majority (66%) approved of the Supreme Court's ruling that racial segregation in public transportation was unconstitutional, a strong majority (64%) also disapproved of these freedom rides (Gallup, 1972: 1723). White Americans were giving simultaneous approval to the *principle* of integrated buses and disapproval to the *process* of integrating the buses.

In 1963, a quarter of a million black and white civil rights supporters held a peaceful demonstration in Washington. Prior to this event, only 22% of those who had heard that it was going to happen approved of it (Gallup, 1972: 1836). In 1964, three-fourths of Americans indicated that they thought that mass demonstrations by blacks were more likely to hurt than help the cause of racial equality (Gallup, 1972: 1884). Marx (1969: 15) found, however, that blacks were almost unanimous in thinking that demonstrations had helped.

Part of the explanation of white attitudes toward black protests is that, even though the protestors were peaceful and orderly, there were often violent reactions to them. While such violence against peaceful demonstrators probably increased public support for civil rights, there was also a tendency to blame the peaceful demonstrators for the violence—another example of blaming the victim. Campbell (1971: 16) found that more than a third of whites made no distinction between a "riot" and "non-violent marches and demonstrations." Despite the strictly nonviolent approach of the protestors in the early 1960s, a majority (58%) of Americans in 1964 viewed the actions blacks had taken during the last year or so as more violent than peaceful (Center for Political Studies). The same survey also showed that 58% thought that the actions that blacks had taken had hurt their cause. Further, in 1966 only a minority of whites (36%) felt that Martin Luther King was helping the cause of civil rights (Erskine, 1967: 661).

The negative attitude of Americans toward protest activities is further demonstrated by a final point: many Americans tend to view protests as the work of a Communist conspiracy. The logic seems to be that since everything is basically fine in the United States, these people would not be demonstrating unless they were being pushed to do it by Communist agitators. In 1964, almost half (47%) of Americans agreed with the idea that "most of the organizations pushing for civil rights have been infiltrated by the Communists and are now dominated by Communist trouble-makers" (Free and Cantril, 1968: 196). Further, in a 1965 survey, a majority (51%) indicated that they thought that Communists had been involved "a lot" in the civil rights demonstrations and another 27% indicated "some" Communist involvement (Erskine, 1967: 664). Even though the motivations for a protest are straightforward, some people seem to want to avoid confronting the issue of racial equality; instead, they ignore the issue by attributing the cause of the protest to Communists. This type of attitude is not limited to black protests; for example, it occurred to some extent with regard to the antiwar protests of the 1960s. It can be expected that some people will blame the Communists for just about any protest movement.

In sum, Americans generally have a very negative attitude toward protest activities. This has had consequences for movements for which the protest was a primary political tool. Nevertheless, protest activities can, when used skillfully, sometimes be influential in changing the attitudes of the public.

SUMMARY AND CONCLUSIONS

There has been a tremendous change in public attitudes toward greater support for equality for black Americans during the last twenty or thirty years. This support for equality, however, lies along a spectrum, with almost unanimous support for integration and equality in some areas (e.g., jobs) and very little support for equality and integration in other areas (e.g., interracial marriage). Support for equality seems to be greatest in those situations in which contacts among people are the least personalized and lowest in situations in which contacts are more personal in nature.

Many white Americans have been disturbed, especially during the 1960s, by what they perceive as an excessively fast pace of integration. They appear to want integration to proceed at a very gradual pace with a minimum of disruption.

Many white Americans tend to deny the existence of racial discrimination against blacks. They can acknowledge that there are differences in income, education, housing, and employment between whites and blacks, but they do not necessarily attribute the cause of such differences to racial discrimination. Instead, many people place the blame for such conditions on blacks themselves.

White Americans tend to give lukewarm support for laws and government actions designed to achieve racial integration. It appears that they would prefer such integration to come about by itself on a voluntary basis. One form of activity, busing to achieve school integration, is extremely unpopular even though there is a consensus in favor of school desegregation.

White Americans have held negative views toward the tactic of the protest demonstration, even though this was basically the only political tool that blacks could use during the early 1960s. White Americans don't seem to like confrontation situations—especially if there is any possibility that violence might occur—no matter what the goals of such confrontations are.

The legal battle for equality for blacks is basically over. Even so, it will be a while before blacks can enjoy full equality even in this sense. There are many ways to get around the laws and there is still discrimination against blacks. Public attitudes still do not support full equality and integration for blacks along the full spectrum of social, political, economic, and personal activities. Segregation has been replaced by economic concerns as the biggest problem for blacks. And, as noted before, whites have no intention of making much effort to compensate for three hundred years of black inequality. Most whites will support "equal opportunity" for blacks from now on, but they will not acknowledge that the disadvantages—economic, social, physical, and psychological—incurred by blacks for many generations past will preclude true "equality of opportunity" for blacks for several generations hence.

5

Support for Equality for Women

BACKGROUND

Introduction

The movement for sexual equality involves a wide range of areas of life: job hiring and promotion, property rights, credit, educational opportunities, political rights, and many other areas. Aside from these areas which have some legal aspect to them, the movement also encompasses matters of human dignity and respect: the person—whether male or female—must be treated as an individual human being rather than ascribing certain roles or traits on the basis of gender.

This chapter concerns the American public's support for equality for women. The primary focus of the "women's movement" is on the abolition of discrimination against women. However, to some extent the term *women's movement* is misleading; it is more accurate to refer to it as the "movement for sexual equality." The success of the movement will involve a redefinition of roles for both men and women, and both are involved in the movement. Although most obvious sexual discrimination is directed against women, there are also certain situations (e.g., divorce proceedings and the draft for the military) in which there can be discrimination against men. Further, the pressures for men in American society to conform to certain roles constitutes an abridgment of their individuality. The conflict in this struggle is not between men and women; it is a conflict between those who support sexual equality (both men and women) and those who do not (both men and women).

The Earlier Movement

The movement for sexual equality in the United States is not a recent movement; it goes back a long way. For example, the first women's rights convention, the Seneca Falls Convention, met in 1848 and developed a Declaration of Sentiments concerning equality for women which was modeled after the Declaration of Independence (Kraditor, 1968: 183). Prior to the Civil War, such women as Susan B. Anthony and Elizabeth Cady Stanton worked to obtain equality and freedom for both women and blacks. After the war, black *males* received the right to vote, but women's suffrage was rebuffed. Hole and Levine (1971: 10) argue that this setback caused the women's movement to set suffrage as its first priority, although this goal had been only a part of a wider range of goals. When the goal of suffrage for women was achieved in 1920, the movement collapsed.

With the passage of the 19th Amendment the majority of women activists as well as the public at large assumed that having gained the vote woman's complete equality had been virtually obtained. . . . The woman's movement virtually died in 1920 and with the exception of a few organizations, feminism was to lie dormant for forty years [Hole and Levine, 1971: 14].

The New Movement

In *Rebirth of Feminism*, Hole and Levine (1971) indicate that such rebirth took place in the 1960s. This was a time of renewed desire for equality for a number of groups, women included, and some progress was made. There was a variety of important victories for the cause of sexual equality. For example, the 1964 Civil Rights Act, which was tremendously important in the black civil rights movement, also contained one victory for women: Title VII prohibits employment discrimination on the basis of sex (as well as race, color, religion, and national origin). The movement also began to take on an organizational structure again. There are now a number of different organizations within the movement, such as the Women's Equity Action League (WEAL), the Professional Women's Caucus (PWC), Federally Employed Women (FEW), and others. The best known organization, however, is the National Organization for Women (NOW), which was formed in 1966.

During the early 1970s, opponents of sexual discrimination were finally able to get Congress to propose the Equal Rights Amendment (ERA). This proposed amendment, which had been introduced in Congress yearly since 1923, reads as follows:

Equality of rights under the law shall not be denied or abridged by the United States or by any State on account of sex.

This proposed amendment has not yet been ratified and might not be. Although the movement for sexual equality has met with some success in a number of areas of discrimination, it is argued that the ERA is needed in order to make a clean sweep of the morass of laws and policies which form the legal basis for sexual discrimination.

Earlier Attitudes

Let's take a look at information available from the early surveys concerning women—although these surveys were not based on strict probability samples and are, therefore, likely to be less accurate than more recent surveys. In 1937, during the Depression, a whopping 82% of Americans disapproved of a woman earning money in business and industry if she had a husband capable of supporting her, and 74% approved of the idea of a law which would prohibit married women from working if their husbands earned a certain amount per month (Cantril, 1951: 1044–1045). Evidently support for discrimination against married women was greater than for unmarried women, the assumption being that married women had husbands who could support them. In 1938, 50% approved of the policy which some schools had of hiring only unmarried teachers (presumably only women) and firing them if they got married (Cantril, 1951: 856).

In terms of political matters, it was indicated in chapter 3 that in 1937, only 31% were willing to vote for a qualified woman candidate for President. Also, in 1937, almost a third (31%) opposed allowing women to serve on juries (Cantril, 1951: 1052), and in 1945, almost half (48%) opposed having a woman in the President's Cabinet (Cantril, 1951: 1053).

Lastly, a majority of 60% in 1943 indicated that women's morals should be stricter than men's (Cantril, 1951: 483). This is an indication of the double standard which has so often been used in judging the behavior of men and women.

Women and Blacks

There are certain similarities and certain differences in the situations of women and blacks in the United States; sometimes these similarities and differences have led to cooperation and sometimes they have led to conflict. In the first place, both women and blacks are in a similar situation in that both have faced discrimination on the basis of biological/physical characteristics. They are also similar in that the discrimination has covered a very wide range of areas of life rather than being limited to a few specific situations. Also, members of both groups have been treated to some degree as if they were perpetual children with less capacity for reasoning and responsibility than white male adults.

There are other parallels which could be drawn between the situations of women and blacks in American society; however, there are also some important differences which have implications for their respective movements for equality. In the first place, women are a slight majority of the population, whereas blacks are a minority of about 11%. Nevertheless, some (e.g., Hacker, 1974; Lessard, 1976) have discussed women in terms of the characteristics of a minority group because of their disadvantaged status. Another difference between women and blacks is that the general standard of living of most women has not been so bad as that of most blacks. In terms of general standard of living (housing, clothes, food, transportation, medical care, etc.), white males have it best, then white women, then black men, and then black women. The average woman (combining both white and black women) has a higher standard of living than the average black (combining both male and female blacks). As we shall see later, this does not apply to all aspects of the economic situation. The fact of the general economic deprivation of so many blacks has given the black movement an added dimension which is not perceived with regard to the women's movement. This probably helps to account for a third difference: women are less likely to perceive the discrimination against women than blacks are to perceive discrimination against blacks.

In discussing sexual and racial discrimination in American society, it is apparent that white males face the least discrimination and black females face the most. In between, white females face greater discrimination in some situations than black males do, black males face greater discrimination than white females in some situations, and both are equally disadvantaged in some situations (e.g., a club which only admits white males). Amundsen (1977: 42) concludes that blacks have made greater progress than women have. As an example, she states:

The insistence on using the term *girls* when speaking to or about adult females illustrates this point very well. The time has long since passed that anyone dared call a black male "boy." Both terms are equally insulting when applied to mature adults; yet the designation of women to the ranks of the childlike is still widespread [Amundsen, 1977: 42].

As a final note, when Representative Shirley Chisholm from New York sought the 1972 Democratic nomination for President, she expressed the view that she had faced greater discrimination as a result of being a woman than she did as a result of being black.

PERCEPTION OF DISCRIMINATION

Denying Discrimination

To what extent do Americans perceive that there is discrimination against women? In chapter 3 we saw that a 1977 survey indicated that only 31% felt that there was discrimination against women. Table 5.1 presents further information, and the results once again demonstrate that many people refuse to acknowledge the existence of discrimination against particular groups in society. In 1973, only

TABLE 5.1
Perception of Discrimination against Women, in Percentages

Women are discriminated against in our society. (*1973*)

Applies to	Males	Females
None or only a few women	32	29
Some women	32	33
Many women	19	16
All or most women	16	19
Don't know	1	3

Do you feel that you've been *personally* discriminated against as a woman in any way? (*Women respondents only, 1973*)

	Males	Females
No	—	79
Yes	—	20
Don't know	—	1

Do you think women in your country have equal job opportunities with men, or not? (*1976*)

	Males	Females
Yes	46	49
No	50	46
Don't know	4	5

SOURCES: 1973 data, Institute for Social Research 1973 Fall Omnibus Survey, University of Michigan; 1976 data, *Gallup Opinion Index*, March, 1976, p. 28.

35% felt that many, most, or all women were discriminated against; more than 62% felt that discrimination only affected some, a few, or no women. Further, there is very little difference in the responses of males and females to this question. The next question, asked of females only, demonstrates a very important point: only 20% of women felt that they had *personally* been discriminated against as a woman in any way.

The third question in Table 5.1 indicates that both males and females are roughly split half and half on the question of whether men and women have equal job opportunities in the United States. Thus, these results and the others in the table demonstrate that there is not widespread perception of discrimination against women and that women themselves share the prevailing views of society in this regard.

Women and Responsibility

In chapter 4, it was demonstrated that many Americans refuse to acknowledge that blacks face discrimination. It was also indicated that the conflict between this denial of discrimination and the fact of the unequal conditions of blacks was often resolved by "blaming the victim," by placing the responsibility for the condition of blacks on blacks themselves. Further, many blacks themselves share these views. The situation with regard to women is similar in that there is a widespread denial of discrimination against women and that women themselves share in this denial. The situation is different, however, in that there is not a widespread perception of a gap between the conditions of men and women which must be explained away. When asked whether men or women have a better life, Americans are very much split on the question. Roughly a third of both men and women think men have a better life, roughly a third think women have it better, and roughly a third think both men and women have it the same (*Gallup Opinion Index*, April, 1975: 19). Thus, although a majority would probably agree that blacks have a worse life than whites, there is only minority support for the view that women have a worse life than men.

It is apparent that the view shared by both men and women is that women have less responsibility than men do. Further, going along with the tendency to treat women as being more childlike and less capable than men and the tendency to believe that women are placed on a pedestal, many people—both men and women—believe that women have less responsibility than men and that this is the right and proper order of things. Women are viewed primarily as housewives or future housewives, even when they have full-time jobs. The housewife role is often paid great tribute—especially by those who oppose sexual equality—but perhaps the real value which Americans place on the role is better indicated by the fact that those who perform this role on a paid basis (housekeepers, maids, etc.) are usually minority women who are paid low wages.

The housewife role is seen as one which is easier and requires less responsibility than the role of the man who works. At the same time, those women who work at a job outside the home face a similar situation. Women will be considered more childlike and less capable; therefore, they will usually be guided toward jobs which are perceived to require less responsibility. The attribution of childlike qualities to women who work is demonstrated by the role of the secretary. In the first place, the secretary will almost always be a woman. In the second place, the wages will usually be rather low. In the third place, bosses (males) will speak glowingly about the performance and loyalty of their secretaries. But, no matter how old the woman is and no matter how skillful and responsible she is, she will commonly be referred to as "the girl in the office." Further, she will probably reinforce this type of attitude rather than object to it.

Women against Women

The fact that so many women share negative views of themselves is of considerable importance. Amundsen (1977) casts the question of equality for women in terms of Myrdal's *An American Dilemma*, which was originally formulated in reference to blacks. Americans pay tribute to a number of ideals concerning equality, but these ideals are not held to be applicable to women. Amundsen (1977: 99) points out that with respect to blacks, Myrdal ignored one problem:

How the members of a group suppressed so gravely for so long were to overcome the feelings of inferiority and the habits of deference inculcated in them throughout their lifetime; for one of the most debilitating effects of racial prejudice . . . is that the victims come to believe in and even cherish their "inferiority."

Amundsen notes that the "Uncle Tom" mentality had to be changed before blacks could begin to achieve equality; this was not an easy task since blacks had been taught to believe in and accept their inferior status. Amundsen argues that this applies equally well to women: women have been taught to accept certain roles in society and even to feel good about their inferior status. Freeman (1976: 241) also makes this point:

Yet until very recently, most women have refused to recognize their own oppression. They have openly accepted the social definition of who and what they are. They have refused to be conscious of the fact that they are seen and treated, before anything else, as women. Many still do. This very refusal is significant because no group is so oppressed as one which will not recognize its own oppression.

Hacker (1974: 128) discusses the "majority of American women who have no wish to be liberated." Liberation involves a changing of the roles of men and women in society. Many women—especially older women—who are established in the homemaking role are comfortable in the role and would be upset by any substantial change in their circumstances. Further, they might resent any implication that their role is not the most desirable role for women to fulfill. On the other hand, there is also opposition from some successful business and professional women. As long as there are only a few women who have succeeded in their areas, they occupy a certain unique status, and they might want to keep it relatively unique by keeping other women out.

The finding that women share prejudice against other women can be amply demonstrated. In chapter 3 it was noted that the percentage of Americans who indicated a willingness to vote for a qualified woman for President had increased quite substantially over the last twenty or thirty years. A point not mentioned earlier is that the most substantial changes in attitudes have occurred among women themselves. From 1958 to 1969, men were more willing to vote for a woman for President than women were. Somewhere between 1969 and 1972, the differences between men and women on this issue faded (Ferree, 1974: 393). Thus, until relatively recently, women were more opposed to a woman being President than men were. As we shall see later, women have also been more opposed to ratification of the Equal Rights Amendment than men have. Goldberg's (1968) experiment indicated that, at least under certain circumstances, women would automatically rate the work of women lower than the work of men—even when it was the same work. Two groups of women students were given the *same* essay to evaluate with only one difference: one group was told that the author of the essay was "John McKay" and the other group was told the author was "Joan McKay." The "John" essay was rated higher than the "Joan" essay. However, further research along these lines has indicated that such a pattern occurs in relatively limited circumstances. On the other hand, another study of student attitudes (Corbett *et al.*, 1977) found that female students were no more supportive of sexual equality (as measured by a series of questions concerning sex roles in society) than males were. Further, the main organized opposition to the ratification of the Equal Rights Amendment has been led by women (e.g., Phyllis Schafly).

In sum, Americans have a tendency to deny the existence of discrimination against women, and women themselves often share in this denial. A big task for those involved in the movement for sexual equality has been "consciousness raising," a process of getting men and women to realize the ways in which sexual discrimination affects their lives. It appears that such efforts made some progress during the 1970s. Table 5.2 presents some indication of this and further evidence will be presented later. Between 1972 and 1976, the percentage of those concurring with the idea that it is sex discrimination which keeps women from top jobs jumped from 35% to 48%. This is a substantial change for a four-year period. Thus, the trend appears to be toward a greater degree of perception of sexual discrimination.

TABLE 5.2
Trend in Perception of Sexual Discrimination

Respondents select the statement with which they agree more.	*1972*	*1976*
"It's more natural for men to have the top responsible jobs in a country."	65%	52%
OR		
"Sex discrimination keeps women from the top jobs."	35%	48%

SOURCE: Center for Political Studies, University of Michigan.

ATTITUDES TOWARD EQUALITY

Equality in Jobs

Equality in employment situations is a goal which many disadvantaged groups share. Myths surrounding affirmative action programs have led some people to believe that "reverse discrimination" is now prevalent in employment situations, that women and blacks— and especially black women—have the best job and promotion prospects. This picture is probably partially correct in a very limited number of situations, but overall it is grossly misleading. Overall, as Thurow (1976) indicates, women have *not* made progress toward equality with men in jobs; unemployment, for example, remains much higher among women than among men. Boles (1979) demonstrates that with regard to pay, women have actually lost ground in relation to men. In 1955, the median income of full-time female workers was only 64% as high as the median income of full-time male workers. By 1974, this ratio had *dropped* to only 57% (Boles, 1979: 49), and it has remained at about this level. In 1974, the median salaries of full-time workers by sex and race were (Boles, 1979: 50):

White men	$12,104
Nonwhite men	8,524
White women	6,823
Nonwhite women	6,258

These figures suggest that sex is more of a disadvantage than race in terms of wages and salaries.

Returning to Table 5.1, we see that 50% of males and 46% of females believed that women do not have equal job opportunities with men in the United States. These respondents were further asked whether women *should* have equal job opportunities; the overwhelming majority of both males (78%) and females (83%) said "yes" (*Gallup Opinion Index*, March, 1976: 28). Thus, only a small proportion of the American public disagrees in principle with the overall idea of job equality for women. However, when this type of question is broken down into more specific components, there is a different picture. Results in Table 5.3 indicate attitudes toward three aspects: hiring, equal pay for equal work, and promotion. A majority of Americans support discrimination against women in hiring for jobs. Note that support for such discrimination against

TABLE 5.3
Attitudes toward Job Discrimination against Women, 1970

	Males	Females
Do you think it is necessary to give preference to men over women in hiring for jobs? (*Yes*)	50%	53%
Do you think it is necessary to pay a man more than a woman for doing the same kind of work? (*Yes*)	16%	21%
Do you think it is necessary to consider men first for promotion, before women? (*Yes*)	28%	38%

SOURCE: CBS survey reported in Robert Chandler, *Public Opinion Attitudes on Contemporary Political and Social Issues* (New York: R. R. Bowker, 1972), pp. 48–49.

women is slightly higher among females (53%) than among males (50%). Support for equality in employment situations is highest for the idea of equal pay for equal work; only a fifth of Americans supports the idea that males and females should be paid differently for the same work. With regard to promotion, a minority of males (28%) and a somewhat larger minority of females (38%) support the idea of considering males first. In all three of these questions, female respondents were more supportive of discrimination against women than males were, a finding that can be very perplexing to those working for sexual equality.

We see, then, that many Americans do support discrimination against women in employment; further such discrimination does actually exist on a widespread basis (Blau, 1976). In certain types of situations, majorities of Americans do recognize that such discrimination exists; for example, in 1970, a majority of both men and women said "no" to the question of whether a woman with the same ability as a man has as good a chance to become the executive of a company (*Gallup Opinion Index*, September, 1970: 6). On the other hand, also in 1970, a substantial proportion of Americans supported discrimination in this type of situation; 39% agreed that an employer was better off to hire a man instead of a woman for an executive position because women usually don't think as logically as men do (Chandler, 1972: 49).

Another aspect of the employment situation that has been a great problem to women and minorities is that any progress made during normal times can be very quickly wiped out during times of economic recession. In occupations which were customarily filled by white males in the past, women and members of minority groups are the ones with the least seniority, and the "last hired, first fired" rule works against them. Even putting this aside, however, 36% of Americans in 1976 agreed with the idea that an employer who has to lay off workers should first lay off those women whose husbands have jobs (Center for Political Studies 1976 Election Study).

Equality in Careers

The focus here is different from attitudes toward job equality; here the concern is with society's attitude toward a woman having a job outside the home. In 1977, almost two-thirds (65%) of Americans agreed that it is "much better for everyone involved if the man is the achiever outside the home and the woman takes care of the home and family" (National Opinion Research Center). In that same survey, a majority (55%) also agreed with the statement: "It is more important for a wife to help her husband's career than to have one herself." In a 1976 survey, however, a majority (60%) agreed with the statement: "Our society, not nature, teaches women to prefer homemaking to work outside the home" (Center for Political Studies 1976 Election Study). While all three sets of results indicate the prevailing norm that the more appropriate role for women is in the home, the last set of results at least does not attribute this to any natural order of things.

Earlier it was indicated that some changes in attitudes toward the role of women in society took place during the 1970s. Table 5.4 presents results from two questions which indicate a small trend. In 1974, 34% agreed with the idea of a woman running the home while men ran the country; by 1978, the percentage agreeing with this idea was down to 31%. This is a small change, but it ties in with the overall pattern of changes. As indicated before, in 1937, 82% of Americans disapproved of a married woman working in business or industry if she had a husband capable of supporting her. By 1972, the proportion disapproving was down to 34%, and in 1978, only 26% disapproved. The change of 8 percentage points between 1972 and 1978 is another piece in a pattern of changing attitudes. While society still encourages women to follow the homemaker role, attitudes are changing in the direction of greater freedom of choice.

TABLE 5.4
The Home Base Trend, 1972–1978, in Percentages

Women should take care of running the home and leave running the country up to men.

	1974	1978
Agree	34	31
Disagree	62	66
Not sure	4	3

Do you approve or disapprove of a married woman earning money in business or industry if she has a husband capable of supporting her?

	1972	1975	1978
Approve	64	70	72
Disapprove	34	29	26
Don't know	2	1	1

SOURCE: National Opinion Research Center, University of Chicago.

Equality in Education

In 1976, only 8% of Americans felt that women did not have equality of educational opportunities with men in the United States (*Gallup Opinion Index*, March, 1976: 27). Further, big majorities of both males (71%) and females (65%) disagreed in 1970 with the idea that males should be given preference over females in admissions to universities and professional schools (Chandler, 1972: 49). Educational opportunities are probably roughly equal for males and females today, although some qualifications would have to be made to this statement. For example, women students who wish to pursue a program of education in order to prepare for a career which has traditionally been occupied almost exclusively by males will probably encounter resistance from some teachers and from some other students. This was much more prevalent not so many years ago. Another problem is that some male professors sometimes discriminate against female students. On the whole, however, it can be said that access to educational opportunities is roughly the same for males and females now and that the public basically supports this equality.

Equality in Politics

In terms of elective or appointive public offices, women have not yet begun to achieve equality. There has never been a female President or Vice-President, and there have been very few women in Congress. As noted earlier, however, 76% of Americans in 1978 expressed a willingness to vote for a woman for President. Further, in 1976, 88% of Americans said they would be willing to vote for a woman for Congress; 81% would vote for a woman for governor; and 83% would vote for a woman for mayor or top official of their city or community (*Gallup Opinion Index*, March, 1976: 7–9). Given the apparent willingness of the American public to vote for women candidates and given the actual success in recent years of a number of women in gubernatorial, congressional, and mayoral races, it might be expected that the tiny proportion of women officeholders will increase substantially during the 1980s.

ATTITUDES TOWARD THE MOVEMENT

Support for the ERA

Table 5.5 shows that in 1980 a majority of both males (61%) and females (54%) supported the ratification of the Equal Rights

Amendment. Other surveys have worded the question differently and this produces different results; the results in Table 5.5 probably constitute the most conservative estimate of the degree of support for the ERA. For example, the Center for Political Studies in 1976 found 70% in favor of the ERA, and the National Opinion Research Center in 1977 found 67% favoring the ERA. Despite differences in question wording, a solid majority of Americans supports ratification of the ERA.

An examination of Gallup results (*Gallup Opinion Index*, 1980: 4) for 1975–1980 indicates that support for the ERA has remained stable; there has been no pattern of decreasing support. Nevertheless, the ERA might not be ratified. Legislatures in three-fourths of the states must ratify the amendment. While a majority of Americans support the ERA, the majority in a particular state might not. Also, legislative majorities are not necessarily reflective of the majority in the population. In Illinois, for example, despite the fact that the majority of the population favors the ERA, the state legislature has not ratified the amendment.

Note also from Table 5.5 that males are somewhat more likely to support the ERA than females are; this finding has also been verified by other surveys. Further, nonwhite respondents are more likely to support the ERA than whites are.

TABLE 5.5
Support for the Equal Rights Amendment, 1980, in Percentages

Have you read or heard about the Equal Rights Amendment to the Constitution which would give women equal rights and equal responsibilities? (*If "yes"*) Do you favor or oppose this amendment?

	Favor	Oppose	No Opinion
Total sample	58	31	11
Males	61	28	11
Females	54	34	12
Whites	55	34	11
Nonwhites	73	16	11

SOURCE: *Gallup Opinion Index*, June, 1980, p. 4.

Support for Women's Liberation

In 1973, 58% of males and 50% of females indicated that they approved of "women's liberation" (Institute for Social Research 1973 Fall Omnibus Survey). Table 5.6 presents other information from a series of questions which use the term *women's liberation*. In

1970, a majority of males (55%) but only a minority of females (41%) indicated that they sympathized with the overall objectives of women's liberation. Thus, overall, it appears that a bare majority of Americans who have an opinion have a favorable attitude toward the concept of women's liberation. These results add further evidence to the statement made earlier that the movement for sexual equality is not a conflict between males and females, but rather a conflict between those who believe in sexual equality and those who do not. In many situations, the proportion of males favoring sexual equality is higher than the proportion of females favoring such equality.

TABLE 5.6
Attitudes toward Women's Liberation
Movement by Sex, 1970, in Percentages

	Males	Females
Generally, do you sympathize with the overall objectives of women's liberation, or not?		
Yes	55	41
No	40	51
No answer	5	8
What about their methods, do you approve or disapprove of them?		
Approve	42	29
Disapprove	50	60
No answer	8	11
Do you, yourself, take the women's liberation movement seriously, or not?		
Yes	35	23
No	63	73
No answer	2	4
Do you think it is probable, or not, that a woman could achieve the same goals of women's liberation for herself, without joining the movement?		
Can	73	77
Cannot	23	19
No answer	4	3

SOURCE: CBS survey reported in Robert Chandler, *Public Opinion: Changing Attitudes on Contemporary Political and Social Issues* (New York: R. R. Bowker, 1972), p. 50.

The next question in Table 5.6 indicates majority disapproval (50% of males and 60% of females) of the methods of women's liberation. Only 29% of females approve of the methods of women's liberation. This is rather puzzling, since the methods of the women's liberation movement do not appear to be unusual. It is possible that many people are reacting to methods *attributed* to women's liberation (such as the mythical "bra burnings") rather than the actual methods.

The next question also presents a puzzling set of results: a strong majority of both males (63%) and females (73%) indicate that they do not take the women's liberation movement seriously. Perhaps this means that the goals are not taken seriously, but the responses to the previous questions do not seem to support this type of explanation. Perhaps it means that they don't expect the movement to succeed or perhaps they don't think an organized movement is necessary. Responses to the next question seem to indicate that many people feel an organized effort is not needed. Strong majorities of both males and females feel that a woman could achieve the same goals of women's liberation for herself without joining the movement. This again demonstrates the idea presented in chapter 3 that, with regard to solutions for the problems of disadvantaged groups, Americans tend to stress individual action (work hard, get a good education, and mind your own business) rather than collective action to abolish the basis of discrimination for the whole group. In the same survey, when women were asked whether they belonged to a women's liberation group, only 1% said "yes"; when asked whether they would join such a group if they had the chance, 80% said they would not join (Chandler, 1972: 51).

Overall, the results in Table 5.6 indicate weak majority approval of women's liberation, disapproval of their methods (or alleged methods), a rejection of the seriousness of the movement, and a feeling that the goals of the movement can be achieved on an individual basis without an organizational effort. However, these results probably underestimate the degree of support for sexual equality in most situations. The problem is that the term *women's liberation* is used in all these questions, and this term has apparently taken on some symbolic meaning in the mind of the public which is distinct from the specific issues involved. One study (Corbett et al., 1977) found that student attitudes toward "the women's liberation movement" were not much related to the students' attitudes toward specific sexual equality issues (e.g., job equality). Another study is even more revealing on this point. Jacobson (1979) asked students to rate four terms: *equal rights for women, feminism, women's lib,* and *women's liberation.* On a logical basis, it might be argued that all four terms mean essentially the same thing. However, there were substantial differences in how the students rated the four terms. *Equal rights for women* received the most positive response from the students and *women's liberation* received the most negative response. *Women's lib* came in second and *feminism* came in third.

It might be argued, then, that the term *women's liberation* has a somewhat negative connotation in the United States that has nothing to do with the fundamental, specific issues involved in the movement for sexual equality. Thus, the results in Table 5.6 probably underestimate the degree of support which Americans hold for the underlying issues of sexual equality.

SUMMARY AND CONCLUSIONS

There have been tremendous changes in the American public's attitudes toward the role of women in society since around the time of World War II, and the evidence suggests that there have been small but steady changes recently toward greater support for sexual equality. Further, the "rebirth of feminism" during the 1960s has given the movement an organizational structure again. Also, there is a solid majority of Americans in favor of ratification of the Equal Rights Amendment, which would demolish the legal foundations of discrimination against both men and women on the basis of sex. Americans also give majority support to sexual equality in educational opportunities and to at least certain aspects of employment situations. Trends in public opinion and actual election results also indicate that women's chances of getting elected to public offices will increase in the coming years.

On the negative side, the examination of public attitudes also indicates some rather large obstacles to sexual equality. In the first place, the norms of society still strongly emphasize the homemaker role for women, thus making it difficult for a woman to make a free choice. In the second place, a very important aspect of the problem is that many Americans simply will not acknowledge the existence of any discrimination against women. Third, many women have accepted their traditional roles in society so completely that they themselves do not perceive the discrimination. Fourth, a majority of Americans do support discrimination against women in certain situations (e.g., hiring for jobs), and substantial minorities support discrimination in a wide range of situations. Fifth, women themselves are more likely than men are to support such discrimination in many situations. Finally, there is not much support among either men or women for organized efforts to end discrimination against women; rather, the feeling seems to be that each individual woman is to overcome discrimination through her own vigorous efforts.

These findings indicate that progress has been made toward sexual equality, but they also indicate that there is a long way to go. Americans are willing to accept such equality in certain situations, but they are far away from accepting sexual equality along the full spectrum of social, economic, political, and personal aspects of life.

6

Tolerance in Context

INTRODUCTION

So far we have been examining *levels* of tolerance in the American public, both in terms of support for First Amendment rights and support for equality. In general, levels of tolerance are low in some situations, medium in some, and high in others. It is also apparent that different individuals have different levels of tolerance. Some people are very tolerant regardless of the situation, and some are very intolerant regardless of the situation. For most people, however, the level of tolerance depends upon the situation, the context.

In this chapter and the following chapters, the concern will be with the ways in which a person's level of tolerance is related to other types of factors. In this chapter, several questions will be examined concerning the attitudes of tolerance/intolerance and the context of such attitudes. First, the question of the extent to which attitudes are translated into actual behavior is briefly discussed. Are attitudes and behavior consistent with one another? Flowing from this, an examination will be made of the question of the extent to which attitudes themselves are consistent with one another. Next, the "group-relatedness" of tolerance will be examined: to what extent does an individual's level of tolerance depend upon who (what individual or group) is to be tolerated? Finally, the extent of overlap between tolerance as support for First Amendment rights and tolerance as support for equality will be examined. A person might be highly supportive of First Amendment rights but oppose equality for particular groups, and vice versa. Some U.S.

senators, for example, are staunch defenders of the First Amendment and also staunch opponents of efforts to achieve equality for women and blacks.

ATTITUDES, BEHAVIOR, ATTITUDES

Attitudes vs. Behavior

In the early 1930s, La Piere (1934) performed a simple experiment, the results of which have been cited widely in discussions of the link between the attitudes of people and their actual behavior. La Piere traveled throughout the United States accompanied by a Chinese couple; they stayed at 66 sleeping places and ate at 184 eating places. During this trip, the Chinese couple was refused service at only one place. After returning from the trip, La Piere sent a questionnaire to the proprietors of all the sleeping and eating places he and the Chinese couple had patronized; the questionnaire asked whether the proprietors would accept members of the Chinese race as patrons in their establishments. The proprietors of 92% of the sleeping places and 93% of the eating places responded that they would *not* accept the Chinese as patrons.

The results of La Piere's study provide a classic example of inconsistency between attitudes and behavior. In this case, the proprietors were more tolerant in their actual behavior than in their expressed attitudes. There are probably many situations in which people are more tolerant in an actual situation than their expressed attitudes would indicate; conversely, people might also be less tolerant in many situations than their expressed attitudes would indicate. To what extent, then, can we expect that the behavior of people will be in accord with the attitudes they express? Gross and Niman's (1975) review of the research on this question indicates clearly that expressed attitudes are not generally a very good means of predicting the actual behavior of people. They argue that the link between expressed attitudes and actual behavior is affected by the nature of the particular situation in which behavior occurs. Crespi (1971: 334) suggests that a person's expressed attitude is a good predictor of the person's actual behavior when the person has reliable expectations of the behavioral situation; i.e., the situation is one which related to the actual past experiences of the person. If the person has already been through the type of situation which the attitude concerns, then there will probably be a high correspondence between attitude and behavior.

As an example, let's take the question: "If blacks came to live next door to you, would you move?" As indicated in chapter 4, in 1978, only 13% of whites said they would move. It can be expected that if these 13% were in an actual situation in which blacks moved next door, some would move and some would not. Further, it is likely that some who said they would not move would actually move in such a situation. Based on what Crespi is saying, the best correspondence between attitude and behavior for this issue should be found among those who had been closer in their past experiences to this type of situation—at some point a black family had lived next door or at least near to them. The worst correspondence between attitude and behavior could be expected among those who had never come close to being in this type of situation.

Any situation may draw upon a number of attitudes which a person holds; behavioral consistency with one of these attitudes might conflict with another attitude (Lane and Sears, 1964: 14). Let's say that Joe and Mary Jones said they would not move if a black family moved next door. Then a black family does move next door, and contrary to their previously expressed attitude, Joe and Mary decide to move. When asked about this inconsistency, our hypothetical couple responds:

Well, it's not that we're racists or anything like that. We personally don't mind it a bit having a black family next door. And they seem like very nice people. The thing is that we've got a lot of money tied up in this house, and it looks like the property values are going to go down in this neighborhood. If we don't sell now, we won't ever get our money back out of this house. It's a real shame, but that's the way it is.

We come back again, then, to the matter of priorities. If a particular attitude has a high priority, then a greater correspondence between attitude and behavior can be expected. If an attitude has a low priority, then behavior in a situation will more likely be determined by other, higher priority attitudes. In the situation above, the economic value has higher priority than the racial integration value. Conversely, the same emphasis on the economic value might lead to just the opposite behavior in a somewhat different context: Sam and Judy Smith, who had said they would move if blacks moved next door, decided not to move when the situation actually occurred simply because the costs of relocating would be so high.

The social context is very important in determining whether behavior will be consistent with attitudes. With regard to discrimination, Dworkin and Dworkin (1976: 79) suggest that the willingness of most Americans to discriminate in actual situations will depend

upon "the specific social circumstances in which they find themselves: the kind of pressures they are under, and from whom."
This suggests that the attitudes which people hold concerning the
importance of friendships, peer pressures, and other social relationships have a higher priority in a person's hierarchy of values
than do beliefs concerning whether discrimination is right or
wrong. Let's take two hypothetical examples. First, Joe Smith does
not believe in racial discrimination, but he works in an environment in which racial discrimination is openly advocated and practiced. Let's say that he works with a group of men in a small
Southern town, that cooperation with the other men in the group
is important in this job, and that outside social activities are carried
on primarily with his co-workers and their families. In this situation, it seems highly likely that Joe Smith's *behavior* will be in
accord with the norm of discrimination rather than his own belief
in nondiscrimination. For the second example, let's say that Mary
Jones does believe in racial discrimination, but she works in an environment in which the norms oppose discrimination both in policy
and in practice. In this situation, her *behavior* will probably be determined by the norm of nondiscrimination rather than by her own
belief in discrimination. Peer pressures can override personal beliefs in determining behavior. This is, of course, not always the
case. If the personal belief has high priority in the person's hierarchy of beliefs, then the person might act in accord with this belief
in spite of the possible costs in the social environment.

In sum, behavior is not necessarily consistent with the attitudes
a person holds. If a particular attitude has a high priority in the
person's hierarchy of beliefs, then behavior is more likely to be
consistent with the attitude. If the attitude has lower priority, then
behavior will probably be consistent with other, higher-priority attitudes.

Attitudes vs. Attitudes

When researchers deal with the gap between behavior and attitudes, the attitudes are ordinarily those expressed in a survey
situation. When these attitudes indicated in interviews do not cor-
respond to actual behavior, the usual explanation given is that
there is a gap between the interview situation and the real world.
Schuman (1972: 345) argues that this explanation overestimates the
gap between the interview situation and the real world and it also
overestimates the correspondence between one expressed attitude
and another in the same interview situation. It has already been

indicated that a person can hold different attitudes that can conflict with one another in particular situations. Schuman argues that *within* the interview situation, there are attitudinal inconsistencies as sharp as the inconsistency *between* the expressed attitude and actual behavior. Schuman's explanation for the inconsistencies among attitudes expressed in interviews is that the respondent is attempting to reconcile two or more positively held values in conflict. This is basically the same type of explanation discussed earlier.

Using data from three questions, Schuman (1972) provides a strong example of the effects of context on attitudes of tolerance. First, an overwhelming majority (85%) agreed to the idea of racial equality in jobs as implied in the statement that "employers should hire men for top management without paying any attention to whether they are white or Negro." In another question, however, a specific context alters the results. Respondents are told that two department heads don't want to work with a Negro engineer. When asked about this situation, 39% of the respondents agreed with the idea that the personnel director would be right to refuse to hire a Negro engineer in order to avoid friction with the two department heads. Thus, the value of "harmony" overrides the value of racial equality for many of the respondents.

In the third question, 50% of the respondents agreed with the idea that the personnel director could make the decision on hiring the Negro engineer on the basis of majority feeling in the company. Here, the value of "majority rule" wins out over the value of racial equality. The 85% who agreed to the general principle of racial equality in job hiring might be very sincere in their belief in this ideal; however, when other values are introduced into the context, the value of racial equality for some of the respondents is not so strong as some of the other values they hold. Schuman (1972: 353) concludes:

Faced with issues that seem to call forth other values and goals—"a good education for their children," "business success," "paying attention to the opinions of one's neighbors," "keeping law and order in the city"—the principle of nondiscrimination often loses out.

It should be clear by this point that we must be very careful in attempting to predict how people will behave in real-life situations on the basis of particular attitudes they express. On the other hand, we should not simply dismiss the importance of attitudes. For example, people might be very inclined to act more in accord with their attitudes—for better or worse—in situations requiring little effort or cost to themselves (e.g., voting for candidates or voting in a referendum). Further, when certain attitudes are widely held, the very fact that such attitudes exist might have a substantial effect on the behavior of many people. For example, it seems logical to assume that a person who holds unpopular views would be more likely to express those views in a society which at least makes the claim to be tolerant than in a society which makes no such claim. Further, it seems reasonable to assume that the amount of intolerant behavior would be less in a society which affirms tolerant principles—even simply as slogans—than one which does not.

Westie's Experiment

By now, you are well aware that many Americans who agree with general, abstract principles of tolerance are not so tolerant in specific contexts. What happens when they are confronted with this inconsistency? Complete answers cannot be given to this question, but one study has produced some very interesting results. Westie (1965) set out to test certain aspects of the theory presented in Gunnar Myrdal's *An American Dilemma* (1944). The dilemma is that Americans embrace on the one hand the Christian-democratic tenets of the "American Creed" and on the other hand—with regard to blacks—certain un-Christian, undemocratic attitudes. In Myrdal's theory, the resolution of his dilemma could take two forms: (1) the American Creed could be extended to cover blacks or (2) the Creed itself could be abandoned. Using a sample of Indianapolis citizens, Westie (1965) asked three separate sets of questions. First, respondents were asked to agree or disagree with each of ten *general* statements concerning equality (e.g., "Everyone in America should have equal opportunities to get ahead"). Second, respondents were asked to agree or disagree with ten *specific* statements concerning racial equality. Each of the ten specific statements corresponded to one of the ten general statements. Third, respondents were shown, side by side, their response to a general statement and their response to the corresponding specific statement. Then they were asked: "Any comment?" At this point, many respondents would attempt to reconcile any contradiction between their general response and their specific response. If they did not, they were asked: "Do you see any contradiction?" Most of those who perceived a contradiction gave an explanation for it, but if they did not, they were asked: "Any explanation?"

Several results from Westie's study are of interest here. First, as expected, the level of agreement with the more general statements of equality was much higher than the level of agreement for the more specific statements of racial equality. For example, 98% agreed that everyone in America "should have equal opportunities to get ahead," but only 60% would be willing "to have a Negro as my supervisor in my place of work."

A second important finding is that when respondents were shown their response to the general statement and their response to the specific statement side by side, they usually recognized on their own any contradiction between the two. In this situation, the respondents who were inconsistent were able to perceive their own inconsistency; they recognized the "dilemma."

Third, when respondents recognized the contradiction between their support for equality in the abstract, general statements and their lack of support for racial equality in the specific statements, they tended to resolve the dilemma in favor of the general ideal of equality; they changed their intolerant response on the racial equality statement to conform to their tolerant position on the general statement. Thus, there was a definite tendency to extend the American Creed to encompass blacks as well as whites; Myrdal's fear that Americans might resolve the dilemma by abandoning the American Creed appears to be unfounded. As indicated earlier, the civil rights movement led by such leaders as Martin Luther King during the early 1960s seemed to be based on the idea that Americans would resolve the dilemma in favor of equality for blacks if Americans could be confronted with the gap between equality in ideals and the actual state of inequality in which blacks existed.

A fourth finding of importance from Westie's study is that many of the explanatory comments made by the subjects were made by those who were consistent in supporting equality in both the abstract and the specific applications. Those who were taking a stand in favor of racial equality often felt a need to justify such a stand. This again demonstrates the importance of the social context; in an environment in which the support for specific applications of tolerance is relatively low, those who support tolerance might feel a need to defend their position.

Westie's experiment indicates that when people are confronted with a contradiction between their support for a general principle of tolerance and their opposition to tolerance in a specific context, many will resolve the contradiction in favor of the tolerant general principle. It must be noted, however, that these results are based on an interview situation and might not be reflective of the types of attitude changes that would occur in more normal contexts. Further, many people will simply deny the existence of any contradiction, or they will attempt to justify their position in some way.

THE GROUP-RELATEDNESS OF TOLERANCE

A very important part of the context in which tolerance or intolerance exists is the person or group to be tolerated. People might be very tolerant of certain groups and very intolerant of certain other groups, depending upon their attitude toward the particular group involved. When tolerance depends on attitudes toward the particular group involved, it is "group-related" tolerance. This idea has already been implied previously, but it will be demonstrated more fully in this section. The focus here is on tolerance as support for freedom of expression, but tolerance as equality is also involved.

Chapter 2 contained a description of the study (Sullivan *et al.*, 1979) in which respondents were asked to select the group they liked the least. Respondents were very intolerant of their least liked group; for example, only 34% would allow their least liked group to hold a public rally. While this type of finding and the findings from the Stouffer (1955) and related studies strongly suggest that tolerance is highly group-related, there is another possible explanation: perhaps most respondents would not allow a particular group to engage in a particular political act (e.g., a demonstration) simply because they would not allow *any* group to engage in that political act. We can't be sure from this type of result whether the intolerant respondents are intolerant because of the group involved or because they simply do not approve of the political act at all.

We also saw in Chapter 2 (Table 2.2) that many people do not approve of such political acts as speech making, demonstrating, and petitioning. However, in Table 2.4, we saw that the percentage who would allow a group to demonstrate or petition varied quite a bit depending upon the group involved. For example, 81% would allow a group of their neighbors to demonstrate, but only 41% would allow a demonstration by a group calling for the legalization of marijuana. These results, then, more clearly demonstrate the group-relatedness of tolerance.

Other results from the Lawrence (1976) study further demonstrate both (1) the group-relatedness of tolerance and (2) the inconsistency between support for a political act (demonstrations or petitions) in the abstract and support for this political act when carried out by a particular group. First, let's note that 59% of the respondents indicated that they would "always" approve of petitioning and 47% would "always" approve of peaceful demonstrations. Only 5% would "never" allow petitions and 17% would "never" allow demonstrations.

Having determined the respondent's attitudes toward the political act ("always," "sometimes," or "never" allow), Lawrence went on to ask whether the respondent would allow the political act by each of a series of particular groups. Since the pattern of results is basically the same for both acts, the focus here will be limited to attitudes toward demonstrations. Also, those who said that they would "sometimes" allow the political act are excluded from the discussion because it cannot be determined whether they are consistent or not.

Part of the results are presented in Table 6.1. Two points are clear from the results. First, the group-relatedness of tolerance is further demonstrated. For example, among those who said they would *always* allow demonstrations, 95% would allow demonstrations by a group concerned about crime, but only 63% would allow a demonstration by a group calling for the legalization of marijuana. Also, 33% of those who said they would *never* allow demonstrations would allow a demonstration by a group concerned about crime.

The second finding is already implicit in what has been said above: the abstract stance on the political act is not necessarily in accord with the stance on the political act in a more specific con-

TABLE 6.1
Percentages "Always" or "Never" Allowing a Demonstration
Who Would Allow a Particular Group to Demonstrate

Group	Attitude toward Demonstrations[a]	
	Always Allow	*Never Allow*
A group concerned about crime in their community	95	33
A group of your neighbors	95	30
A group of black militants	81	3
A group calling for the government to make sure that blacks can buy and rent homes in white neighborhoods (*white respondents only*)	77	2
A group calling for the legalization of marijuana	63	2

SOURCE: Adapted from Table 7 in David G. Lawrence, "Procedural Norms and Tolerance: A Reassessment," *American Political Science Review*, 70 (March, 1976), p. 92.

[a] In this 1971 survey, respondents were asked whether people should be allowed to hold peaceful demonstrations to ask the government to act on some issue. For purposes of this table, those who answered "sometimes" are omitted.

text. Among both those who would "always" allow and those who would "never" allow a demonstration, many people will deviate from their general stance depending on who it is that will be doing the demonstrating. The context can determine the level of tolerance or intolerance.

In Table 6.2, results from my own study (Corbett, 1980) of "Middletown" (Muncie, Indiana) further demonstrate the group-relatedness of tolerance. Respondents were asked to indicate their attitude (favorable, neutral, or unfavorable) toward each of eight groups; then they were asked whether each of these groups should be allowed to give a speech concerning its political views in the community. The results clearly demonstrate that those with a favorable attitude toward a group are much more likely to allow the group to give a speech than are those with an unfavorable attitude toward the group. For example, 93% of those with a favorable attitude toward conservatives would allow conservatives to give a speech; only 45% of those with an unfavorable attitude toward conservatives would allow them to speak. Only in one case (the liberal group) would a majority of those with an unfavorable attitude toward a group allow it to give a speech.

The results in the Total column of Table 6.2 also indicate one other point, a finding which is also substantiated by Sullivan *et al.* (1979): tolerance toward left-wing groups is not greatly different

TABLE 6.2
Percentage Allowing a Group to Give a Speech
by Attitude toward Group: Muncie Survey[a]

Group	Favorable		Neutral		Unfavorable		Total
Conservatives	93%	(150)	78%	(85)	45%	(15)	79%
Liberals	98%	(102)	73%	(86)	59%	(46)	76%
NAACP	97%	(116)	68%	(81)	44%	(31)	72%
Women's liberation	96%	(104)	71%	(67)	44%	(47)	69%
Atheists	96%	(25)	63%	(74)	21%	(37)	43%
Homosexuals	88%	(22)	64%	(51)	22%	(48)	37%
Communists	78%	(7)	87%	(26)	26%	(72)	33%
Ku Klux Klan	64%	(7)	42	(14)	30%	(81)	32%

SOURCE: 1978 Muncie Survey by the author; $n = 364$.
[a] Respondents were asked to indicate their general attitude toward each group on a 5-point scale going from very favorable to very unfavorable. Then they were asked: "Suppose that each of the groups below wanted to give a speech in your community concerning their political views. Please indicate for each group whether you yourself feel that the police should allow or should not allow the speech."

overall from tolerance of right-wing groups—although, of course, different people will be tolerant or intolerant toward different kinds of groups. Overall, the left-right aspect of the political dimension does not seem to be the important consideration in determining the level of tolerance toward a particular group; rather, it appears that tolerance is greatest for those groups that are closer to mainstream American political values and decreases as the values espoused by the group deviate further from prevailing norms.

TOLERANCE AND TOLERANCE

Tolerance has been discussed in terms of support for First Amendment rights and in terms of support for equality. Here the concern is with two types of questions. First, to what extent is tolerance in one area related to tolerance in the other area? Is there any connection between the level of support a person holds for First Amendment rights and the person's level of support for equality? Second, within an area, how broad or narrow is tolerance? If a person is tolerant toward one group, will that person also be tolerant toward other groups? Such questions have already been partly answered, but they will be discussed further here. Available research does not allow precise answers to such questions, but some imprecise generalizations can be formulated based on the information available.

The first generalization is that people cannot simply be categorized in any absolute sense as either "the tolerant" or "the intolerant." Most people are tolerant in some situations and intolerant in others. People are not, of course, equally tolerant; some people are much more tolerant than others. Further, a small minority of people are so tolerant under such a wide range of circumstances that it would not be too inaccurate to refer to them as tolerant in an absolute sense; on the other side, there are some who are so intolerant in such a wide variety of circumstances that they could be said to be intolerant in an absolute sense. But the great bulk of people are tolerant or intolerant by degree, depending upon the particular context. They might be tolerant toward certain persons or groups and intolerant toward others. Nunn et al. (1978: 57) note as an example the finding that anti-Semitism and racial prejudice are not usually connected; if a person is intolerant of Jews, we cannot safely predict that the person will also be intolerant of blacks, and vice versa.

Freedom of Speech across Groups

Despite the lack of a necessary connection between tolerance of one group and tolerance of another group, there might nevertheless be patterns or tendencies of such attitudes toward a variety of groups. Many people who are intolerant toward a particular group might also tend to be intolerant toward a variety of other groups. My analysis of questions from the 1977 NORC survey in Table 6.3 demonstrates this tendency with regard to support for freedom of speech for four groups: Communists, homosexuals, atheists, and racists. The results in this table (and other results from this analysis not shown) indicate that the overwhelming majority (generally about 80%) of those who would allow a speech by any one of these groups would allow a speech by another group (but not necessarily all other groups). For example, 79% of those who would allow a

TABLE 6.3
Tolerance of Speech for One Group by Tolerance of Speech for Another Group, in Percentages[a]

Allow Speech by	Allow Speech by Atheist?		Allow Speech by Racist?	
	Allow (n = 952)	*Not Allow* (n = 566)	*Allow* (n = 893)	*Not Allow* (n = 605)
Communist				
Allow	79	18	75	31
Not Allow	21	82	25	69
Homosexual				
Allow	83	31	81	40
Not Allow	17	69	19	60
Atheist				
Allow	—	—	84	33
Not Allow	—	—	16	67
Racist				
Allow	79	26	—	—
Not Allow	21	74	—	—

SOURCE: 1977 General Social Survey by the National Opinion Research Center, University of Chicago.
   [a] The basic question asked for each group was: "If such a person wanted to make a speech in your community favoring . . . should he be allowed to speak, or not?" See appendix for the full wording of the questions. The undecided respondents are excluded in the computations of the above percentages.

speech by an atheist would also allow a speech by a Communist. Further, although we associate racism with the right wing in politics and Communism with the left wing, 75% of those who would allow a speech by a racist would also allow a speech by a Communist, and 79% (result not shown in table) of those who would allow a Communist speech would also allow a racist speech. Thus, those who support freedom of speech for one of these groups also tend to support it for other groups.

The converse of the above conclusion is also true, but to a somewhat lesser extent: those who oppose freedom of speech for one of these groups also tend to oppose it for another of these groups. For example, 82% of those who would not allow an atheist to speak also would not allow a Communist speech. As another example, 60% of those not allowing a speech by a racist also would not allow a homosexual to speak. However, this latter example also demonstrates that we are dealing with tendencies rather than precise, fixed patterns; 40% of those who would not allow a racist to speak would allow a homosexual to speak.

Questions concerning tolerance of five groups (the four listed in Table 6.3 plus militarists) were included in NORC's 1977 survey. My analysis of responses to these questions indicates that one-third (33%) of the respondents were consistently tolerant in allowing a speech by each of the five groups, and 17% were consistently intolerant in not allowing a speech by any of the five groups. The remaining 50% would allow some groups to speak but would not allow others to speak, thus demonstrating this aspect of the contextual nature of tolerance for many Americans.

Equality across Groups

There is not adequate information available to delve very deeply into the question of whether support or opposition concerning equality for one group is associated with similar attitudes toward other groups. However, it can be speculated that generally there are tendencies, weak or strong depending upon which groups are involved, for those who are more supportive of equality for one group to be more likely to support equality for other groups. This type of tendency with regard to blacks and women is demonstrated by my analysis of the 1977 NORC data in Table 6.4. Of those who favor the ERA, 80% oppose laws against racial intermarriage; however, 65% of those who oppose the ERA also oppose laws against racial intermarriage. This particular tendency, then, is not very strong. Willingness to vote for a woman for President is a bet-

TABLE 6.4
Sex-Role Attitudes by Racial Attitudes, in Percentages[a]

	Attitude toward Equal Rights Amendment		Willing to Vote for a Woman for President		Women Should Run Homes, Men Run the Country	
	Favor (n = 877)	*Oppose* (n = 319)	*Yes* (n = 1177)	*No* (n = 307)	*Agree* (n = 569)	*Disagree* (n = 921)
Laws against Interracial Marriage						
Favor	20	35	23	49	67	25
Oppose	80	65	77	51	33	75
Whites Have a Right to Keep Blacks out of Neighborhoods						
Agree	34	50	36	65	63	30
Disagree	66	50	64	35	37	70
Blacks Shouldn't Push Themselves Where They're Not Wanted						
Agree	66	81	69	85	87	64
Disagree	34	19	31	15	13	36

SOURCE: 1977 General Social Survey by the National Opinion Research Center, University of Chicago.
[a] For full questions, see appendix. Undecided respondents are excluded in the computation of the above percentages.

ter predictor of racial attitudes. For example, only 36% of those willing to vote for a woman for President (as compared to 65% of those not willing) agreed with the idea that whites have a right to keep blacks out of their neighborhoods. There also appears to be a fairly strong connection between racial attitudes and attitudes toward the idea that women should run their homes while men run the country. For example, 67% of those who want women to stay in the home favor laws against racial intermarriage, as contrasted with only 25% of those who reject the stay-at-home role for women.

In sum, there is a tendency for those who take a tolerant position on sexual equality issues to take a tolerant position on racial equality issues. This is, however, only a tendency. In the first place, only a minority of the respondents were consistently tolerant or intolerant on either the three sexual equality issues or the three racial equality issues. Only 39% took the tolerant position on all three sexual equality issues, and only 19% took the tolerant position on all three racial equality issues. In the second place, it is apparent that support for equality for one of these groups does not completely translate into support for equality for the other group. In the third place, the findings would be further complicated if information were available concerning equality for other groups. Nevertheless, these limited findings do suggest that there is some degree of generalizability to attitudes toward equality.

Freedom of Expression and Equality

The available information does not allow a specification of how tolerance of First Amendment rights for any particular group might be related to support for equality for all conceivable groups. Again, however, there are at least some tendencies which are apparent from the information available. It can be generalized that those who support First Amendment rights for unpopular minorities are more likely to support equality for various groups. My analysis in Table 6.5 shows a connection between support for freedom of speech for atheists and racists on the one hand and support for sexual and racial equality on the other hand. Further, although the results are not shown, the same type of pattern also holds up with regard to support for freedom of speech for Communists, homosexuals, and militarists.

The results in Table 6.5 demonstrate a tendency for those who are more supportive of freedom of speech to be more supportive of sexual and racial equality. For example, 85% of those who would

TABLE 6.5
Tolerance of Speech Attitudes by Sex-Role and Racial Attitudes, in Percentages[a]

	Allow Speech by Atheist?		Allow Speech by Racist?	
Attitude toward the Equal Rights Amendment	*Allow* ($n = 952$)	*Not Allow* ($n = 566$)	*Allow* ($n = 893$)	*Not Allow* ($n = 605$)
Favor	77	65	76	70
Oppose	23	35	24	30
Willing to Vote for a Woman for President				
Yes	85	69	83	74
No	15	31	17	26
Laws against Racial Intermarriage				
Favor	14	53	19	41
Oppose	86	47	81	59
Whites Have a Right to Keep Blacks Out of Their Neighborhoods				
Agree	32	61	36	52
Disagree	68	39	64	48

SOURCE: 1977 General Social Survey by the National Opinion Research Center, University of Chicago.
[a] For full wording of the questions, see appendix. Undecideds are excluded from the computations of the percentages above.

allow an atheist speech would be willing to vote for a woman for President, as compared to 69% of those who would not allow an atheist speech. Thus, there is a tendency, although not a really strong tendency, for support of First Amendment rights for unpopular minorities to go hand in hand with support for sexual equality. This tendency is somewhat stronger with regard to racial equality. For example, only 14% of those who would allow an atheist to speak—as compared to 53% of those who would not allow such a speech—favored laws against racial intermarriage. Interestingly enough, those who are less racist are more likely to be among those who support the right of a racist to speak: support for laws against racial intermarriage is more than twice as high (41% as

compared to 19%) among those who would not allow a racist to
speak as among those who would.

Overall Support

So far tolerance has been viewed in terms of responses to single
questions. A better picture can be provided by examining the number of tolerant responses an individual makes to several different
questions. The 1977 NORC survey asked people whether they
would allow a speech by each of five persons: an atheist, a racist, a
Communist, a militarist, and a homosexual. For these five questions, a person could make from zero (not allow any of the five to
speak) to five (allow all five to speak) tolerant responses. Similarly,
a person could make from zero to three tolerant responses on the
three sexual equality questions (willingness to vote for a woman for
President, support for the ERA, and disagreement with the idea
that women should run their homes while men run the country). A
person could also make from zero to three tolerant responses on
the three racial equality issues (disagreement with the idea that

TABLE 6.6
Distribution of Tolerant Responses on Sexual Equality, Racial
Equality, and Freedom of Speech Questions, in Percentages[a]

Number of Tolerant Responses	Three Sexual Equality Questions	Three Racial Equality Questions	Five Freedom of Speech Questions	All Eleven Questions Combined
None	12	30	17	3
One	21	24	14	6
Two	28	27	11	8
Three	39	19	11	9
Four			14	9
Five			33	8
Six				8
Seven				10
Eight				10
Nine				10
Ten				10
Eleven				9

SOURCE: 1977 General Social Survey by the National Opinion Research Center,
University of Chicago.
  [a] For full wording of the questions, see appendix.

whites have a right to keep blacks out of their neighborhoods, opposition to laws against racial intermarriage, and disagreement with the idea that blacks shouldn't push themselves where they're not wanted).

My analysis in Table 6.6 presents the distribution of tolerant responses (as opposed to intolerant, undecided, or no response at all) for the three sexual equality questions, the three racial equality questions, the five freedom of speech questions, and all eleven questions combined. No claim is made that these questions are perfect indicators of sexual equality, racial equality, or freedom of speech attitudes; they do not, however, need to be perfect in order to demonstrate the points which follow.

This analysis indicates that 39% took a completely tolerant position on the three sexual equality issues, 19% were tolerant on all three racial equality questions, and 33% would allow all five persons to speak. Only 9% of the respondents, a tiny minority, gave the tolerant response for all eleven questions; on the other hand, only 3% failed to give even one tolerant response for the eleven questions. Thus, there is a great deal of diversity in tolerance among people for each of the three issue areas and for all three combined. This further demonstrates the point that while some people are either very tolerant or very intolerant in a wide variety of situations, most people are either tolerant or intolerant depending upon the particular situation.

SUMMARY AND CONCLUSIONS

How tolerant are Americans? It depends a lot on the context. The same person can be very tolerant in some situations and very intolerant in others. It depends a lot on who is to be tolerated. It also depends on how abstract or specific the situation is; people are much more tolerant in terms of abstract ideals which have a sloganistic aura than when asked about much more specific situations. It can also depend on what kind of tolerance we're talking about. Some who are very tolerant in terms of freedom of expression are not tolerant in terms of equality, and vice versa. In a sense, it also depends on whether we are talking about tolerant attitudes or tolerant behavior. In some situations, people might be more tolerant in their expressed attitudes than they are in actual practice; in other situations, people might be more tolerant in real-life contexts than you would expect on the basis of the things they say.

While the results examined in this chapter indicate that the level of tolerance of an individual can vary quite a bit depending on the context, the evidence also clearly indicates that some people are generally more tolerant than others. For example, for the eleven questions used from the 1977 NORC survey, 29% of the respondents gave tolerant responses to at least nine questions; on the other hand, 26% gave three or fewer tolerant responses. These results demonstrate quite well that there are different general levels of tolerance among different individuals. In the following chapters, an attempt will be made to give some explanations for why some people are more tolerant than others.

7

The Distribution of Tolerance

INTRODUCTION

In this chapter an examination will be made of relationships between tolerance and a variety of social and political background
characteristics of people. Tolerance is not evenly divided throughout society; people with certain background characteristics tend to
be more tolerant than people with other characteristics. What kinds
of people tend to be more tolerant or less tolerant? For example,
are males or females more tolerant?

Most of the characteristics to be examined in this chapter are social characteristics. With regard to sex, race, and age it might be
objected that these are biological/physical characteristics rather
than social characteristics. The point, however, is that such characteristics (along with other characteristics such as income or region of residence) lead to different types of social experiences.
These differences in social experiences, rather than the social characteristic itself, can lead to different levels of tolerance among individuals.

It might be useful at the beginning to provide an organizing
concept for the consideration of the effects of various social characteristics on political tolerance. Diversity seems to be the crucial concept. Tolerance itself implies an acceptance of diversity; an exposure to diversity, in turn, should contribute to the growth of tolerance among individuals, an idea suggested by Stouffer (1955),
McClosky (1964), and Nunn et al. (1978). Different social characteristics of people can lead to a greater or lesser diversity of social ex-

periences. For example, do males or females have more diverse social experiences? If we answer that males have more diverse experiences, then males could be expected to be more tolerant than females. Do rural residents or urban residents have more diverse social experiences? If we agree that urban residents ordinarily have more diverse experiences than rural residents, then we would expect urban residents to be more tolerant. This focus on social characteristics in terms of the degree of diversity of social experiences is limited in its usefulness, but it should be more helpful than simply considering each social characteristic in isolation with no theoretical link between it and political tolerance.

In addition to such social characteristics as age, sex, race, education, income, region of residence, the urban-rural difference, and occupation, other characteristics which include beliefs will also be considered. The focus will be primarily on general political orientations (e.g., political party preference) and religious orientations. Both these types of belief characteristics are, of course, tied in with social characteristics.

TOLERANCE AND SOCIOECONOMIC CHARACTERISTICS

Education

Considering all the social characteristics of people, many would agree with the contention of Williams et al. (1976: 397) that education is the most important in the development of tolerance. Education has been found to be related to tolerance in many studies (e.g., McClosky, 1964; Stouffer, 1955; Nunn et al., 1978; Greeley and Sheatsley, 1974). Those who have higher education are more tolerant regardless of whether tolerance is defined in terms of support for freedom of expression or in terms of support for equality. Presumably education exposes people to greater social diversity, and it also leads to greater learning of democratic norms.

Because of the importance attributed to education in the development of tolerance, education and learning will be discussed more fully in the next chapter; at that point it will be seen that there are some possible theoretical problems in the tolerance-education relationship. In this chapter, the relationship between tolerance and education will be briefly demonstrated, leaving fuller discussion to the next chapter. However, education will serve another use in this chapter. With regard to the relationships between tolerance and certain social characteristics such as income, it has been suggested that the really important, underlying factor contributing to tolerance is not the social characteristic (e.g., income) but rather the education level. For example, if people with higher income are more tolerant, this might actually be due to the higher education level of people with high income. Thus, in examining the relationships between tolerance and certain social characteristics, the possible influence of education on the relationship will also be considered.

Table 7.1, based on my analysis of the 1977 NORC survey, demonstrates a clear pattern of connection between tolerance and education level. Those who have higher education are more tolerant in terms of freedom of speech, sexual equality, and racial equality. With regard to freedom of speech, for example, 80% or more of those with some college or a college degree would allow

TABLE 7.1
Percentages Tolerant by Education Level

	8 years or Less (n = 265)	9–12 Years (n = 799)	1–3 Years of College (n =237)	4 or more Years of College (n = 219)
Allow atheist to speak	30	63	80	84
Allow racist to speak	44	58	69	77
Allow Communist to speak	26	55	71	83
Allow militarist to speak	23	50	64	78
Allow homosexual to speak	34	64	79	83
Willing to vote for a woman for President	63	79	88	91
Favor the ERA	64	74	76	76
Disagree that women should run their homes while men run the country	29	62	80	83
Oppose laws against racial intermarriage	38	72	89	90
Disagree that whites have a right to keep blacks out of their neighborhoods.	34	57	65	77
Disagree that blacks shouldn't push where they're not wanted	14	21	35	52

SOURCE: NORC General Social Survey, 1977. See appendix for full wording of the tolerance questions.

an atheist to speak; this percentage goes down to 63% of those with nine to twelve years of school, and drops drastically—to 30%— for those with eight years or less of school. With regard to sexual equality, 91% of college graduates expressed a willingness to vote for a woman for President—as opposed to 88% of those with some college, 79% of those with nine to twelve years of school, and 63% of those with eight years or less. With regard to racial equality, at least 89% of those with some college or a college degree oppose laws against interracial marriage; this percentage drops to 72% of those with nine to twelve years, and the percentage drops drastically to 38% of those with eight years or less. For all eleven questions, the percentage tolerant always rises with each educational level. Thus, there is a very clear tendency for greater tolerance to go with greater education.

The differences in tolerance among the different education categories are even more dramatic when a combination of questions concerning tolerance is used, rather than individual questions one at a time. For example, 64% of those with a college degree took the tolerant positon on all five freedom of speech questions—as opposed to 49% of those with some college, 28% of those with nine to twelve years of school, and a tiny 8% of those with eight years or less. This same general type of pattern prevails with regard to sexual equality and racial equality issues. Thus, there is a distinct pattern of differences in tolerance among the different education categories when a single question is used; when a combination of questions is used, the pattern is even more distinct. No claim is made that these particular questions are the perfect questions to measure tolerance, but they do not need to be perfect in order to demonstrate this pattern.

Income

Generally, people with higher incomes usually have a greater exposure to social diversity than people with lower incomes. Thus, on the basis of the idea that greater exposure to social diversity leads to greater tolerance, people with higher incomes could be expected to be more tolerant than people with lower incomes. My examination of the eleven tolerance questions from the 1977 NORC survey indicates that for all eleven questions those in the highest income category ($20,000 or more per year) were the most tolerant and those in the lowest income category (under $10,000) were the least tolerant. Six of these questions are presented in Table 7.2. As an example, 85% of those in the highest income category opposed laws against racial intermarriage—as compared to 74% to 77% of those in the middle income categories and only 59% of those in the lowest category. To demonstrate the point further, almost half (49%) of those in the highest income category would allow a speech by all five hypothetical persons (atheist, racist, etc.), but only 20% of those in the lowest income category would allow speeches by all five. Although people with lower income tend to support the "liberal" position on economic issues (e.g., medical care, housing programs, efforts of the government to provide jobs), they tend to take a nonliberal position on noneconomic issues (Erikson *et al.*, 1980: 158). Lipset and Raab (1970: 435–439) indicate that lower income whites are more racist and more anti-Semitic than higher income whites. People with lower income are also less supportive of equality in job opportunities for homosexuals (*Gallup Opinion Index*, October, 1977: 3).

TABLE 7.2
Percentages Tolerant by Income Level

	Under $10,000 (*n* = 512)	$10,000– $14,999 (*n* = 288)	$15,000– $19,999 (*n* = 217)	$20,000 or More (*n* = 381)
Allow atheist to speak	49	67	72	76
Allow racist to speak	49	65	64	68
Willing to vote for a woman for President	72	82	83	88
Favor the ERA	72	74	73	77
Disagree that whites have a right to keep blacks out of their neighborhoods	49	56	61	71
Oppose laws against racial intermarriage	59	74	77	85

SOURCE: National Opinion Research Center 1977 General Social Survey. See appendix for full wording of the tolerance questions.

While the research demonstrates that tolerance is lower among lower income groups, the reasons for this are not completely clear. In the first place, much of this relationship between income and tolerance can be accounted for by the higher education level of those with higher income and lower education level of those with lower income. Thus, it can be argued that income per se really doesn't have much effect on tolerance. On the other hand, at least some of the differences in tolerance among different income groups cannot be accounted for on the basis of differences in education. For example, if differences in tolerance among different income categories are examined *within* one education category, the differences in tolerance among the different income groups are not so great; however, there are still differences. Within a given education category, there is still a tendency for those with higher incomes to be more tolerant. To take a specific example, among the 1977 NORC survey respondents with one year or more of college education, 86% of those in the highest income category would allow a speech by an atheist, compared to 83% of those in the middle income categories and 72% of those in the lowest income category. Thus, when education is taken into account, the differences in tolerance among the different income categories are not so sharp, but there is still a tendency for those with higher incomes to be more tolerant.

It seems reasonable to assume that the greater capability to deal with the world produced by a higher income and the probable greater exposure to social diversity would contribute to the development of tolerance in an individual. The greater income could also lead to a greater sense of personal security and well-being which could translate into a greater willingness to tolerate others. Based on Maslow's (1954) concept of a "need hierarchy," Shingles and Walrath (1981) propose a psychological explanation of why people with higher income should be more tolerant. Basically, Maslow suggests that humans must fulfill certain physiological needs (hunger, shelter, etc.) first. Once these needs have been fulfilled, the individual seeks to fulfill nonmaterial needs (e.g., love, self-esteem, self-actualization). Shingles and Walrath (1981) suggest that when people have done relatively well in material terms (as indicated, for example, by higher income), needs related to self-development will lead to greater tolerance; the need for self-development (or self-actualization) entails a great deal of freedom. People in lower income brackets feel less secure because they are still more concerned with fulfilling material needs; therefore, they do not place as much value on self-development or on human freedom. In sum, Shingles and Walrath (1981) propose that material security leads to support for freedom. Material security, however, is a psychological concept as well as an economic concept. The 1977 NORC survey asked respondents: "During the last few years, has your financial situation been getting better, getting worse, or has it stayed the same?" There is not much difference in tolerance between those who indicated that their financial situation had stayed the same and those who said it had gotten worse. However, those who said that their financial situation had gotten better were more tolerant on all eleven of the tolerance questions discussed before. For example, 72% of the "getting better" group would allow an atheist to speak, as compared to approximately 57% of the others. This is an indication that the individual's perception of his or her financial situation can have an effect on how tolerant the individual is.

In sum, there is a relationship between income and tolerance: those with higher incomes are more tolerant. Some of this relationship, however, can be accounted for by the higher education of those with higher incomes. On the other hand, it appears that there is at least some effect on tolerance which is due to the income itself.

Occupation

When occupation is used as a variable in research, it is usually condensed into broad categories such as "white-collar vs. blue-collar," or "manual vs. nonmanual," or a set of about four to seven categories (e.g., business and professional, clerical and sales, worker and service, and farm). The usual finding is that those in the upper status occupations are more tolerant than those in the lower status occupations. Lipset and Raab (1970: 435, 439), for example, find that racism and anti-Semitism are greatest among those in the "farm" and "worker and service" occupations and lower in the "clerical and sales" and "business and professional" categories. Manual workers are less supportive than nonmanual workers of equality in job opportunities for homosexuals (*Gallup Opinion Index*, October, 1977: 3). Stouffer (1955) and Nunn *et al.* (1978) found that white-collar workers are more tolerant than blue-collar workers in terms of support for freedom of expression for atheists, socialists, and Communists. Thus, there is an overall pattern of greater tolerance among those in the higher status occupations and lower tolerance among those in the lower status occupations.

Lipset's (1960: 100) concept of "working-class authoritarianism" needs to be mentioned. Lipset proposes that members of the working class (basically manual workers) share an authoritarian, intolerant set of attitudes which is produced by their working-class situation. These intolerant predispositions are primarily due to such factors as low education, low participation in voluntary associations, little reading, isolated occupations (e.g., farming), economic insecurity, and authoritarian family practices. This concept has generated some support (e.g., Grabb, 1979) and a great deal of criticism (e.g., Lipsitz, 1965; Miller and Riessman, 1961), and no attempt will be made here to resolve the issue of whether "working-class authoritarianism" actually exists or not. Basically, this type of approach suggests that there is a whole series of factors surrounding occupational status which lead to the lower tolerance of working-class individuals.

It appears that the connection between occupation and tolerance is due primarily to differences in education among the various occupations. Nunn et al. (1978: 62) demonstrate that individuals with similar education levels have similar levels of tolerance, regardless of their occupation. Individuals with similar occupations, however, do not have similar levels of tolerance if their education levels are different. While Nunn et al. (1978: 63) emphasize that differences in education account for most of the differences in tolerance among different occupations, they also indicate that some of the effects on tolerance might be due to "the power and control over one's environment afforded by high occupational position." In short, occupation by itself does not appear to have a great effect on the development of tolerance, but it might have some effect.

TOLERANCE AND SOCIOBIOLOGICAL CHARACTERISTICS

Sex

Despite the divergent social experiences of males and females in American society, there are few differences in the political opinions of men and women. With the exception of a small number of political issues (e.g., gun control legislation), research has indicated little difference between the political views of men and women, even on such issues as the Equal Rights Amendment and abortion (Erikson et al., 1980: 186). Men and women do not differ greatly in levels of tolerance, either in terms of support for freedom of expression or support for equality.

To the extent that differences in tolerance between men and women do exist, the usual finding is that men are a little more tolerant. In terms of tolerance of atheists, socialists, and Communists, males were found to be somewhat more tolerant than females (Stouffer, 1955; Nunn et al., 1978). Further, women were less tolerant than men even when other social characteristics (e.g., education, occupation, age) were taken into account. The somewhat greater tolerance among men, then, is not due to such factors as their higher education levels. Nunn *et al.* (1978: 119) suggest that the greater tolerance of men is due to the greater diversity of social experiences of males which grows out of the sexual inequality in society.

My analysis of the 1977 NORC survey indicates rather minor differences between males and females with regard to support for freedom of expression for an atheist, a Communist, a racist, a militarist, or a homosexual. Males are just slightly more tolerant. Overall, 36% of the males, as compared to 31% of the females, would allow all five hypothetical persons to give speeches. For the six racial and sexual equality questions, males and females are almost exactly the same in terms of support for equality.

In sum, there is little difference in tolerance between men and women. To the extent that there is a difference, men tend to be a little more tolerant, due perhaps to their greater diversity of social experiences.

Race

Race, as might be expected, is relevant for many types of political opinions. Monroe (1975: 92) argues that race constitutes the greatest social cleavage in America as far as political opinions are concerned. Laurence (1970) demonstrates that there are differences in political attitudes—including tolerance issues—between white and black children and that these differences increase with age. Laurence suggests that these differences in attitudes exist because of selective socialization and that differences in socialization exist because white children and black children occupy different positions in society.

Based on the idea of exposure to social diversity, whites could be expected to be more tolerant than blacks. Compared to blacks, whites have advantages in terms of education, income, occupation, and general cultural background. These advantages should lead to a greater diversity of social experiences and, therefore, to a greater degree of tolerance. On the other hand, blacks have suffered as a result of intolerance and might therefore be more supportive of tolerance. The effects of these divergent influences on tolerance seems to produce a mixed picture with regard to whether whites or blacks are more tolerant. In the first place, my analysis of the 1977 NORC survey indicates that differences in tolerance between whites and blacks are not great (Table 7.3). In the second place, it appears that whites are somewhat more tolerant than blacks. In

TABLE 7.3
Percentages Tolerant By Race[a]

	Whites (n = 1339)	Blacks (n = 176)
Allow atheist to speak	64	55
Allow Communist to speak	57	50
Allow racist to speak	61	49
Allow militarist to speak	52	46
Allow homosexual to speak	65	56
Willing to vote for a woman for President	80	78
Disagree that women should run their homes while men run the country	63	55
Favor the Equal Rights Amendment	72	82

SOURCE: National Opinion Research Center 1977 General Social Survey. See appendix for full wording of the tolerance questions.
[a] The questions concerning racial equality were not asked of black respondents.

terms of freedom of speech, for example, whites were more willing than blacks to allow each of the five hypothetical persons to speak. Overall, 34% of whites, as compared to 24% of blacks, would allow all five persons to speak.

There are qualifications to be made concerning the apparent tendency of whites to be more tolerant than blacks. First, on some issues blacks are more tolerant than whites—in addition to the obvious issue of racial equality. Table 7.3 indicates, for example, that support for the Equal Rights Amendment is greater among blacks than among whites, although blacks were somewhat less supportive of sexual equality on the other two issues. Blacks also seem to be somewhat more supportive of equality in job opportunities for homosexuals (Gallup Opinion Index, October, 1977: 3) and less supportive of discrimination against Jews (Quinley and Glock, 1979: 58). Thus, while whites are more tolerant than blacks on almost all the questions in Table 7.3, this does not mean that whites are more tolerant in all types of situations.

The second qualification that needs to be made is that other socioeconomic characteristics and differences in the entire cultural background need to be taken into consideration. Blacks have lower income, education, and occupational status than whites, and such characteristics are related to the development of tolerance. Considering these conditions, it is remarkable that blacks are so similar to whites in tolerance. Thus, status as a deprived group in American society appears to have both negative and positive effects on the development of tolerance among blacks.

There are large patterns of sociocultural differences in the backgrounds of blacks and whites which can lead to the mixed picture of tolerance. The factor of education alone, for example, is not sufficient to explain these differences. Nevertheless, the tolerance questions were examined by education level for whites and blacks. These results can be briefly summarized without presentation. First, among both whites and blacks, tolerance increases with education. Second, the differences in tolerance among the education categories are greater than the differences between the race categories; thus, education is more important in explaining differences in tolerance than race is. Third, within education categories the mixed picture concerning race and tolerance persists; whites are more tolerant than blacks on most of the questions, but blacks are more tolerant on some. Education alone is not a sufficient concept to delineate the large patterns of sociocultural differences in the backgrounds of whites and blacks.

In sum, there are differences in tolerance between whites and blacks, but these differences are not large. Whites tend to be more tolerant than blacks on many, but not all, issues.

Age

Among children, as will be discussed more fully in the next chapter, tolerance increases with age (Zellman, 1975). Apparently this increase in tolerance among children as they age is partly due to increased knowledge, but it has been suggested that the child simply does not have the cognitive ability to be very tolerant until a certain level of maturity is reached (Patterson, 1979; Zellman, 1975).

Among adults, older people are less tolerant than younger people. This is demonstrated by my analysis of the 1977 NORC survey in Table 7.4. For example, the percentage of those under thirty who would allow an atheist to speak—81%—is more than twice as high as the percentage of those sixty or older—36%—who would allow an atheist to speak. With regard to both the freedom of speech questions and the sexual and racial equality questions, those in the younger age brackets are more tolerant than those in the older age brackets.

The greater tolerance of younger people has been demonstrated in many studies. Younger people are more supportive of racial

TABLE 7.4
Percentages Tolerant by Age

	Under 30 (n = 368)	30–39 (n = 303)	40–49 (n = 255)	50–59 (n = 267)	60 or Older (n = 330)
Allow atheist to speak	81	77	61	57	36
Allow racist to speak	66	71	62	56	43
Allow Communist to speak	71	65	57	56	33
Allow militarist to speak	66	65	48	49	27
Allow homosexual to speak	75	74	63	68	39
Willing to vote for a woman President	89	87	79	83	60
Favor the ERA	83	74	68	76	65
Disagree that whites have a right to keep blacks out of their out of their neighborhoods	70	63	61	53	41
Oppose laws against racial intermarriage	88	83	74	66	47

SOURCE: National Opinion Research Center 1977 General Social Survey. See appendix for full wording of the tolerance questions.

equality (e.g., Campbell, 1971; Chandler, 1972; Greeley and Sheatsley, 1974), and they are less anti-Semitic (Lipset and Raab, 1970). Welch's (1975) study of women's attitudes toward sexual equality adds further evidence to the finding that younger people are more supportive of sexual equality. Younger people are more supportive of equality in job opportunities for homosexuals (*Gallup Opinion Index*, October, 1977: 3). Many other studies could be cited to demonstrate that younger people are more equalitarian, less prejudiced, and more supportive of civil liberties.

One possible explanation of the differences in tolerance between younger people and older people is that younger people have higher education levels. Education has greatly expanded in American society in the last few decades. For example, in the 1977 NORC survey, 39% of those in the under thirty age bracket had one or more years of college—as compared to only 20% of those over fifty years of age. While the higher education levels of the younger age brackets do account for some of the greater tolerance among younger people, this is not the complete explanation (Nunn *et al.*, 1978: 80). Within education categories, those in the older age brackets still tend to be less tolerant. For example, in the NORC 1977 survey, among those who had one or more years of college, 91% of the under-thirty age bracket would allow an atheist to speak compared to only 64% of those over fifty years old. Among those with nine to twelve years of school, 67% of those under thirty—as compared to 48% of those over fifty—disagreed with the idea that whites have a right to keep blacks out of their neighborhoods. Thus, the higher education of younger people accounts for some of their greater tolerance, but not all of it. Even within a particular education level, younger people are more tolerant than older people.

There are two fundamental explanations for the greater intolerance among older people. First, the "Life Cycle Model" assumes that people change toward less tolerant views as they age (Zellman, 1975: 38). It is argued that people become less flexible and more cautious as they grow older, and they are consequently less tolerant than they were when they were younger. In this veiw, aging processes lead to attitudinal changes in a less tolerant direction.

Second, the "Generational Model" assumes that attitudes formed early in life remain fairly stable over the lifetime of the individual; the basic attitudes do not change as the person grows older (Zellman, 1975: 38). There is a certain time period in the lives of people— basically between puberty and age thirty—when the basic political orientations are crystallized for the individual. Once these political orientations are formed, they remain basically unchanged throughout the life of the individual.

Which of these explanations seems to account for the finding that older people are less tolerant than younger people? Longitudinal research (comparisons of survey results from different points in time) supports the Generational Model. Zellman's (1975) review concludes that the Generational Model is more appropriate in explaining the relationship between age and tolerance. To put it simply, older people are more intolerant now because they were more intolerant when they were younger—*not* because they became less tolerant as they grew older.

Davis (1975), Cutler and Kaufman (1975), and Nunn *et al.* (1978) all compare results from surveys in the 1970s with the baseline established by the 1954 tolerance study by Stouffer (1955). All these studies find that American society has become much more tolerant since 1954, at least with regard to the rights of atheists, socialists, and Communists. Further, and very importantly, all age brackets have become more tolerant. For example, those presently in the forty to forty-nine age bracket are more tolerant than the forty to forty-nine age bracket was in 1954. Thus, there has been a trend in American society toward greater tolerance for these groups (atheists, socialists, and Communists), and this tolerance is higher among all age brackets. The most crucial finding for the Generational Model, however, is that people at a given age level are not less tolerant than their age cohort in 1954. For example, those who were fifty years old in 1974 were thirty years old in 1954 when Stouffer did his study. The results indicate that people age fifty in 1974 were not less tolerant than people age thirty in 1954. Thus, people in a given age bracket did not become less tolerant as they moved into higher age brackets.

These results provide strong evidence for the Generational Model. Let's take one age bracket to demonstrate. Those in the thirty to thirty-nine age bracket in 1954 were fairly tolerant in comparison with the older age brackets. By 1974, these people are now in the fifty to fifty-nine age bracket. The Life Cycle Model would predict that they are now less tolerant. By comparison with the younger age brackets, they are no longer so tolerant. But they have not changed toward a less tolerant position as they grew older; on the contrary, they are somewhat *more* tolerant than when they were younger. But American society as a whole has become much more tolerant. Thus, in relation to younger people, they are now *relatively* lower in tolerance.

As a final note, Cutler and Kaufman (1975: 80) do not entirely rule out the possibility that the aging process can have some effect on tolerance. Older people did not become less tolerant in these studies; they became somewhat more tolerant. However, the *degree* of change among the older people as American society became more tolerant was smaller than the degree of change in the younger age brackets. This suggests that the aging process might produce less inclination to change attitudes. Foner (1974), however, demonstrates that people's political attitudes do not become rigid as they grow older; not only do older people change their political attitudes, but they can change toward a more liberal direction.

TOLERANCE AND RESIDENCE

Region

With regard to tolerance as either support for freedom of expression or as support for equality, the basic pattern is that residents of the

West are the most tolerant, followed closely by Northeasterners; Midwesterners are in the middle, and Southerners are the least tolerant. This pattern prevails with regard to the region in which people presently live and the region in which they grew up. Table 7.5 demonstrates this pattern with regard to the region in which a person lived at the age of sixteen, based on my analysis of the 1977 NORC survey.

TABLE 7.5
Percentages Tolerant by Region at Age Sixteen[a]

	South (n = 499)	Midwest (n = 469)	Northeast (n = 312)	West (n = 177)
Allow atheist to speak	49	66	69	82
Allow racist to speak	52	63	63	71
Allow Communist to speak	42	63	63	73
Allow militarist to speak	40	54	60	67
Allow homosexual to speak	48	69	73	82
Willing to vote for a woman for President	76	80	84	84
Favor the ERA	69	72	79	76
Disagree that whites have a right to keep blacks out of their neighborhoods	45	58	64	73
Oppose laws against racial intermarriage	50	77	80	90

SOURCE: National Opinion Research Center 1977 General Social Survey. The full wording of the tolerance questions is given in appendix.
[a] Respondents were asked what state they lived in when they were sixteen years old. See appendix for the states included within each region.

Differences in tolerance among the regions have been found in a number of studies, and the basic rankings of the regions in tolerance are almost always the same: West, Northeast, Midwest, and South. This pattern is demonstrated in terms of support for freedom of expression (e.g., Wilson, 1975; Nunn et al., 1978; Stouffer, 1955), racial equality (e.g., Campbell, 1971; Lipset and Raab, 1970), sexual equality (Table 7.5), and support for equality in job opportunities for homosexuals (Gallup Opinion Index, October, 1977: 3). A partial exception is that Northeasterners are the most tolerant in terms of anti-Semitism issues (Lipset and Raab, 1970: 439).

Different educational levels among the regions could account for some of the differences in tolerance. Westerners and Northeasterners are the most tolerant and they also have the highest education levels; Southerners are the least tolerant and also have the lowest education level. Again, however, education alone does not account for all the differences. As Table 7.5 indicates, for example, only 49% of Southerners would allow an atheist to speak. However, my analysis indicates that 71% of Southerners with at least one year of college would allow an atheist to speak; thus, at least part of the lower tolerance of Southerners appears to be due to their lower education levels. At a given education level, the differences in tolerance among respondents from different regions are not as dramatic as they appear when education is not taken into account. Yet, there are still differences, even when education is taken into account (Stouffer, 1955; Nunn et al., 1978). In the example above, although 71% of Southerners with at least one year of college would allow an atheist to speak, 85% of those outside the South with one or more years of college would allow an atheist to speak.

These results suggest that there might be cultural variations from one region to another which account for differences in tolerance. The term *culture* refers to the shared patterns of behaviors and attitudes within a society. Such patterns include the entire range of human concerns: political, economic, social, religious, moral, and so on. Within society, there are dominant themes about what should be done, how it should be done, and how the individual should think. Within any society, however, there can also be any number of subcultures; the members of a subculture usually share some of the patterns of attitudes and behaviors of the general culture, but they also have some patterns which are different from the general culture. Thus, there might be regional subcultures which are relevant to the differences among the regions in tolerance.

Putting tolerance issues aside for the moment, an examination of regional political views on a variety of substantive political issues by Erikson et al. (1980: 181) indicates that regional differences in political issues are disappearing, and it is also suggested that any differences that remain can be explained on the basis of different group compositions of the regions rather than on the basis of different political cultures. Thus, a possible explanation for regional differences in tolerance is that the populations of the different regions are different in terms of such characteristics as income, education, urbanism, and so on.

While the above explanation might account for regional differences for many types of political issues, it does not appear to account for all the regional differences in tolerance—at least not with regard to differences between the South and the rest of the nation. In the first place, both Stouffer (1955) and Nunn *et al.* (1978) found that there were differences in tolerance for atheists, socialists, and Communists between the regions even after differences in education and urbanism were taken into account. For example, people with a high school education living in an urban area in the West are more tolerant than people with a high school education living in an urban area in the South.

In the second place, research indicates that there are regional variations in political culture—and even distinct variations among the states (Patterson, 1968). Basically this means that a particular region has a tendency to hold certain sets of political orientations, and these orientations are passed on from generation to generation. This does not, of course, mean that the political cultures of the regions are entirely different from one another; it does mean that there can be some substantial differences in the political cultures of the different regions. It also does not mean that everyone in the region shares the dominant political values. What is suggested is that people in a given region are more likely to adopt certain political orientations than people in another region. One of the chief studies to indicate that regional subcultures exist is that by Middleton (1976) who compared racial attitudes in the South with the rest of the country. Even after taking into consideration whether people lived in urban or rural areas, what their education levels were, and their status on some economic variables, Middleton (1976: 110) concluded that racism is still higher in the South than in the rest of the nation. This indicates that there is a distinct Southern subculture and that differences in tolerance are not just due to such factors as the lower levels of education, income, and urbanism in the South.

In terms of changes in tolerance that have occurred in the regions in recent years, two different observations can be made. First, Greeley and Sheatsley's (1974: 245) analysis indicates that support for racial equality increased in all regions between 1963 and 1972. Further, although Southerners were still the lowest in support for racial equality, their rate of change toward a prointegration position was the highest; thus, there is more change in racial attitudes going on in the South than in the rest of the country. Greeley and Sheatsley (1974: 245) optimistically predict that there may soon be no differences between the regions on the issue of racial equality.

The second observation concerning regional changes in tolerance presents a somewhat different picture. Nunn *et al.* (1978: 103) demonstrate that tolerance of atheists, socialists, and Communists increased in each region since 1954 by about the same amount. Since all regions increased in tolerance by about the same amount, the gaps in tolerance among the regions remained basically the same. For example, although the South became more tolerant, the West also became more tolerant, and the differences between the South and the West remained as great as they were in 1954.

In sum, geographic region continues to be a predictor of levels of tolerance. Although the social composition differences (e.g., education, income, urbanism) among the regions appear to account for some of the differences in tolerance, there also appear to be at least some subculture patterns within the regions which lead to higher or lower levels of tolerance.

Size of Area of Residence

The population size of the area in which people live usually has an effect on the degree of social diversity to which they are exposed, and this could be expected to have an effect on their levels of tolerance. My analysis of the 1977 NORC tolerance questions in Table 7.6 indicates responses by the size of residence of people at age sixteen, presumably an important time period in the crystallization of political opinions. There is a definite pattern to the results. First, those who lived on farms are clearly the least tolerant on all five of the freedom of speech questions and on the racial and sexual equality questions (including two questions not presented in the table). Second, the next least tolerant group consists of those who lived in rural areas but were not involved in farming. Third, the differences in tolerance between the two categories of cities (under 50,000 and over 50,000) are rather small. However, although the breakdown in the table does not show it, residents of small towns are less tolerant than residents of cities. Fourth, those who lived in the suburbs near large cities (250,000 or more) are the most tolerant on almost all the questions. Over half (58%) of those living in suburbs near large cities gave tolerant responses to all five freedom of speech questions— compared to 37% of the urban residents, 28% of the rural nonfarm residents, and only 17% of the farm residents.

Urban-rural differences in tolerance have been demonstrated in many studies. Lipset and Raab (1970: 436, 439) find racism and anti-Semitism to be highest among the residents of farms and small towns and lowest in large cities and their suburbs. Stouffer (1955: 113) and Nunn et al. (1978: 97) found tolerance of atheists, socialists, and Communists to be lowest among farm residents, next lowest among residents of towns under 2500 population, higher among residents of 2500 to 100,000, and highest in cities of 100,000 or more and their suburbs.

TABLE 7.6
Percentages Tolerant by Size of Residence at Age Sixteen

	Farm (n = 344)	Rural Nonfarm (n = 170)	City under 50,000 (n = 534)	City over 50,000 (n = 398)	Suburb near Large City (n = 88)
Allow atheist to speak	42	59	67	72	85
Allow racist to speak	49	57	62	62	80
Allow Communist to speak	36	49	61	68	75
Allow militarist to speak	32	49	57	57	77
Allow homosexual to speak	44	58	68	76	79
Willing to vote for a woman for President	68	82	82	83	90
Favor the Equal Rights Amendment	64	70	77	78	72
Disagree that whites have a right to keep blacks out of their neighborhoods	43	59	58	66	72
Oppose laws against racial intermarriage	51	68	77	82	85

SOURCE: National Opinion Research Center 1977 General Social Survey. See appendix for the full wording of the tolerance questions.

The analysis by Nunn *et al.* (1978: 97–101) indicates two other important findings. First, in comparison with Stouffer's (1955) results, the gap in tolerance between farmers and large-city residents increased between 1954 and 1973. Although both groups increased in tolerance since 1954, the urban residents increased more than the farm residents did. The second finding is that the relationship between tolerance and size of place of residence is not due completely to urban-rural differences in such factors as education or region. For example, a Midwesterner with a high school education who lives in a city is more likely to be tolerant than a Midwesterner with a high school education who lives on a farm. Rural residents have lower education levels than urban or suburban residents, and this probably contributes to the lower tolerance among rural residents; but even when such factors as education are taken into account, rural residents are still less tolerant.

Nunn *et al.* (1978: 101) attribute the greater tolerance of urban residents to the greater likelihood that they will encounter new ideas and situations and thus expand their awareness of alternatives. Exposure to the greater diversity of ideas and people within the urban-suburban environment should lead to a greater acceptance of differences among people and to greater tolerance. Additionally, based on the work of Shingles and Shoemaker (1979), a cultural explanation of differences in tolerance between rural areas and urban-suburban areas can be suggested. Tolerance requires that people put aside their personal likes and dislikes of other ideas or people and abide by certain principles, or rules, concerning freedom of expression and equal treatment. This is related to the concept of "rule by law." Shingles and Shoemaker (1979: 401) suggest that the concept of rule by law is least accepted in small towns and rural areas. Formal, universal principles of tolerance and laws give way in the rural or small-town culture to the local norms. The integration and homogeneity of rural and small-town communities makes it possible to reach consensus on desired rules of behavior and to enforce such rules on a basically informal basis—regardless of whether such rules are consistent with broader principles or laws of the larger political system. The greater diversity within the large urban and suburban populations makes consensus on rules and informal enforcement unworkable. Thus, people come to accept the necessity of formal rules based on more universal principles, and they are more likely to realize that there are legitimate differences in views about what the rules should be.

The urban-rural difference makes a lot of difference in terms of levels of tolerance. The fundamental explanation seems to be that people in rural areas are exposed to less diversity of people and ideas and, therefore, have no necessity to learn to tolerate differences.

TOLERANCE AND RELIGIOUS ORIENTATIONS

General Religious Preference

My analysis of the 1977 NORC survey presented in Table 7.7 indicates a definite association between religious preference and political tolerance. In accord with many other studies (e.g., Lipset and Raab, 1970; Campbell, 1971; Nunn et al., 1978), these results indicate that Protestants are the least tolerant, Catholics are somewhat more tolerant than Protestants, and the most tolerant are—depending upon the particular issue—either Jews or those who are not religious. This pattern persists for support for freedom of expression, support for sexual equality, and support for racial equality. With regard to freedom of speech, for example, only 28% of the Protestants gave tolerant responses to all five questions—as compared to 34% of the Catholics, a majority (57%) of Jews, and a very strong majority (72%) of those with no religion.

TABLE 7.7
Percentages Tolerant by Religious Preference

	Protestant (n = 1004)	Catholic (n = 373)	Jewish (n = 35)	None (n = 93)
Allow atheist to speak	58	66	83	95
Allow racist to speak	56	61	69	91
Allow Communist to speak	51	60	80	89
Allow militarist to speak	48	51	69	82
Allow homosexual to speak	59	71	83	87
Willing to vote for a woman for President	77	82	97	87
Favor the ERA	71	76	88	87
Disagree that whites have a right to keep blacks out of their neighborhoods	54	58	77	78
Oppose laws against racial intermarriage	67	77	91	88

SOURCE: National Opinion Research Center 1977 General Social Survey. See appendix for the full wording of the tolerance questions.

In the United States today, there are not great differences between Protestants and Catholics in such social characteristics as education and income. Further, there are not great cultural differences between them. Both share in the commitment in the abstract to such political concepts as democratic government, majority rule, and minority rights. Both also share in the belief in individual achievement buttressed by the "Protestant Ethic," a religious-social-economic belief that people should work hard and achieve success. The Protestant Ethic and certain other religious beliefs have helped to reconcile religious beliefs with political and economic beliefs. Hard work is virtuous and material success is an indication of virtue. In order to give everyone a fair chance of success, there is a certain level of support in the abstract for the idea of equality of opportunity. The emphasis on individualism also leads to a certain degree of support for freedom of expression. Thus, some of the basic cultural beliefs shared by Protestants and Catholics lead to the development of a certain degree of tolerance. These same beliefs, however, can also lead to limitations on tolerance. A commitment to individual achievement and to the existing political-economic system is not in conflict with a certain range of freedom of expression; however, this commitment might lead to intolerance of viewpoints which suggest fundamental changes in the system (e.g., a redistribution of wealth). Further, a belief in the system coupled with the perception that equality of opportunity already exists has implications for concepts of equality. If equality of opportunity does exist, then those people who are low in income, education, or occupational status must have something wrong with them (e.g., laziness, lack of motivation). Their lack of success is their own fault and they do not deserve equality.

The greater tolerance among Jews might be partly accounted for by their higher income, education, and occupational status; however, the crucial factor seems to be the unique features of the Jewish subculture. First, the tremendous amount of persecution inflicted upon Jews throughout history has probably played a very important role in their development of subcultural norms stressing tolerance of minority groups and minority viewpoints. Second, the Jewish subculture places a great emphasis upon a humanitarian viewpoint. Although the average income of Jews is higher than that of either Protestants or Catholics, Jews have been much more supportive of liberal programs to help the disadvantaged. This viewpoint has no doubt contributed to the greater support among Jews for equality for such groups as women and blacks. Thus, the historical circumstances of Jews and certain parts of the Jewish subculture have led to the higher levels of tolerance in terms of both support for freedom of expression and support for equality.

One further finding needs to be discussed with regard to differences in tolerance among Protestants, Catholics, and Jews. In the study mentioned before in which survey respondents were asked to select their own "least liked" group, further analysis by Piereson et al. (1980) found that there were no differences in tolerance among Protestants, Catholics, and Jews. Jews were not more tolerant than the others when they were asked questions about their individual least liked group. Piereson et al. (1980) argue that previous research had shown that Jews were more tolerant simply because the questions concerned tolerance of left-wing groups, and Jews are more tolerant of left-wing groups than Protestants or Catholics are. But when Jews pick their least liked group, they are likely to pick a right-wing group (e.g., Nazis). This research indicates that Jews are just as intolerant toward their individual least liked group as Protestants or Catholics are. While this is a legitimate point, it should not be overgeneralized. For understandable reasons, the least liked group of many Jews will consist of Nazi or fascist people; it is also understandable why many Jews might not feel tolerant toward such groups. It would be a mistake, however, to say that because Jews are not more tolerant of "least liked" groups than Protestants or Catholics are, they are not more tolerant than Protestants or Catholics at all. The evidence presented in Table 7.7 and in other parts of the discussion indicates clearly that Jews are more tolerant than Protestants or Catholics are on a range of both left-wing (e.g., atheists and Communists) and right-wing (e.g., racists and militarists) groups and on issues of racial and sexual equality.

The findings of Piereson et al. (1980) did substantiate the higher levels of tolerance among those who are not religious, even when it involved toleration of their least liked group. Perhaps the explanation for the greater level of tolerance among atheists and agnostics lies in the fact that they are themselves nonconformists and have, therefore, gained an appreciation for tolerance of nonconformity.

Protestant Denominations

Obviously, most people in the United States are Protestants, and there are a number of different denominations and sects. These denominations can vary in terms of geographical distribution (e.g., the high number of Baptists in the South), in terms of socioeconom-

ic characteristics (e.g., the higher education and income of Episcopalians), and they can vary in terms of beliefs and orientations
(e.g., degree of fundamentalism). Several studies (e.g., Glock and
Stark, 1966; Lipset and Raab, 1970) have demonstrated that such
differences among denominations can lead to different levels of
tolerance.

Certain denominations (e.g., Presbyterian and Episcopalian)
tend to attract people who are higher in education and income and
lower in religious fundamentalism. These denominations tend to be
more tolerant. On the other end of the spectrum, Baptists (especially Southern Baptists) are usually higher in religious fundamentalism but lower in education and income, and they tend to
be less tolerant. For example, my analysis of the 1977 NORC survey indicates that tolerant responses were given to all five freedom
of speech questions by:

- 49% of the Episcopalians
- 39% of the Presbyterians
- 33% of the Lutherans
- 28% of the Methodists
- 20% of the Baptists

To take another example, less than half (45%) of the Baptists
opposed laws against interracial marriage, but 100% of the Epis-
copalains who answered the question opposed such laws. Baptists
were the least tolerant and Episcopalians were the most tolerant on
all three tolerance areas (freedom of speech, sexual equality, and
racial equality), and other denominations placed somewhere between them. Although differences among the denominations in
tolerance are probably due in great part to differences in socioeconomic characteristics, one aspect of religious beliefs—fundamentalism—will be discussed which might have a bearing on
tolerance levels among different denominations.

Religious Commitment

Religious commitment can be conceptualized and measured in various ways. One way is simply to ask people how strong their religious preference (general religious preference and denomination)
is. My analysis of the 1977 NORC survey in Table 7.8 indicates that
strength of religious preference is related to tolerance: those with
strong religious preference tend to be less tolerant. Those whose
religious preferences are not very strong are the most tolerant.

TABLE 7.8
Percentages Giving All Tolerant Responses in
Each Tolerance Area by Religious Commitment

	Percentages Tolerant on		
	All 3 Sexual Equality Questions	All 3 Racial Equality Questions	All 5 Freedom of Speech Questions
Strength of religious preference			
Strong (*n* = 581)	33	15	25
Somewhat strong (*n* = 111)	39	18	24
Not very strong (*n* = 715)	43	20	36
Frequency of church attendance			
Never (*n* = 212)	44	17	40
Several times yearly (*n* = 520)	43	21	38
1–3 times a month (*n* = 251)	41	22	27
Every week (*n* = 415)	38	17	29
Several times weekly (*n* = 123)	22	15	25

SOURCE: National Opinion Research Center 1977 General Social Survey. See appendix for the wording of the questions.

Another method of indicating religious commitment is the frequency of church attendance. The results in Table 7.8 indicate that those who attend church more often are less tolerant, a pattern also found by Stouffer (1955) and Nunn *et al.* (1978).

There are not many studies which examine the relationship between church attendance—or other forms of church involvement—and tolerance. There are, however, a number of studies which examine the relationship between church involvement and *prejudice* against such groups as Jews, atheists, Catholics, and blacks. Some of the ideas involved in the prejudice research are helpful for the discussion of political tolerance.

First, if we divide people into two categories, church attenders vs. nonattenders, Gorsuch and Aleshire's (1974) extensive review of the research clearly demonstrates that those who do not attend church are less prejudiced than those who do. However, this distinction is too crude. Gorsuch and Aleshire (1974: 285) argue that there is a "curvilinear" relationship between religious activity and racial prejudice: those who are not involved at all in religious activities and those who are highly involved are both low in prejudice, while those in the middle levels of religious commitment are more racially prejudiced. Those in the middle—the typical church members—are simply conforming to community norms, and they are higher in prejudice for the same reason: they are simply conforming to the widely accepted norm of racism. It needs to be noted that when Gorsuch and Aleshire refer to the highly religious, they do *not* mean the fundamentalist. On the contrary, as will be demonstrated, the fundamentalists are less tolerant.

When Gorsuch and Aleshire distinguish between those who are high and those who are low in religious commitment, they do so on the basis of the intrinsic-extrinsic religious orientations proposed by Allport and Ross (1967). Basically, those with an extrinsic orientation *use* their religion to achieve such values as "security and solace, sociability and distraction, status and self-justification" (Allport and Ross, 1967: 434). A person might attend church often, for example, simply to socialize with other members, to build social status within the community, or to receive hope that the burdens they bear now will be compensated later. Further, a person might be very "religious" in order to criticize others or to relieve personal anxieties. On the other hand, persons with an intrinsic religious orientation *live* their religion; they believe in and practice their religious creed as a value in itself rather than as a means to achieve other goals. Allport and Ross (1967) propose that, among church members, it is those with the extrinsic orientation who are high in prejudice; those with an intrinsic orientation are low in prejudice. This is an interesting idea, but it has not yet been tested adequately in actual research.

Somewhat along these same lines, Stark and Glock (1969: 87) argue that persons with Christian ethical commitment are lower in prejudice against Jews, atheists, and blacks. However, they also make two other points. First, the majority of church members are prejudiced. Second, the ethical commitment is somewhat higher among those church members who attend church less frequently and do not take part in church activities. Thus, while those with greater Christian ethical commitment may be less prejudiced, those with greater *church* commitment are more prejudiced.

Religious Fundamentalism

Glock and Stark (1966: 208) define religious orthodoxy as commitment to a literal interpretation of traditional Christian dogma. A person who is religiously orthodox, for example, believes that all the miracles described in the Bible actually happened and that everything in the Bible is literally true and accurate. For present purposes, the terms *religious orthodoxy* and *religious fundamentalism* will be used somewhat interchangeably, although experts in this area of study would object. Religious fundamentalism might be thought of as an extreme form of religious orthodoxy.

Glock and Stark (1966: 208) argue that religious orthodoxy leads to particularism, the belief that one's own religion represents the *only* religious truth. Those who take a literal, traditional view of religious doctrine tend to develop the attitude that their religion is the only true religion and that all others are wrong. Particularism in turn leads to prejudice against religious outsiders—those with a different religious faith and those who are not religious. Glock and Stark (1969) find that these types of attitudes are related to anti-Semitism and intolerance of atheists.

Lipset and Raab (1970: 434) and Quinley and Glock (1979: 109) argue that religious beliefs are second only to education in their influence on anti-Semitism. However, some (e.g., Middleton, 1973) argue that the relationship between religious attitudes and prejudice is better explained in terms of the social characteristics or personality traits of the church members rather than by their religious attitudes. Roof (1975) suggests that both the religious attitudes (orthodoxy and particularism) and the prejudice are caused in common by other types of orientations people hold. The issue is not yet resolved.

A number of studies have shown that fundamentalists tend to be more prejudiced than nonfundamentalists against blacks (e.g., Glock and Stark, 1966; Maranell, 1967), atheists (e.g., Whitt and Nelsen, 1975), and Jews (e.g., Glock and Stark, 1966). Tedin's (1976) study indicates that women involved in anti-ERA groups tend to hold fundamentalist religious beliefs, and these beliefs are more related to their views on the Equal Rights Amendment than are such social characteristics as education, family income, and urban-rural residence. An interesting finding with regard to tolerance of atheists, socialists, and Communists is that those who believe that the Devil actually exists are less tolerant than those who do not (Nunn *et al.*, 1978: 139).

My own study (Corbett, 1978) of Muncie, Indiana, supports the idea that religious fundamentalists are less tolerant—with regard to support for freedom of speech and support for equality for such groups as blacks, women, atheists, and homosexuals. For example, only 55% of those who agreed with the idea that all the miracles in the Bible actually happened ($n = 188$) would allow a speech by a women's liberation group; by contrast, 94% of those who disagreed with the literal interpretation of the Bible ($n = 58$) would allow a women's liberation speech. My analysis of the relationships between tolerance and religious fundamentalism in this Muncie study indicated that part of the relationship was due to such factors as the lower education and income of the fundamentalists. However, even after these social characteristics and some personality traits were taken into consideration, religious fundamentalism still apparently has some effect on levels of tolerance. Further, religious fundamentalism by itself was a better predictor of levels of tolerance than education was. While it might be unclear as to what causes what, it is clear that religious attitudes, tolerance attitudes, and education are all strongly interrelated.

A number of intolerant groups have no difficulty in a psychological reconciliation of intolerance and religious fundamentalism. Such groups as the Ku Klux Klan and the Nazis seem to attract people who are both intolerant and religiously fundamentalistic. Such groups currently appear to be gaining strength. Further, it appears that even more people are being mobilized by groups which are somewhat milder, such as the "Moral Majority." While many of these right-wing, fundamentalist groups appeal to people with little education, not all of them do. Some, such as the Christian Anti-Communist Crusade, pull their members from the relatively affluent strata of society. It also needs to be stressed that not all people who are religiously fundamentalistic are intolerant. It might be inferred, in line with Rokeach's (1960) concepts, that both the intolerance and the attraction to a fundamentalistic religious viewpoint are both born out of a need to view the world in a fixed, simplified, unchanging manner. Religion in the mind of an intolerant person has an extrinsic purpose: it becomes a tool to use in order to express hostilities against others.

TOLERANCE AND POLITICAL ORIENTATIONS

Political Party Preference

One of the most fundamental political orientations in the American political system is, of course, political party preference. Given the importance of political parties in the American system and the importance attached to political party preference, it might be expected that such a fundamental orientation would be related to levels of tolerance among individuals. During particular time periods, the elected officials of one party might be viewed as being more tolerant or more supportive of legislation which promotes tolerance. For

TABLE 7.9

Percentages Tolerant by Political Party Preference

	Strong Democrat (n = 275)	Not Very Strong Democrat (n = 400)	Independent (n = 505)	Not Very Strong Republican (n = 226)	Strong Republican (n = 107)
Allow atheist to speak	52	62	70	67	50
Allow racist to speak	52	59	64	60	62
Allow homosexual to speak	53	65	72	63	56
Willing to vote for a woman for President	76	81	82	81	64
Favor the ERA	75	77	74	69	62
Disagree that whites have a right to keep blacks out of their neighborhoods	49	54	64	64	44
Oppose laws against racial intermarriage	53	71	79	77	66

SOURCE: National Opinion Research Center 1977 General Social Survey. See appendix for the full wording of the questions.

example, the Democratic Party is currently thought of as being more supportive of racial equality than the Republican Party is. The political parties do not, however, ordinarily stress clear-cut, opposing stands on issues of tolerance; further, this does not appear to be the type of issue which ordinarily distinguishes the two major parties in the minds of most people. Thus, putting aside any differences which exist between the elected officials of the two parties, it is not to be expected that there would be large differences in levels of tolerance between Democrats and Republicans in the general public.

With regard to tolerance of atheists, socialists, and Communists, Stouffer's (1955: 211) study indicated that Republicans in the general population were somewhat more tolerant than Democrats. My analysis of the eleven questions from the 1977 NORC survey, however, presents a somewhat more complicated picture. Results from some of these questions are presented by party preference in Table 7.9. First, there is a tendency for those who classify themselves as independents to be somewhat more tolerant than either Democrats or Republicans on most of the eleven tolerance questions, especially the freedom of speech questions; however, some distinctions need to be made among those in the independent category later. In summary form, 42% of the independents would allow all five persons to give speeches as compared to 20% of the strong Democrats, 31% of the weak Democrats, 34% of the weak Republicans, and 29% of the strong Republicans. With regard to freedom of speech, then, there is a relationship between tolerance and *intensity* of party identification: independents are the most tolerant; the weak party identifiers are in the middle, and the strong party identifiers are the least tolerant. Overall, there is little difference in levels of tolerance for these speech questions between the weak Democrats and the weak Republicans; strong Republicans are a little more tolerant than strong Democrats.

With regard to sexual equality issues, there are not any substantial overall patterns of differences among the five political party preference groups except that strong Republicans seem to be somewhat less supportive of sexual equality than the others. With regard to racial equality, the strong party identifiers—either Democrats or Republicans—share a lower level of support for racial equality than that expressed by the independents and weak party identifiers. Additionally, with regard to equality for homosexuals, a Gallup poll (*Gallup Opinion Index*, October, 1977: 3) indicated that independents (60%) were somewhat more tolerant than Democrats

(55%) or Republicans (54%) with regard to equality in job opportunities for homosexuals.

In short, differences in tolerance between the Republicans and Democrats are not very impressive. The more important consideration appears to be the intensity of party identification. The independents (about which more needs to be said below) are the most tolerant, the weak party identifiers are second, and the strong party identifiers are the least tolerant. Thus, the *degree* of party identification appears to be more important than the *direction* of party identification, although this statement will be somewhat qualified below. The question of why this is so cannot be answered here, but the answer might have to do with the handling of certainty. Perhaps there is a tendency for those who need to have reality resolved into either-or categories to attach themselves strongly to one political party or the other; these same people might also take an either-or view with regard to what is right or wrong in terms of freedom of expression issues and equality and limit tolerance to a narrow range of situations. It needs to be stressed that not all strong party identifiers are intolerant or rigid; on the contrary, it is highly probable that some of the most tolerant people are strong party identifiers. It also seems, however, that a disproportionate number of those who are less tolerant are likely to classify themselves as strong party identifiers.

Now the idea that independents are more tolerant than party identifiers needs to be qualified somewhat. The independent category in Table 7.9 actually includes three groups: straight independents, independents who lean toward the Democratic Party, and independents who lean toward the Republican Party. While it is correct that this whole group of independents is more tolerant as a category than the party identifiers, distinctions need to be made about the three categories of independents. Table 7.10, based on my analysis of the 1977 NORC survey, presents the percentage of each party identification group which gave all tolerant responses within each of the three tolerance areas being considered (sexual equality, racial equality, and freedom of speech). First of all, it is apparent that the straight independents are *not* more tolerant than the party identifiers on the sexual and racial equality issues, and they are not much more tolerant on the freedom of speech questions. Thus, the straight independents are not distinctly higher in tolerance than the party identifiers are. However, the independents who lean toward one party or the other are more tolerant than the straight independents. On freedom of speech questions, there is little difference between the Democratic leaners and the Republican leaners, and both are more tolerant than any other group. On sexual and racial equality issues, the Republican leaners are more tolerant than the straight independents, but the Democratic leaners are the most tolerant of all. The Democratic leaners are more tolerant on all three sets of tolerance issues. In sum, straight independents are not distinctly more tolerant than party identifiers, but those independents who lean toward one party or the other—especially the Democratic leaners—tend to be more tolerant than the party identifiers.

TABLE 7.10
Percentages Giving All Tolerant Responses in Each Tolerance Area by Political Party Identification

	Percentage Tolerant on		
	All 3 Sexual Equality Issues	All 3 Racial Equality Issues	All 5 Freedom of Expression Issues
Strong Democrats (n = 275)	33	13	20
Not very strong Democrats (n = 400)	43	16	31
Independents leaning toward Democrats (n = 200)	50	30	44
Independents (n = 175)	37	18	38
Independents leaning toward Republicans (n = 130)	43	21	43
Not very strong Republicans (n = 226)	38	24	34
Strong Republicans (n = 107)	28	12	29

SOURCE: National Opinion Research Center 1977 General Social Survey. See appendix for the wording of the questions.

Liberalism and Conservatism

It might be expected that those who classify themselves as "conservatives" would be less tolerant than those who classify themselves as "liberals." However, this relationship could be complicated by differences in perceptions concerning what the two terms mean, by the different bases on which people classify themselves, and by the fact that many people place little meaning at all on the terms *liberal* and *conservative*.

Recall from chapter 1 that the basic branch of political philosophy we today call "conservatism" is usually the classical liberalism formulated by John Locke with its emphasis on individual freedom. In terms of political philosophy, liberalism today and conservatism today are distinguished more by their views on the role of the government in the economy than anything else. In the general population, however, a person might think of himself or herself as a "liberal" or a "conservative" on the basis of any of various types of issues—economic issues, civil liberties issues, "social issues" (e.g., morals, crime control, life-styles), and so on. Thus, Joe Doe might classify himself as a liberal on the basis of economic issues, such as medicare, social security, unemployment compensation, and so on. Mary Smith, however, classifies herself as a liberal because of civil liberties issues. Thus, different people might have different reasons for classifying themselves as "liberal" or "conservative." To further complicate the matter, there is a tendency for those who are "liberal" on economic issues to be " conservative" on noneconomic issues, and vice versa (Erikson *et al.*, 1980: 158).

Because of the problems indicated above, it is not to be expected that there would be really sharp, dramatic differences in levels of tolerance between self-classified liberals and conservatives. There are, however, some differences. With regard to freedom of speech, my analysis of the 1977 NORC survey in Table 7.11 indicates that self-identified liberals (no matter what degree of liberalism) are more tolerant than self-identified conservatives and moderates. The same basic pattern also prevails with regard to the racial and sexual equality issues. On the whole, the strong conservatives are the least tolerant; there is little difference between those who are slightly conservative and the moderates; the liberals are the most tolerant.

While there is a definite pattern of differences in tolerance between self-identified liberals and conservatives, these differences are not terribly impressive. Generally, the percentage tolerant in the liberal group is only about 15% to 20% higher than the percentage tolerant in the "conservative or extremely conservative" group. (It should be noted that the amount of error in surveys, usually about 3%, is higher when discussing subgroups of the sample; thus, the real differences might be greater or lesser than this.) This indicates that the problems discussed earlier with regard to the bases on which people classify themselves are very relevant. While there are group differences in tolerance between self-identified liberals and conservatives in the general public, these differences do not amount to an ideological gulf.

TABLE 7.11

Percentages Tolerant by Self-Identification on the Liberalism-Conservatism Dimension

	Liberal or Extremely Liberal (n = 206)	Slightly Liberal (n = 214)	Moderate, Middle of the Road (n = 564)	Slightly Conservative (n = 251)	Conservative or Extremely Conservative (n = 218)
Allow atheist to speak	73	70	63	63	53
Allow racist to speak	66	67	56	63	54
Allow homosexual to speak	74	71	64	63	56
Willing to vote for a woman for President	85	81	84	79	69
Favor the Equal Rights Amendment	80	82	76	65	61
Disagree that whites have a right to keep blacks out of their neighborhoods	64	67	56	60	48
Oppose laws against racial intermarriage	83	77	70	74	66

SOURCE: National Opinion Research Center 1977 General Social Survey. See appendix for the full wording of the questions.

Political Alienation

Political party identification and self-classification on the liberalism-conservatism dimension represent preferences. Neither of these preferences helps a great deal in predicting how tolerant a person is. Political alienation is not a preference; it represents an attitude toward the political system itself. Gilmour and Lamb (1975: 5) define political alienation in terms of a combination of three types of feelings. First, those who are politically alienated have little political trust; they do not trust government and politicians. Second, they tend to feel that electoral politics and political choices are not really meaningful; e.g., they feel that it doesn't matter who gets elected, things will go on the same. Third, they have low political efficacy; they do not feel that they can have any influence on political matters. Here the connections between tolerance and two components of political alienation—political trust and political efficacy—will be briefly examined in order to demonstrate that political orientations other than political party preference and the liberalism-conservatism dimension might be useful in predicting levels of political tolerance. ance.

First, several studies provide some evidence to indicate that those who are higher in political trust are more tolerant. For example, racial tolerance is higher among those with higher political trust (Martin and Westie, 1959), even when differences in education are taken into account (Aberbach and Walker, 1970). Herson and Hofstetter's (1975) Ohio study indicated that those who are higher in political trust are more tolerant of both the right wing and the left wing.

Second, my analysis of the NORC 1977 survey in Table 7.12 indicates that political tolerance is higher among those with higher political efficacy, although political efficacy is indicated with just a single questionnaire item here, and this might produce misleading results. There is a definite pattern of differences among those who agreed (lower political efficacy) and those who disagreed (higher political efficacy) with the statement: "Most public officials are not really interested in the problems of the average man." Those who agreed are less tolerant than those who disagreed. The results in the table and other results not shown indicate that the more politically efficacious are more tolerant toward each of the five hypothetical persons (atheist, racist, Communist, militarist, and homosexual) in terms of allowing a speech by the person, allowing the person to teach in college, and the issue of whether a book written by the person should be removed from the public library; they are also

TABLE 7.12
Percentages Tolerant by Attitude toward Public Officials

Most public officials are not really interested in the problems of the average man.

	Agree (n = 955)	Disagree (n = 517)
Allow atheist to speak	59	71
Allow militarist to speak	47	63
Willing to vote for a woman for President	78	84
Favor the Equal Rights Amendment	70	79
Disagree that whites have a right to keep blacks out of their neighborhoods	52	68
Oppose laws against racial intermarriage	66	82

SOURCE: National Opinion Research Center 1977 General Social Survey. See appendix for the full wording of the tolerance questions.

more tolerant on each of the sexual and racial equality issues which have been used from the NORC survey.

These results and the studies mentioned earlier suggest that political tolerance is higher among those who have higher political trust and higher political efficacy, which constitute two components of the concept of political alienation/nonalienation. This pattern of higher tolerance among those who are apparently not alienated (at least in terms of political trust and political efficacy) is bolstered by findings concerning the connection between tolerance and political interest and participation. Nunn et al. (1978: 164) find that tolerance of atheists, socialists, and Communists is higher among those with greater interest in current events. Presumably those with greater interest have more knowledge about democratic norms, have a greater exposure to diversity of people and ideas, and feel less alienated from the political system. This is in accord with Wilson's (1975: 73) finding of greater tolerance among those who read more books and magazines. Further, tolerance is higher among those who demonstrate nonalienation by actual participation in political activities such as voting, working for or contributing to candidates, going to political rallies, and so on (Wilson, 1975: 73; Herson and Hofstetter, 1975: 1029).

These bits of evidence, then, suggest that political alienation constitutes an orientation toward the political system which has consequences for the level of tolerance. With regard to two of the components of political alienation, political tolerance is higher among those with higher political trust and higher political efficacy;

those who are more distrustful and less efficacious toward the political system are less likely to support the freedom and equality of other people. This also suggests that there might be other political orientations that are useful in predicting levels of political tolerance among people.

SUMMARY

In this chapter, the distribution of tolerance among people has been examined on the basis of certain social characteristics and certain religious and political orientations. Tolerance is not evenly distributed throughout society; it varies on the basis of other characteristics which people have.

Since the social background of a person can affect the development of attitudes, possible connections between tolerance and a series of social characteristics were examined first. As an organizing idea, it was suggested that social characteristics of people which tend to expose them to a greater diversity of people and ideas will lead to higher tolerance; conversely, social characteristics of people which tend to restrict their exposure to diversity will impede the development of tolerance.

Some of the social characteristics examined are clearly related to tolerance. There is a very strong pattern of connection between education and tolerance—although some cautions about this relationship will be discussed in the next chapter—and the possible effects of education on other relationships need to be kept in mind. Race is related to tolerance, but the relationship seems to be mixed as two countervailing influences (the lower socioeconomic status of blacks vs. their historical status as a deprived minority) push against one another. On the whole, whites tend to be somewhat more tolerant than blacks, but the differences are not great. Further, blacks are more tolerant than whites on some issues. Age is an important correlate of tolerance, but the evidence suggests that age is more important as an indicator of the political values of the nation during particular time periods than as an indicator of changing attitudes due to the process of growing older. Region of residence (especially the distinction between the South and the rest of the nation) is an important predictor of tolerance attitudes, which suggests that there are different regional subcultures. The size of the population in which one lives or in which one grew up—especially the urban-rural distinction—partly determines the amount of diversity to which one is exposed, and tolerance is strongly related to this characteristic.

The relationships between tolerance and some social characteristics are not completely resolved. This pertains primarily to economic characteristics having to do with income and occupation. Although it is clear that people with higher income and higher occupational status are more tolerant, it is not clear why this is so. Those with higher income and higher occupational status usually have higher education; thus, it is possible that income and occupation really do not influence tolerance much. On the other hand, higher income and high occupational status produce a greater capability to deal with the world and fulfillment of material needs, and presumably they would tend to produce greater personal security; these factors could produce a greater willingness to accept diversity among people and greater support for individual freedom in order that needs concerning self-fulfillment might be met. While the evidence suggests that education is the more crucial variable, it also appears that at least some of the effects on tolerance are due to income and occupational characteristics.

Perhaps surprisingly, sex apparently has little effect on levels of tolerance, even when the topic is sexual equality. On the basis of the many distinctions in social roles which are made on the basis of gender, it might be expected that differences in social experiences would lead to differences in tolerance. Such differences, however, are very small; there is just a slight tendency for men to be more tolerant than women.

Tolerance is related to certain religious orientations which people hold. In terms of religious preference, Jews and those who are not religious tend to be more tolerant than Protestants or Catholics. Within the Protestants, denominations which tend to draw their membership from people with relatively low education and income tend to be less tolerant than those whose membership is higher in social status. Those who are more strongly attached to their religious preference and who are more involved in church attendance tend to be less tolerant than those whose involvement is more casual. Finally, religious fundamentalists are less tolerant than nonfundamentalists. There are, then, strong connections between tolerance and religious orientations.

In terms of political orientations, connections between tolerance and two fundamental political orientations—political party preference and the liberalism-conservatism dimension—were examined first. Despite the apparent fundamental nature of such orientations, tolerance is not strongly related to either. With regard to party identification, tolerance appears to be more related to the intensity of identification than to the direction of identification: strong party identifiers are the least tolerant, weak party identifiers are in the middle, and independents are the most tolerant. An examination of the independents, however, indicates that the straight independents are not much different from the party identifiers; it is the independents who lean toward one party or the other—especially the Democratic leaners—who are more tolerant. With regard to self-identification on the liberalism-conservatism dimension, liberals are more tolerant than conservatives, but the differences are not large. An examination of two components (political trust and political efficacy) of political alienation indicates the possibility that other types of political orientations people hold might be strongly connected to their levels of political tolerance. On the whole, Americans are not ideological, and this seems to account for the lack of a clear connection between political tolerance and such fundamental orientations as political party preference and self-identification on the liberalism-conservatism dimension.

Thus, it is clear that people with different backgrounds vary in terms of political tolerance. In the next chapter, an examination will be made of the process by which different levels of tolerance or intolerance are learned.

Tolerance and Learning

INTRODUCTION

Obviously, tolerance and intolerance are learned. In this chapter, the learning of such attitudes will be examined. To begin, a fuller examination of the effects of education on tolerance will be undertaken, taking into consideration some of the problems in this relationship and in the schooling process itself. Education represents a formal learning process; learning will also be examined in terms of several less formal learning processes. First, tolerance will be discussed in terms of personality development; within this focus, the concern will be with tolerance/intolerance as part of a personality pattern and with the effects of certain other personality traits on levels of political tolerance. Second, the learning of tolerance will be viewed in terms of social learning theory; thus, the focus will turn to the effects of the environment on the individual's level of tolerance. Third, the learning of tolerance will be viewed in terms of cognitive development, in terms of the development within the individual of the ability to deal with abstractions such as tolerance. Finally, the learning of tolerance will be viewed in terms of direct experiences individuals have which might shape their attitudes.

TOLERANCE AND EDUCATION

Basic Relationships

In chapter 7, it was demonstrated that tolerance and education are strongly related. Evidence of such a relationship can be found in

162

many other studies; for example, Hyman and Wright (1979) present a veritable catalog of survey research findings to support the connection between tolerance and education. In a later section, there will be a discussion of some reservations which need to be made concerning the idea that greater education produces greater tolerance. At this point, several aspects of the tolerance-education relationship need to be reiterated.

First, those who have higher education are more tolerant. As indicated in chapter 7 and in such studies as Hyman and Wright (1979), this applies to tolerance in terms of support for freedom of expression and tolerance in terms of support for equality.

Second, the gap between the better educated and the less educated becomes wider when questions about tolerance are combined to produce an overall measure of tolerance. In chapter 7, it was seen that the better educated were more likely to allow a speech by each of the five hypothetical persons (atheist, racist, Communist, militarist, homosexual); when the question of how many would allow all five of these persons to give speeches was examined, the differences in tolerance between the different education categories were even greater. This same type of pattern also applies to attitudes toward allowing these five persons to teach in college and to attitudes toward removing a book written by one of these persons from the public library. The same type of pattern also applies to the series of sexual and racial equality issues.

Third, as indicated by Lawrence (1976), the gap in tolerance between the better educated and the less educated becomes wider as the context becomes more specific. When general, abstract principles of tolerance are involved, there is little difference between the better educated and the less educated because support for such principles is extremely high throughout the population. In questions concerning specific applications of such principles, when the context is more specific, the gap between the better educated and the less educated widens. Later, however, a challenge to this proposition will be considered.

There are, then, strong connections between political tolerance and the number of years of schooling completed by individuals. Before getting into possible reasons why this connection exists, this idea can be examined from other angles.

Other Connections

Here the tolerance-education relationship will be viewed from two other angles. First, if tolerance is higher for individuals with higher education in the United States, then it might be expected that as the education level of the American population as a whole increases, the general level of tolerance in the population will also increase. Stouffer (1955: 220) predicted that as education increased in the United States, tolerance would also increase. In the United States the general education level has risen very substantially since Stouffer's 1954 survey was conducted. Has tolerance also increased? The replications of Stouffer's study by Davis (1975) and by Nunn et al. (1978) indicate clearly that there has been a substantial increase in tolerance toward the particular groups (atheists, socialists, and Communists) included in Stouffer's questions. Further, Lawrence (1976) argues that tolerance in general has increased, at least in terms of support for freedom of speech. Also, the trends discussed in earlier chapters indicate that tolerance in terms of support for equality has increased. Thus, there appears to have been a substantial increase in tolerance since Stouffer's 1954 study. Recall, however, that Sullivan et al. (1979) found that people were very intolerant toward their "least liked group"; thus, it is possible that Americans have simply switched the targets of intolerance. But even here there is an indication of an increase in tolerance; as Abramson (1980) notes, tolerance of the least liked group is higher than tolerance of Communists and atheists was in 1954.

At a minimum, it can be said that tolerance toward the groups studied by Stouffer (1955) has increased quite substantially. Is this increased tolerance due to higher levels of education in the United States? Having analyzed the data, Davis (1975) comes to the conclusion that some of the increase in tolerance is due to increased education, but most of the increase in tolerance is not due to education. In fact, Davis has no specific explanation for most of the increase; Americans have become more tolerant toward certain groups, but it is not clear what accounts for most of the increase. Some of the change, however, is apparently due to increased education levels in the United States. Thus, it appears that an increase in the education levels of Americans does produce an increase in tolerance, but the degree of additional tolerance which can be attributed to education is not so great as was expected.

A second angle by which to view the tolerance-education relationship is to look at the connection among students. More will be said on this later, but there are some points which are relevant here. First, tolerance among students does increase as they progress through school, including college. Nunn's (1973: 301) review of research and his own study indicate that support for civil liberties—including freedom of expression—increases among college students as they progress from their first year to senior year. As will be discussed later, this pattern also holds with regard to students in elementary school on up. Second, tolerance is also related to the student's link with the schooling process. Langton and Jennings (1968) found that high school students who planned to go to college were more tolerant than those who didn't plan to go to college. Zellman and Sears (1971) discovered this same type of pattern for students in grades five through nine. With regard to college students, Nunn's (1973: 307) research indicates that intolerance is greatest among those students who feel that college has had little impact on them. In terms of achievement, Bullock (1976: 280) presents evidence to indicate that students who do better in school (including college) are higher in racial tolerance. With regard to democratic norms, Quinley and Glock (1979: 41) found that knowledge of such norms (as indicated by answers to two questions concerning the First Amendment) is associated with greater tolerance toward Jews. Presumably these norms had been learned in school at some level. In sum, tolerance does appear to be related to the student's connection to the educational process as well as simply the number of years of school. This is an additional indication that it is education which accounts for the education-tolerance relationship, rather than other underlying factors.

Why Should Education Increase Tolerance?

Nunn *et al.* (1978: 61) offer three reasons why education can be expected to increase political tolerance. First, it is expected that greater schooling will lead to a greater probability of learning specific knowledge about civil liberties, equality, and the democratic process in general. As indicated before, support for general, abstract principles relating to freedom of expression and equality receive strong support in the general population. However, it might be much more difficult for a person to learn to apply these principles in specific situations. The suggestion here is that greater schooling increases the probability that the individual will gain knowledge which is helpful in learning to apply the principles.

Second, it is expected that increased education will lead to "increased awareness of the varieties of human experiences that legitimize wide variation in belief, values, and behavior" (Nunn *et al.*, 1978: 61). The education process exposes people to a diversity of people and ideas, and presumably this exposure will lead to a greater acceptance of the legitimacy of diversity.

Third, it is expected that greater schooling will lead to cognitive development that is characterized by flexible, rational thinking which encourages the development of tolerance. Education, then, is expected to produce a capability to think which can overcome the narrow, rigid, illogical way of thinking which is presumed to characterize an intolerant outlook.

Thus, as people progress through schooling, they are expected to learn more about democratic norms in specific applications as well as in terms of general, abstract principles; they are expected to be exposed to people of backgrounds and viewpoints which differ from their own; and they are expected to develop a thinking capability which will help to overcome intolerant attitudes. Education leads to the discovery and appreciation of diversity among people and—if it is successful—to a greater understanding of the cooperative, nonauthoritarian basis of a democratic ideology for a society composed of diverse people with conflicting values.

PROBLEMS IN THE EDUCATION-TOLERANCE RELATIONSHIP

It has been demonstrated that better-educated people give more tolerant responses to questions about freedom of expression and equality issues, and reasons have been given for why education should be expected to produce such tolerance. Now the possibility that education really is not that important in the development of tolerance must be entertained. There are several important questions which have been raised about the existence and importance of the education-tolerance relationship.

The Measurement of Tolerance

The study by Sullivan et al. (1979) and its continuations (Sullivan et al., 1981; Piereson et al., 1980) argue that previous research had not adequately measured the concept of political tolerance. In previous research, the researchers had determined the group (e.g., atheists, socialists, Communists) about whom questions on tolerance were to be asked. Two problems are involved in this procedure. First, it is not known what the respondent's attitude toward the group is; it is not known whether the respondent likes or dislikes the group. Second, the groups selected for research have usually been left-wing groups; it might be that the tolerance-education relationship applies to tolerance of left-wing groups but not to tolerance of right-wing groups. In order to remedy these two problems, Sullivan and his associates asked each respondent to select his or her own least liked group.

When respondents are allowed to choose the group which they most dislike, there is a change in the education-tolerance relationship. In the first place, when just education and tolerance are considered, the relationship still exists, but it is weaker than in other studies (Piereson *et al.*, 1980). The gap between the better educated and the less educated is not so wide when the respondents are being asked to tolerate the group they most dislike. As suggested, it turns out that those with lower education tend to be more intolerant of left-wing groups and those with higher education tend to be more intolerant of right-wing groups.

The results presented in chapter 7 indicated that the better educated were more tolerant toward both the left (atheists and Communists) and the right (racists and militarists). However, it appears that when people are allowed to choose the group which they least like, the effects of education on tolerance are weakened.

Lack of a Direct Relationship

As indicated above, when just education and tolerance are considered, the education-tolerance relationship is weaker in terms of tolerance of the least liked group than in other studies of tolerance in which respondents reacted to groups selected by the researcher. Further, Sullivan *et al.* (1981) indicate that education has no *direct* effect on political tolerance at all; instead, education has an effect on personality variables (psychological security) which in turn has an impact on political tolerance. Thus, education does not directly increase political tolerance; instead, it increases the psychological security of people and the psychological security increases political tolerance. Furthermore, it appears that education is not the most important determinant of psychological security. Overall, then, this analysis attributes much less importance to education's impact on political tolerance than might be expected. Two reservations need to be expressed concerning these results. First, the statistical-mathematical analysis used by Sullivan *et al.* (1981) is very complex, and critical analysis of the study might lead to revisions in the conclusions. Second, even if the conclusions of the study are upheld, the results are still limited to tolerance of the least liked group. The lack of a strong direct or indirect relationship between political tolerance and education for least liked groups does not mean that such a relationship would not exist for other types of groups. The results so far, however, certainly indicate that education's effects on tolerance are not terribly strong in situations in which people are reacting to a group which they extremely dislike. Further, in such situations, the person's sense of psychological security seems to be the direct influence on tolerance, and this psychological security can be influenced by any number of factors other than education.

Response Set

When asked questions of the "agree-disagree" type of format, some people are automatically predisposed to answer in the affirmative and some people are predisposed to answer in the negative. Such a predisposition is called a response set. Jackman (1973) points out that the less educated are more likely to give affirmative answers and the better educated—perhaps because they are more likely to see possible exceptions to statements—are more likely to give negative responses. Thus, Jackman argues that questions concerning tolerance which use the agree-disagree format might produce misleading results concerning the education-tolerance relationship. On this basis, it can be said that some results have exaggerated the degree of relationship between education and political tolerance. However, studies using different types of question formats (e.g., Lawrence, 1976) have also found a strong relationship between education and tolerance. Thus, while this type of criticism serves as a caution, it is apparent that the relationship between education and tolerance is not just due to response set.

Selection

So far, the interpretation of the education-tolerance relationship has been that increases in education produce increases in tolerance. However, it is possible that the relationship might be at least partly the other way around. It is possible that those who are more tolerant are the ones who are more attached to schooling or are considered to be more suitable for higher education and are therefore encouraged to go on. This is the problem of selection. Those who are already more tolerant might be the ones who are selected to receive more education. Earlier it was mentioned that students in high school (Langton and Jennings, 1968) and in elementary school (Zellman and Sears, 1971) who planned to go on to college were more tolerant than those who did not. It is possible that those who are more tolerant are more likely to be guided by teachers or parents toward increased education. It is also possible that those who are more tolerant are simply more comfortable with the learning process; perhaps the same type of flexible thinking which leads to tolerance also leads to a greater affinity for schooling. Thus, there are three possibilities: (1) education produces tolerance; (2) tolerance produces a tendency to continue schooling; and (3) the two factors might interact together to produce some sort of mutually reinforcing effect. A fourth possibility is that both education and tolerance are produced by some other unknown factor, such as some personality trait which contributes to both. While it seems reasonable to think that education leads to greater tolerance, this issue cannot be resolved on the basis of the available research.

Social Desirability

As indicated previously, the problem of social desirability in research refers to the tendency of people to give the answer which they think is the most socially acceptable. For example, if you asked people whether they voted in the last election, many of those who didn't vote would say that they did; it is not socially acceptable to fail in such citizenship duties. Jackman (1978) argues that this type of problem has an effect on the tolerance-education relationship. With regard to general principles of tolerance, Jackman (1978: 322) argues that the better educated are more likely to recognize the socially accepted answer—the "right" answer. The less educated are less able to give the socially accepted answer, and they therefore appear to be less tolerant than the better educated. Jackman (1978: 322) then suggests that the better educated, while more likely to give tolerant responses to the general questions, are not more likely than the less educated to respond in a tolerant direction for questions involving more specific situations. Jackman (1978: 323) argues that the better educated have learned the general principles better than the less educated have, but this learning is superficial:

Such learning, however, is not very deeply embedded. In an applied situation, those principles are no more likely to influence the orientation of the well educated than of the poorly educated.

Thus, Jackman charges that the better educated are more likely to know the socially acceptable answer to general questions concerning tolerance, but they don't extend these principles to specific situations any more than the less educated do. This conclusion is contrary to the proposition presented earlier that the gap between the better educated and the less educated *increases* as the context becomes more specific. There are two fundamental problems in Jackman's study. First, there are serious problems in the questions used to measure tolerance in the abstract and specific applications (Corbett, 1980; Kuklinski and Parent, 1979). Jackman's questions concerning tolerance consisted of two questions to measure general attitudes toward racial integration and two questions to measure specific applications of the general principle. Both the applied tolerance questions concerned the role of the government in Washington in bringing about racial integration or equality; Kuklinski and Parent's (1979) critique indicates that respondents might be reacting to the issue of the role of the federal government as well as to the issue of racial equality. In short, methodological problems seriously undermine Jackman's conclusions. Further, Lawrence (1976) has demonstrated that the better educated are even more tolerant in specific applications of principles of tolerance than the less educated are—as contrasted with general principles in which the gap is smaller between the better educated and the less educated.

The second problem in Jackman's conclusions is a logical problem. It seems that the gap between the better educated and the less educated in tolerance should logically be smaller for the general principles of tolerance since such principles exist as slogans which almost everyone endorses; if the better educated have an advantage in giving the socially accepted answer, then this advantage should show up the most in specific situations where their advantage is much greater. A great deal of evidence has been provided to indicate that the better educated are more tolerant in specific contexts than the less educated are—except that this pattern is weakened when the respondents are reacting toward their least liked group. A charge that might be made—exactly the opposite of Jackman's charge—is that the better educated are simply better able to give the "right" answers in specific contexts because of their greater knowledge of norms of tolerance. It might also be that in terms of actual *behavior*, the better educated are no more tolerant than the less educated. There is no research yet which can resolve this issue.

Group-Relatedness of Tolerance

As indicated earlier, most research on tolerance has not taken into consideration the respondent's attitude toward the person or group to be tolerated. When tolerance depends on the attitude toward the group to be tolerated, such tolerance is said to be group-related. Three national studies (Lawrence, 1976; Jackman, 1978; Sullivan *et al.*, 1979) have taken the concept of group-relatedness into consideration to one degree or another. Does education decrease the group-relatedness of tolerance? Are people who are more educated more likely to tolerate people they dislike? The study by Sullivan and his associates (Sullivan *et al.*, 1979; Piereson *et al.*, 1980) indicated that when respondents chose their least liked groups, the relationship between tolerance and education was weakened. Jackman's (1978) study also indicated that there was little relationship between education and tolerance toward blacks when the attitude of the respondents toward blacks was taken into consideration; e.g., among those who disliked blacks, there was little difference in tolerance between those with higher education and those with lower education. Lawrence (1976) also asked respondents to indicate their attitude toward the group to be tolerated before asking whether the group should be tolerated, and his results largely support the idea that the better educated are not much more tolerant toward groups they dislike than the less educated are. Tolerance is, as indicated before, group-related; people are less tolerant toward groups they dislike. Further, the group-relatedness of tolerance exists among those with higher education as well as among those with lower education.

The above conclusion might, however, be somewhat time-bound. Sullivan and his associates (1979; Piereson *et al.*, 1980) did find that the better educated were somewhat more tolerant of their least liked group. The research on which Lawrence (1976) and Jackman (1978) based their conclusions was carried out in the early 1970s, when American memories of the turmoil of the 1960s were still fresh. My own study (Corbett, 1980) of Muncie, Indiana, carried out in 1978 indicated a clear tendency for the better educated to be more tolerant than the less educated were of disliked groups. Future national studies will be needed in order to determine whether this result represents a national trend. Another finding of the Muncie study is interesting: the less educated disliked more groups than the better educated did. This suggests that education has a substantive effect on tolerance in a different sense. Even if the better educated and the less educated are equally intolerant toward groups they dislike, the better educated will still be more tolerant generally because they dislike fewer groups. This finding, however, could be due to the particular groups used in the study.

In short, the research based on national surveys indicates that the better educated are not more likely than the less educated to be tolerant toward the people they dislike. One national study (reported in Sullivan *et al.*, 1979 and Piereson *et al.*, 1980), however, indicates that the better educated are somewhat more tolerant toward their least liked group, and a local level study (Corbett, 1980) indicates that the earlier studies might have been influenced by the particular events of the 1960s. On the whole, there is no substantial evidence of a clear-cut pattern for the better educated to be greatly more tolerant of people they dislike.

Incompleteness

Some of the problems that must be considered in viewing the relationship between education and tolerance have been indicated. There is a relationship, but caution must be used in making assumptions about increased education leading to increased tolerance. As a caution, it needs to be noted that people who have graduated from high school do not have very high levels of tolerance and that people who have graduated from college are not completely committed to specific applications of principles of tolerance. Given all the talk about "equality," "freedom," "democracy," and "citizenship" in the elementary and high schools, why is it that people who have gone through high school have such low levels of tolerance? In order to explore this question, let us consider how democratic principles are approached in the schools.

TOLERANCE AND THE SCHOOLS

Patterns of Tolerance

Similar to studies of adults, studies of high school students have found majority support for general, abstract principles of tolerance along with rather low support for specific applications of such principles (Remmers, 1963). Horton (1963: 57) concludes from a national sample of twelfth graders that a significant proportion of them do not support the freedoms guaranteed by the Bill of Rights. Results from Zellman and Sears' (1971) study of students in grades five through nine demonstrate several points. Although these students are not as tolerant as adults, they follow the same pattern with regard to the gap between general principles and specific applications. A majority (60%) agreed with the statement: "I believe in free speech for all no matter what their views might be." But only small minorities would allow a speech by a Communist (21%), a man who wants to help the Vietcong (28%), or the head of the American Nazi Party (13%). Zellman and Sears (1971: 120) also make the point that the children are not deriving their opinion about the specific situation from their general principle. Only 4%

of those who supported freedom of speech in the abstract would allow a speech in all three of the specific situations. Further, 30% of those who took the tolerant stand on the abstract statement of free speech took the intolerant position on all three of the specific applications. Zellman and Sears (1971: 122) argue that the students' attitudes toward the particular group involved—not their attitudes on the abstract statement of freedom of speech—determined whether they would allow the group to speak. Thus, tolerance among children is very highly group related.

The pattern of tolerance among children, then, resembles several patterns among adults: (1) support for general principles of tolerance is high, although not so high as among adults; (2) tolerance in specific situations is much lower, even lower than for adults; and (3) tolerance is group-related.

Since tolerance among children generally increases with age (Dennis *et al.*, 1968) and since adults are more tolerant than children, it might be presumed that as children mature they progress toward greater political socialization into democratic norms. However, given the levels of tolerance among adults, it is apparent that this political socialization process is never completed for a substantial proportion of the American population.

Teaching Tolerance

Hess (1968: 532) suggests four features of political socialization in the schools which can cause difficulties for the political system. Two of these are relevant here. First, there is the "distaste of children for conflict within the society" (Hess, 1968: 532). The teaching steers children away from conflictual situations; thus, children are not taught how to deal with conflicts in political values in society. This leads to an inability to accept and deal with dissent.

Second, political principles and values are taught as slogans rather than as concepts to be applied to actual social issues (Hess, 1968: 532). This same type of conclusion about the sloganistic nature of political values is expressed by Zellman and Sears (1971: 119):

The data suggest that belief in free expression is taught only as a slogan, not as a generalizable principle, and that children therefore do not learn to apply it to concrete situations.

Zellman and Sears (1971: 120) find that the older, more intelligent, and more politicized children—those who are more likely to be in contact with the mainstream of adult political values—are more likely to support the abstract statement of freedom of speech, but they are not more tolerant than the other children in the specific applications. This further indicates that "abstract civil liberties are taught as slogans, and concrete applications are not taught at all" (Zellman and Sears, 1971: 120). Thus, children—and adults—give high support to tolerance in abstract, general principles because they have been taught such principles as slogans; they are less tolerant in specific applications of these principles because they have not been taught how to apply them.

What about the civics courses in high school? So far, the evidence indicates that such courses usually have almost no impact of any kind on most students (Langton and Jennings, 1968). Students who have completed such courses don't even have much more factual knowledge about the political system than students who haven't taken such a course. The reason seems to be that civics courses simply cover information and principles to which the students have already been exposed. By this point, students have already formed their basic political attitudes to a very great extent. Thus, under usual conditions, civic courses cannot be expected to do much to develop tolerant attitudes.

Why Aren't Specific Applications Taught?

Several reasons can be suggested here as to why children are not taught to apply the general principles of tolerance to specific situations. First, such teaching might be considered to be unnecessary. It might be thought that children can apply the general principles to specific situations without having to be taught to do so. Second, there is the problem of the source of such teaching. There is no reason to believe that teachers are exceptionally tolerant themselves or that their understanding of specific applications is complete. Third, there are teachers who are committed to tolerance in principle and in application who could teach their students specific applications, but it is unlikely that the political environment would support such teaching. Most citizens are not very tolerant in specific situations; most school boards are very sensitive to public opinion in their community; and most teachers will have a rough time if their teaching antagonizes the principal, the school board, or community opinion. Thus, teachers are forced to deal with relatively "safe" topics.

Can specific applications of principles of tolerance be taught? Zellman and Sears (1971) did their study as part of an experimental program to teach a more sophisticated view of political conflict to students in grades five through nine in the Sacramento, California, school district. Using an experimental group and a control group, they found that the experimental program did produce some increases in tolerance. Thus, greater tolerance *can* be taught. Political factors surrounding the typical school system, however, make it unlikely that such efforts will be undertaken on a widespread basis.

The effects of formal education on tolerance have been examined. The focus turns now to an examination of other learning processes on tolerance. It needs to be stressed, however, that these various learning processes are not distinct from one another; the learning process is simply being viewed from different focal points.

TOLERANCE AND PERSONALITY

Personality basically refers to the relatively enduring patterns of attitudes and behaviors of a person. Aspects of personality can be viewed in terms of "deep needs" which deal with the fundamental psychological needs of the individual or in terms of the "surface personality," learned orientations that are not so deeply embedded in the basic core personality. The topic of personality can also be approached in terms of a single personality trait or in terms of a pattern—a syndrome—of characteristics which constitute a personality "type." In order to relate tolerance to personality, the discussion will begin with a brief examination of two general personality patterns, authoritarianism and dogmatism, which are supposed to have their roots in the deep psychological needs of the individual. After that, personality traits with varying degrees of "depth" will be considered.

The Authoritarian Personality

Near the end of World War II, a research team at the University of California began a research project which was subsidized by the American Jewish Committee. Spurred by the treatment of Jews in Germany and by anti-Semitism in the United States, the team's purpose was to determine the psychological roots of fascism. What psychological forces lead to the development of a person who supports antidemocratic, fascist beliefs and movements?

The results of this research were published by Adorno *et al.* (1950) in *The Authoritarian Personality*. The authors argue that the political ideology which supports antidemocratic, fascist beliefs and movements is a result of a certain personality syndrome—the authoritarian personality. This personality is characterized by unquestioning acceptance of authority and conventional values on the one hand and, on the other, a demand for complete obedience from those over whom he or she has authority. Further, those who are high in authoritarianism tend to be anti-Semitic and ethnocentric. Thus, intolerance of Jews and ethnic minorities is part of the authoritarianism syndrome.

Adorno *et al.* (1950) developed a scale—a series of questions—to measure the authoritarian personality syndrome; this scale is called the F (for Fascism) Scale. The authoritarian personality agrees with such F-scale statements as:

- Obedience and respect for authority are the most important virtues children should learn.
- People can be divided into two distinct classes: the weak and the strong.

The crucial aspect of the authoritarian personality syndrome is the person's stance toward authority and obedience. The patterns of responses to the F-Scale questions indicate specific traits within this syndrome, such as conventionalism (rigid adherence to conventional values), authoritarian submission (an uncritical, submissive attitude toward idealized authorities of the in-group), and authoritarian aggression (a tendency to watch for, condemn, and punish people who violate conventional values).

There are other personality traits associated with authoritarianism. For example, the authoritarian personality places strong emphasis on status and success and denigrates values concerned with personal intimacy and feelings. The authoritarian has little tolerance for ambiguity, which might be the reason for the strong emphasis on maintaining stereotypical sex roles. For reasons to be discussed below, the authoritarians tend to view their parents as ideal and to have a more favorable evaluation—on the surface—of themselves than nonauthoritarians do.

The authoritarian personality develops in childhood. Due to anxiety about socioeconomic status, the parents attempt to eliminate from their children certain qualities (e.g., emotional tenderness, weakness, passivity) which are seen as impediments to the achievement of success. The elimination of "weakness" is carried out through harsh discipline, including physical punishment. The parents are cold and aloof toward their children. Through the psychological process termed "repression," children eliminate any "weakness" from their self-concept by simply eliminating certain thoughts and feelings from their consciousness; through the psychological process of "projection," the children perceive these weaknesses in other people, especially minority groups.

The discipline administered by the parents leads to aggressive impulses in the children. However, the child cannot direct these aggressive impulses against the parents; this would lead to further punishment. Thus, the child learns to repress any negative or aggressive impulse toward the parents; this is how the parents become idealized. However, the pent-up aggression must be discharged somehow. The solution is to redirect ("displace") these aggressive impulses onto socially accepted targets such as minority groups or nonconformists.

This theory, which has been presented in greatly simplified form, provides a nice explanation for intolerance. There are people who, for deep psychological reasons, place an extreme value on obedience and conformity and who have a strong hostility toward minority groups and nonconformists. Such persons are incapable of understanding the right and value of dissent, and they are hostile toward diversity. Thus, they could be expected to give little support for specific applications of freedom of expression and equality. The work of Adorno et al. (1950) has stimulated literally hundreds of studies which use authoritarianism as a variable, and many of these have demonstrated that authoritarianism and *prejudice* go hand in hand. Further, a few studies have used authoritarianism as a variable to account for differences in levels of tolerance in terms of support for freedom of expression or in terms of support for equality. For example, MacDonald's (1974) study of several student, faculty, and staff samples in West Virginia indicated that support for sexual equality was lower among those who were more authoritarian. Herson and Hofstetter (1975) find that those higher in authoritarianism are less tolerant of the left (Communists) and the right (the Ku Klux Klan). Stouffer's (1955) study included some questions to measure authoritarianism, and those who were more authoritarian were less tolerant of atheists, Communists, and socialists. Thus, there is some evidence to indicate that those higher in authoritarianism are lower in political tolerance.

The picture, however, is not so simple and clear as it first seems; there are several problems. First, even if there were no other problems, the concept of authoritarianism would not account for all the intolerance which exists in American society. Based on my general knowledge of survey results, my *guess* is that the proportion of strongly authoritarian persons in the United States does not exceed 15%. Yet it has been demonstrated that a much higher proportion of Americans than this is intolerant when specific applications of principles of tolerance are involved.

Second there are questions about the methodology employed in studies of authoritarianism. A number of questions have been raised by various researchers (e.g., Christie and Jahoda, 1954). The most serious questions concern the use of the F Scale to measure authoritarianism; two of these problems will be considered here. First, there is the problem of response set. As discussed earlier, some people have a tendency to agree to questions with an agree-disagree format and some people have a tendency to disagree. Further, people with lower education are more likely to agree and people with higher education are more likely to disagree. Since every question on the F Scale is set up so that an agree response represents the authoritarian response, people with lower education come out with higher authoritarianism scores. Do people with lower education get higher F Scale scores because of their lower education or because they really are more authoritarian or because of some combination of these two factors? Attempts have been made to resolve this problem by changing the question format, but the issue of bias has not been completely resolved.

A second problem with the F Scale is that it presumably only measures right-wing authoritarianism (which is what the authors intended) and does not measure authoritarianism of the center or the left wing.

With these and other criticisms of the concept and the measurement of authoritarianism, where does that leave us? Some question the existence of such a personality syndrome. Some believe that the syndrome exists, but the measurement process needs improvement. Some (e.g., Quinley and Glock, 1979: 52) argue that authoritarianism is secondary to education; low education leads to authoritarianism and is more important than authoritarianism in predicting levels of tolerance. Brown's (1965) thorough review of the research on authoritarianism and its relationship to prejudice led him to the conclusion that both personality factors and factors such as education interact together to produce prejudice. Despite the methodological problems in the study of authoritarianism, the numerous studies which find authoritarianism to be important in predicting other attitudes indicate that there is *something* to the concept, but the various factors have not been sorted out adequately. Thus, it cannot be said for certain that there is an antidemocratic, authoritarian personality resulting from deep psychological needs.

Dogmatism

Since the authors of *The Authoritarian Personality* were interested in the right-wing authoritarianism of the potential fascist, this limits the utility of their concept and their measurement scale. Rokeach (1960) attempted to overcome these limitations by developing a broader concept of authoritarianism called "dogmatism," a concept which could be used for authoritarianism of the left wing and the center as well as the right wing. Further, in this expansion of the concept, Rokeach (1960: 6) placed the emphasis on the structure of thinking processes rather than the content: "It is not so much *what* you believe that counts, but *how* you believe." In this more general approach to authoritarianism, a person might even hold a tolerant belief, but hold it in a dogmatic fashion. For example, the following statement could be considered to be dogmatic: "If you don't believe in freedom of speech, then you're just stupid and I'm not even going to talk to you." Thus, the focus here is not on the substance of beliefs so much as on the way in which people hold these beliefs.

Rokeach formulated a continuum of dogmatism, with the open-minded person on one end and the closed-minded person on the other end. The open-minded person is open to new information and ideas and evaluates them on a logical basis; the acceptance or rejection of new ideas is made on the basis of their merit, not on the basis of the psychological needs of the individual. The closed-minded person adopts a closed system of beliefs; this overall system of beliefs is not very susceptible to change because it satisfies some psychological need of the individual. Individual parts of the belief system might be changed, but the basis of the change is usually external. The closed-minded, or dogmatic, person depends on authority figures; when the idealized authority figures change their position, the dogmatic person can easily change particular parts of the belief system. But the overall belief system is not subject to logical evaluation.

Rokeach (1960) developed the Dogmatism Scale in order to measure this generalized concept of authoritarianism. Similar to the situation of the F Scale, the Dogmatism Scale has also received criticism (e.g., the problem of response set also pertains to the Dogmatism Scale). Research using the Dogmatism Scale has indicated that dogmatism is related to prejudice against out-groups, and Sullivan *et al.* (1981) find questions concerning dogmatism to be important in predicting attitudes of tolerance or intolerance of people's least liked groups. Nevertheless, the issue still remains as to whether the Dogmatism Scale adequately measures the basic concept of dogmatism.

Both Rokeach (1960) and Adorno *et al.* (1950) view the genesis of authoritarianism in psychoanalytic terms, in terms of psychological needs of the individual. The dogmatic person develops a system of beliefs which serve as defense mechanisms to protect the ego. These beliefs enhance the position of the in-group and denigrate out-groups; thus, one's own position and ego are viewed more favorably.

Tolerance and Specific Personality Traits

So far the examination has concerned the relationship of political tolerance to overall patterns of personality traits. Here the focus is on two specific traits, self-esteem and anomie, but it can be seen that the basic theoretical propositions are similar to what has already been discussed.

Self-esteem has to do with the attitudes one holds toward one's self; Sniderman (1975: 36) suggests that self-esteem might simply be defined as how favorably or unfavorably a person evaluates his or her self. Wolman (1974: 48) argues that people need to discriminate against others for psychological reasons having to do with self-esteem; they add to their own feeling of importance by adopting a feeling of superiority toward certain groups. People with high self-esteem, on the other hand, feel strong and confident and do not need to raise their own value by undermining the value of other people.

Sniderman (1975: 179) argues that self-esteem also affects the acquisition of the values of a culture. In a democracy, high self-esteem might lead to the greater learning of democratic values; in a nondemocratic political system, high self-esteem might lead to greater learning of the particular nondemocratic values of the political system. Based on Sniderman's (1975: 186–189) analysis, it can be suggested that low self-esteem should produce lower tolerance in individuals in the United States in three ways. First, persons with lower self-esteem will be less likely to learn democratic values—including tolerance—because they have a tendency to interact with other people less and this inhibits social learning. Second, persons with low self-esteem—who by definition think poorly of themselves—also have a tendency to think poorly of other people, and this leads to hostility and suspicion of others, which in turn lead to low tolerance. Third, persons with low self-esteem are more likely to feel that political activity is futile; this leads to a low value on democratic processes and on tolerance of dissent and diversity. In sum, lower self-esteem leads to less democratic commitment in general and less political tolerance in particular. At the other end, Sniderman argues that high self-esteem leads to greater faith and trust in people and, therefore, to a greater acceptance of diversity in the actions and opinions of other people.

Sniderman's (1975: 197) analysis of the same data used by McClosky (1964) reveals that those who are higher in self-esteem are more tolerant. This connection has also been demonstrated in several other studies. For example, Miller (1974) finds that among male college students, those who are lower in self-esteem are less supportive of sexual equality; Zellman and Sears (1971: 127) find that students in their Sacramento sample who have higher self-esteem are more tolerant. Self-esteem is an important component of the psychological security concept found to be so important in the prediction of tolerance of least liked groups in the work of Sullivan *et al.* (1981).

Anomie (also spelled *anomy*) has been defined by Quinley and Glock (1979: 49) as follows:

Anomie refers to feelings of bewilderment, anxiety, and normlessness; it is a state of mind in which the individual feels adrift in life without a sense of purpose or meaning.

McClosky and Schaar (1965) argue that feelings of anomie impede interaction with other people and thus impede socialization into the political norms of a society. This is similar to the idea with regard to the effects of low self-esteem. It can be suggested that any psychological trait which reduces the social interaction (and thus the exposure to diversity of people and ideas) of individuals will tend to impede the learning of democratic norms, including the norms relevant to tolerance.

It might be suspected at this point that there is a pattern to the personality traits which tend to alienate the individual from self and from society. McClosky and Schaar's (1965) research indicates that this is correct. Those who are high in anomie also tend to be high in such traits as rigidity, obsessiveness, intolerance of ambiguity, anxiety, hostility, and other similar traits. Given such personality traits in an individual, it is to be expected that such a person would tend to be intolerant; McClosky and Schaar's study supports this expectation. Other studies (e.g., Zalkind *et al.*, 1975; Herson and Hofstetter, 1975; Quinley and Glock, 1979) also find that there is a tendency for those who are high in feelings of anomie to be less tolerant.

Although anomie is usually measured with a series of questions, the 1977 NORC survey contains just one question which can be used to demonstrate the connection between anomie and tolerance. Respondents were asked to agree or disagree with the statement: "It's hardly fair to bring a child into the world with the way things look for the future." Those who agreed (the anomic response) were less tolerant than those who disagreed on all the freedom of expression questions and all the racial equality and sexual equality questions which have been discussed from this NORC survey. For example, 83% of those who disagreed (the nonanomic) opposed laws against interracial marriage, but only 54% of the anomic opposed such laws.

Maslow's Needs Hierarchy

The research discussed above and other research suggest that the more tolerant personality is psychologically healthy and integrated into the society. The intolerant person, by contrast, is insecure, goalless, distrustful, feels left out of society, and has a negative self-concept. Thus, tolerance appears to be tied in with the satisfaction of the needs of people. Maslow (1954) formulated a hierarchy of need areas for individuals. First, individuals must satisfy physiological needs (e.g., hunger, thirst, sex). It would not be expected that a person who suffers from a severe deprivation of physiological needs—which can have a psychological effect on the person— would be very tolerant. Such people will be primarily concerned with basic needs and cannot give much attention to values which lie outside these needs. Following closely on the physiological needs are safety and security needs which must be satisfied next. Again, it is not to be expected that people who have difficulty satisfying their safety and security needs will be very tolerant. After these first two categories of basic needs are satisfied, the person attempts to satisfy the next two categories, affection and belongingness needs and esteem needs. The final need is self-actualization, which might loosely be described as the self-fulfillment of the individual which proceeds after all other needs have been satisfied. These need areas are listed in the order in which they must be satisfied; all need areas must be satisfied in order to have a totally healthy person.

People can be expected to be more tolerant the higher up they are on the needs hierarchy, and they can be expected to be intolerant to the extent that not even lower-level needs have been adequately met. In the first place, deprivation of basic needs impedes the development of a perspective which can give attention to the needs of other people; people who are just barely getting by need to focus their attention on their own needs. In the second place, tolerance requires a certain degree of psychological security; people who feel insecure or threatened are not likely to be tolerant of other people, especially if they feel that the ideas of others could be dangerous to them. In the third place, certain values such as freedom and democracy are not likely to have much priority in the value system of an individual until that individual has fulfilled other needs; the person who is fulfilling self-actualization needs might place a very high priority on freedom, for example, whereas the person who is attempting to fulfill lower needs might place a much lower priority on freedom.

Maslow's (1954) concept of a hierarchy of needs areas is interesting, and it can be used to encompass many of the other studies concerning personality and tolerance. In addition to encompassing such traits as self-esteem and anomie, it can also be used to cover authoritarianism and dogmatism. In all these situations, intolerance results from a deprivation or a distortion of needs—at one level of the hierarchy or another—of individuals.

Personality and Tolerance: A Final Note

The ideas concerning tolerance and personality seem quite plausible. There are some cautions, however, that need to be emphasized or reemphasized. First, there are problems in the measurement of personality traits or patterns of personality traits; the history of the research on the authoritarian personality demonstrates this problem very well.

Second, there can be a problem in making meaningful distinctions between the effects of psychological needs on the one hand and simple social learning on the other hand. Suppose, for example, a person is intolerant toward blacks. Is this intolerance a means of satisfying some psychological need of the individual, *or* has the individual simply adopted a prevalent norm in the social environment, *or* is the intolerance due to a combination of these and other possible factors? In an area where intolerance of blacks is a social norm, an individual's acceptance of the norm might not have much to do with his or her psychological needs in any deep sense. Goldberg's (1974) exploration of possible connections between prejudice toward women and a variety of personality traits is relevant here. On the whole, Goldberg (1974: 64) found that the personality explanation did not do a very good job in accounting for differences in prejudice against women, and he suggested that the reason for this is that "sexism approaches being a culturally fixed and almost universal attitude." Also, Martin and Westie (1959: 528), while finding that certain personality traits are somewhat related to support for racial discrimination, also stipulate that racial attitudes are to a very great extent simply learned as part of the social norms:

We find in our midst many Happy Bigots whose prejudices are born, not so much of personal psychological difficulties, but rather of the fact that their community and various groups inculcate, expect, and approve of their prejudice.

A third possible problem in the connection between personality and tolerance is that much of this connection might be due primarily to education. Some studies have found that certain personality traits are related to tolerance or intolerance even when such factors as education are taken into consideration; some others (e.g., Quinley and Glock, 1979), however, argue that education is the crucial factor and that personality has no substantial effects on tolerance when education is taken into consideration. On the other hand, the analysis by Sullivan *et al.* (1981) suggests that personality is very important and that education only affects tolerance indirectly by having an effect on personality traits. Further, it needs to be considered that personality characteristics can have an effect on the level of education one attains. In short, the relationship between personality and tolerance becomes more complicated when the factor of education is taken into account.

These cautions indicate that a certain degree of caution should be exercised in discussing the effects of personality on tolerance. A lot of work remains to be done in order to delineate clearly the effects of personality from the effects of other forms of learning.

TOLERANCE AND SOCIAL LEARNING

Social learning theory is based on the idea that learning occurs through the individual's positive and negative experiences in the social environment. Since most of the fundamental social attitudes of an individual are learned during early childhood, the focus of social learning theory is usually on childhood learning, although such learning occurs throughout the life of the individual. Whereas personality theories view intolerance as a result of psychological problems, social learning theory focuses on the learning of social norms—of a culture or a subculture—by well-adjusted as well as maladjusted individuals. Personality factors might, of course, influence which norms are learned and the manner of conformity to the norms. With this social learning focus, however, the development of intolerance in a person does not necessarily represent an aberration; it might simply represent the learning of the particular norms in the individual's particular social environment.

Social learning takes place through the positive reinforcement (rewards) and the negative reinforcement (punishments) of behavior, usually administered by "models" (e.g., parents, teachers, friends). There are several different processes involved in social learning; two of these processes are most important for present purposes. First, in operant (or instrumental) conditioning, a child makes a behavioral response in a situation, and this behavioral response is either positively reinforced (rewarded) or negatively reinforced (punished). For example, suppose a white child proposes to bring a black child home for dinner. The parents' positive or negative reaction (the manner as well as the substance of the reaction) will "teach" the child certain attitudes about racial equality. If, for example, the father angrily says, "You're not going to bring any black kid into this house!" then the child learns that blacks are somehow socially unacceptable.

Operant conditioning requires that a behavioral response be made in a situation before any reinforcement can take place. While this process would account for some social learning, it would usually take a very long time for social norms to be learned by this process. The second social learning process involves identification and imitation. In this process, the child identifies with a model (e.g., a parent) and imitates the attitudes and behavior of the model. To a great extent, this process is self-reinforcing (Campbell, 1979); the child looks up to and admires the model, and imitation of the model adds to the self-esteem of the child. In this process, then, if the model expresses tolerant attitudes, the child could be expected to express tolerant attitudes; if the model is intolerant, then the child will be intolerant.

In terms of general, abstract principles concerning freedom of expression and equality, there are tolerant norms in American society; however, in terms of specific applications, the norm is often one of intolerance rather than tolerance. Thus, social learning often involves the learning of intolerance. Social learning will be discussed in terms of freedom of expression first below, and then it will be applied to matters more related to equality.

It has already been indicated that there is little effort to teach children specific applications of the principles of freedom of expression. In fact, within the family and friendship groups, a great deal of intolerance might be directly taught. For example, a parent says, "They shouldn't allow those damn people to demonstrate; they ought to be in jail." The child learns that certain people should not be allowed freedom of expression. As Zellman (1975: 36) puts it: "So while children learn slogans like 'free speech for all,' they are also learning that often such slogans have no meaning." While children might learn some directly political attitudes through social learning, they can also learn other attitudes which might have an indirect effect on their political attitudes. Zellman (1975: 37) reiterates the point that children are usually presented with a norm which stresses nonconflict. Conflict is usually negatively reinforced; disagreements are to be avoided. Children might be told not to argue with each other or with adults, and arguments among children might be settled arbitrarily by adults— perhaps with negative reinforcement for all the children involved. Thus, the children learn that conflict is to be avoided and that it is legitimate to suppress dissent.

Segall's (1976) theory of ethnocentrism is relevant with regard to social learning of attitudes concerning discrimination and equality. Ethnocentrism here refers to a set of attitudes in which an individual views members of his or her in-group favorably and members of out-groups negatively. Any characteristic of people can be used to separate them into in-groups and out-groups. In Segall's theory, the beginning idea is that civilization imposes restraints on people, and these restraints generate tension and hostility. Since it would be harmful to the in-group to express this aggressiveness (produced by the tension and hostility) within the group, the hostility is displaced toward out-groups. Hostility expressed toward members of the in-group is negatively reinforced; hostility toward members of out-groups is not punished, and it might be positively reinforced. A child begins life with a very self-centered perspective; as the child grows, this perspective expands to include others within the in-group, but not those in out-groups. The child learns to value traits perceived to be held by members of the in-group and to disparage traits perceived to be held by members of out-groups. Ehrlich (1973: 114) states that "children under five years of age begin developing ethnic attitudes even before developing the ability to identify correctly those to whom they are directed." Thus, the in-group–out-group distinctions are made rather early in the life of the child.

In this theory, if the norms of the culture or subculture are intolerant, then there will be a strong connection between conformity and intolerance. Conformity to the norms is positively reinforced by parents, friends, and others within the community. In referring to the conformity to the in-group, it is important to note that the individual's definition of the in-group might be very narrow or very broad. Such factors as education should have an effect on how broad the in-group is conceived to be; it seems probable that the more narrowly the in-group is conceived, the less tolerant the individual will be.

Social learning theory probably accounts for a great deal of the intolerance in American society. In brief, with regard to specific applications of tolerance principles, the norms are often intolerant; the individual simply learns and accepts these norms. On the positive side, as the norms change toward greater tolerance in specific contexts, social learning serves to promote tolerance.

TOLERANCE AND COGNITIVE DEVELOPMENT

You could not teach a two-month-old infant to walk, no matter how hard you tried, because such an infant has not yet achieved the *capability* to learn to walk. Similarly, you could not teach abstract philosophy to an ordinary six-year-old child; the child does not have the ability to deal with abstract concepts. Piaget (1965) and other *stage theorists* maintain that the cognitive development of an individual proceeds through four distinct stages. Cognitive development refers to both (1) the amount and type of information a person has and (2) the level of reasoning a person is capable of using in dealing with such information. In the earliest stage, the individual is only capable of dealing with the immediate environment in terms of immediate needs. In the most advanced stage, the individual has much greater information, a greater level of understanding, and an ability to reason in abstract concepts.

The four stages of cognitive development proceed in a fixed order; a child cannot skip a stage. These stages are age-related in that a child must reach a certain level of maturity—which varies in age from child to child—before the capability to enter a new stage is present. However, even though this capability to enter a new stage must be present before the child can advance to the next stage, the environment still has a very strong impact on cognitive development. Given a stimulating environment, the child might advance to the next stage just as soon as it is physiologically possible. Given a different environment, a child might remain at one stage long after it is possible to move to a more advanced stage. Thus, the cognitive development of a child can be affected by such factors as the surrounding culture (or subculture), the educational environment, and the type of stimulation or experience in the immediate social environment.

In numerous writings (e.g., Kohlberg, 1969), Lawrence Kohlberg has built upon the work of Piaget and others to formulate a stage theory concerning moral development. Moral development follows cognitive development; a certain stage of cognitive development must be achieved before a certain stage of moral development can be achieved. Whereas cognitive development deals with information about the world and the type of reasoning ability the person has to handle such information, moral development concerns the individual's beliefs about what is right and wrong, and it concerns the type of reasoning behind such beliefs. Kohlberg (1971) has formulated three basic stages of moral development; each of these stages contains two substages. These stages and their implications for the development of tolerance (which is a part of moral development) will be discussed briefly.

In the *preconventional stage*, moral judgment is based fundamentally on the immediate consequences to the individual. Moral judgments are not made on the basis of social norms or philosophical considerations. In the *physical power* substage, moral judgments are based on whether an act will be punished or not: "If I do this, will I be punished?" In the *instrumental relativism* substage, moral judgment is based on whether an act will lead to consequences which serve the needs of the individual: "If I do this, will it lead to rewards for me?" Thus, in the preconventional stage, moral judgment is based on an evaluation of the consequences to the individual making the judgment, not on social norms or principles of any sort. No true tolerance can develop at this point; the child is not yet capable of it. "Tolerant" responses might be made by the child simply because making such responses will lead to rewards or because making intolerant responses might lead to punishment. Conversely, intolerance might be rewarded. Given the low level of cognitive development of the child in this stage and given the egocentric outlook of young children, intolerance is the normal stance of young children. When they are "tolerant," it is simply due to a consideration of consequences to themselves. They have not yet developed empathy, the ability to take the role of the other person; thus, they do not yet have the ability to be truly tolerant.

In the *conventional stage*, moral judgments are made on the basis of conformity. In the *interpersonal concordance* substage, moral judgments are determined by whether particular acts will please others and gain their approval. Tolerance would be displayed in this stage when it gained the approval of relevant others (e.g., parents, friends), not because of any principles involved. Conversely, intolerance would be displayed for the same reason. The social environment is the key here in determining whether attitudes are tolerant or intolerant. In the *law and order* substage, moral judgment is based on "doing one's duty (obeying fixed rules), showing respect for authority, and maintaining the given social order" (Tapp and Kohlberg, 1961: 69). Tolerance or intolerance at this stage would be determined by the individual's perceptions of what the official "rules" are. Such tolerance, however, is still not due to philosophical principles; it is due to conformity to rules—or perceptions of rules—formulated by other people.

In the *postconventional stage*, moral judgment moves beyond the self-interest of the individual, and it moves beyond the norms of society; such judgments are now based on the individual's reasoning concerning what is right or wrong. In the *social contract* substage, judgments about individual rights are based on a view of a social system with certain functions, individuals who possess certain rights and responsibilities, and certain procedural processes for settling disputes and making changes. Thus, the individual who reaches this stage has gone beyond conformity and perceives the social system as an abstraction which can be logically analyzed. In the final stage of moral development, which is achieved by a very small percentage of people, the individual in the *universal ethic* substage builds a logical system that is comprehensive, universal, and consistent. This constitutes a whole philosophy about individuals and society.

Tolerance in the postconventional stage is based on reasoning rather than on self-interest or on social norms; in this sense the individual must reach the postconventional stage in order to achieve "true" tolerance. Let's suppose that two people both agree that a Communist should be allowed to give a speech. One might give the tolerant response simply because he or she has been taught that Communists have a right to present their views; the other person might give the tolerant response on the basis of a thought-out rationale about freedom of speech. In one case, the tolerant response might simply be an effect of social learning; in the other case, a deeper thought process is involved and the tolerant response is more autonomous from the norms of the particular society. Therefore, the second person above can independently extend the principle of tolerance to the particular situation; this is tolerance by logic rather than tolerance by rote.

According to Kohlberg, the order of these stages of moral development is fixed; an individual cannot skip a stage. However, it is unlikely that many people will achieve the highest stage. On the contrary, it seems probable that the law and order substage of the conventional stage is the highest level of moral development achieved by most people—and perhaps by some whole societies. The achievement of the postconventional level probably requires higher education and a greater variety of experiences than most people obtain. For most people, then, a tolerant response to a question concerning tolerance probably reflects their perception of what the socially or legally "right" response is.

In practice, it might make little difference whether a person gives a conventional tolerant response or a postconventional tolerant response. However, the level of moral development of an individual might make a difference as to *whether* the response is tolerant or intolerant. Zellman (1975: 37–38) argues basically that children crystallize their civil liberties attitudes during the conventional stage. Since they have not yet fully developed the ability to perceive the role of another person and perceive dissent as legitimate, the attitudes they develop at this stage are more likely to be intolerant rather than tolerant with regard to specific applications of principles of tolerance. These preadolescents are unlikely to acquire skills and knowledge in school or at home which will help them to develop much further in this particular area. If their moral development in this area does not go beyond this stage, then they will continue to hold intolerant attitudes during adulthood. Thus, many adults are at an arrested stage of moral development. Those whose moral development continues (which is more likely among those who obtain higher education or who have a greater diversity of social experiences) will be more likely to be more tolerant. In a small study of elementary school students, for example, Patterson (1979) demonstrated that those students who were in a higher stage of moral development were more tolerant (with regard to freedom of speech for a Communist) and that they were more consistent in applying their stand on the general principle of freedom of speech to a specific context.

In sum, the stage theories concerning cognitive development and moral development have very important implications for the development of tolerant or intolerant attitudes. Individuals must achieve a certain stage of maturity before they can be tolerant or intolerant—in either a norm-oriented, conventional sense or in a reason-oriented, postconventional sense. It appears that the higher the stage of moral development a person achieves, the more likely it is that the person will be tolerant. If a person stops moral development at the conventional stage, it is more likely that the person will be intolerant because the norms of society are not very tolerant with regard to specific applications of principles of tolerance.

TOLERANCE AND DIRECT EXPERIENCES

The learning of tolerance has been examined from several different focal points which overlap one another. Here the focus is on experiences of the individual which might be very relevant for the development of tolerance. Since political experiences usually involve exposure to different viewpoints, an examination of the relationship between tolerance and political participation will be made first. Then, using the example of racial attitudes as a base, an attempt will be made to analyze the effects of experiences (e.g., interracial contact) which are relevant in a very direct way to tolerance.

Tolerance and Political Experiences

Based on moral development theory, it would be expected that those who participate in politics more would be more tolerant (Tapp and Kohlberg, 1971). Exposure to differing viewpoints should provide a greater ability to take the role of the other and understand the position of the other person. For the population as a whole, there is evidence that those who participate more in politics (in terms of voting, contributing money to candidates, working for candidates, and so on) are more tolerant (Wilson, 1975; Herson and Hofstetter, 1975; Nunn et al., 1978). In order to focus more sharply on the relationship between tolerance and political participation and the problems in interpreting this relationship, let us consider differences in tolerance between the general population and political elites. Political elites are those who are occupied with public affairs to an unusual degree; this includes government officials, active political party members, leaders of voluntary associations, political writers, opinion leaders, and others who take a very active role in politics (McClosky, 1964: 364).

Three major studies indicate that political activists are much more tolerant than the general population. First, Stouffer's (1955) study included a sample of the general population and a sample of political activists. The 1500 political activists were selected community leaders (e.g., the mayor, the president of the chamber of commerce, labor union leaders, newspaper publishers) from cities with a population between 10,000 and 150,000; such cities are not, of course, representative of larger cities, rural areas, and smaller towns. The results from this study indicated that the political activists were much more tolerant than the general population. For example, 84% of the leaders would allow a socialist to give a speech in their community, as compared to only 58% of the general population. Further, this type of difference existed no matter what kind of leader was being considered; some groups of leaders (e.g., newspaper editors) were more tolerant than others (e.g., leaders of the Daughters of the American Revolution), but all groups of leaders were more tolerant than the general population. The second major study is the 1973 replication of Stouffer's research by Nunn et al. (1978). This more recent study also indicated that there was a gap in tolerance between leaders and the general population, although both groups had increased in tolerance.

The third major study was carried out in 1956–58 by McClosky (1964). In addition to a national sample, McClosky surveyed a "political influentials" sample consisting of 3020 Republican and Democratic delegates and alternates to the 1956 national party conventions. There was little difference between the leaders and the general population on general, abstract principles of tolerance; both groups gave nearly unanimous support to such abstract ideas. However, in terms of specific applications of the principles of tolerance, the elites were much more tolerant than the general population. For example, 37% of the general population—as compared to 15% of the elites—agreed that a book that contains wrong political views does not deserve to be published. The finding of greater tolerance among elites than among the general population in McClosky's (1964) study applied to both freedom of expression and equality.

As an aside, the finding of greater tolerance among elites and other findings which indicate that elites are generally more committed to a wide range of democratic values than the general population have led some political analysts to the "democratic elitism" position. Dahl (1961) and some others take the position that public policies actually result from the struggle among various conflicting elites while the masses remain relatively apathetic. Since the elites involved in the struggle over public policy represent a wide range of political interests, the public policies which result are pretty much in accord with the public interest. Since the masses are not very committed to democratic norms, it is best to leave them relatively apathetic (e.g., McClosky, 1964: 376; Prothro and Grigg, 1960: 292). *The Irony of Democracy*, an American politics textbook, takes its title from this idea: "Democratic values have survived because elites, not masses, govern" (Dye and Zeigler, 1978: 13). On the other hand, some (e.g., Nunn *et al.*, 1978) argue that increased political participation by the masses would increase their political tolerance and their commitment to other democratic norms; further, if this is not done, the masses might be susceptible to the appeals of an antidemocratic, nontolerant movement during periods of crisis.

Why are elites more tolerant? One of the major explanations is the idea that political participation itself increases tolerance and commitment to democratic norms generally. Prior to serious active involvement in the political process, the person has a certain level of commitment to democratic norms; as the person becomes more politically active, a resocialization to higher levels of democratic commitment takes place. It is argued that there is a unique "political stratum" which resocializes its new members to accept more fully the "rules of the game." Political elites with strong ideas on substantive issues interact with other political elites who also hold strong opinions. Adherence to the democratic rules of the game ensures that the conflicts will be handled more smoothly; thus, the political elites give strong support to these rules of the game. Further, contact and negotiation with other people whose ideas are different from one's own presumably would lead to greater understanding of different viewpoints and to greater tolerance.

All this sounds reasonable, but there is a problem. The question has been raised as to whether political elites actually are more tolerant than people in the general population with similar social characteristics. Political elites are generally recruited from the better-educated segments of society, and people who have higher education tend to be more tolerant. Thus, the greater tolerance of political elites might be due to their social background rather than to their unique experiences as participants in the political process. McClosky's (1964: 373) analysis indicated that political elites of a given education level were still more tolerant than nonactivists of the same education level, thus supporting the idea that political elites are unique in their levels of tolerance. However, Jackman's (1972) reanalysis of Stouffer's (1955) results indicated little difference in levels of tolerance between the community leaders and members of the general population when such background characteristics as education, region, sex, and city size were taken into account. Thus, it appears that much of the additional tolerance of elites in comparison with the general population is simply due to their social backgrounds. Another study provides an interesting finding that is relevant here. Monsma (1971) asked a sample of the residents of Plattsburgh, New York, whether they might be willing at some future time to run for or hold public office. The Potentials (those who would be willing) were more tolerant than the Non-potentials. This suggests that the greater tolerance of political leaders might exist prior to their becoming leaders.

In sum, the evidence concerning political participation and tolerance does not present a clear picture. Those who participate more in politics are generally more tolerant, but it is not clear whether the political participation itself leads to greater tolerance. Other social characteristics (e.g., education) might be more important, or there might be an interaction between such social characteristics and political participation to produce a certain effect on levels of tolerance. Further, the level of tolerance of a person might have a substantial impact on whether the person will become active in politics. Finally, in situations in which the general population is very intolerant on certain matters, it might be that the political leaders who are more intolerant will have a greater chance of success. In an area in which racial intolerance is very high, for example, relatively tolerant political activists might have difficulty in ever becoming political leaders.

Contact and Tolerance

Here the concern is with experiences in situations in which tolerance is involved in a very direct way. The focus is on one specific area, the effects of interracial contact on racial prejudice, but an attempt will be made to generalize from this to other situations.

It is sometimes argued that greater contact between whites and blacks will lead to a reduction in racial prejudice; the evidence, however, indicates clearly that interracial contact alone does not reduce racial prejudice (Allport, 1954; Pettigrew, 1971). If contact alone reduced prejudice, then racial prejudice should be lower in the South than in the rest of the country. Allport (1954: 263) makes the point that in places where segregation is the norm, interracial contacts will be superficial; the contacts are either casual or reflective of superordinate-subordinate relationships. Such contacts do not lead to true acquaintance and knowledge; they simply reinforce existing attitudes.

Allport (1954: 281) suggests that prejudice between groups is most likely to be reduced (provided that it is not deeply rooted in personality needs) if certain conditions are met in the contacts. First, the contacts must be *equal-status* contacts. Within the situation, both parties are interacting on an equal basis, and it is also helpful if they bring equal social status to the situation. For example, the chances of prejudice reduction are greater in contact between two middle-class factory workers performing the same job than they are in contact between a business executive and a clerk. Second, the contacts are more likely to lead to a reduction in prejudice if they occur in the pursuit of common goals. For example, racial prejudice would probably be reduced among the members of a racially mixed group which is enthusiastically pursuing a common goal (e.g., a campaign organization, a basketball team, a neighborhood organization fighting to keep its school from being closed). Third, the probability of contact reducing prejudice would be increased if the contact is approved by institutional supports (laws, custom, the local atmosphere). Fourth, contact is more likely to reduce prejudice if it leads to the perception of common interests and common humanity between members of the groups involved. Let's say that two very different people meet. If the contact focuses on their differences, then their negative attitudes toward one another will probably increase. If the contact brings out their similarities and they are able to perceive these similarities, then it is more likely that a more positive attitude will develop from the contact.

Allport's (1954) conditions concerning contact pertain to the reduction of *prejudice*, rather than to the reduction of *intolerance*. The assumption here is that a reduction in prejudice will also lead in many circumstances to a reduction in intolerance. Further, Allport was concerned primarily with racial and religious prejudice. It appears, however, that Allport's conditions concerning contact can be greatly extended. Given two people who are different in some respect (biologically/physically, socially, or in terms of beliefs), under what conditions will tolerance be increased and under what conditions will tolerance be decreased? Let us take one example of tolerance as support for equality and one example of tolerance as support for freedom of expression.

Obviously, men and women have a great number of contacts with one another, and these contacts do not necessarily lead to greater support for sexual equality. On the basis of Allport's ideas, it is apparent that an extremely high proportion of contact between men and women is not equal-status contact; it is mostly contact between men in a superordinate role and women in a subordinate role. This contact should reinforce the social norms regarding a less important role for women. Equal-status contacts under certain conditions should increase support for sexual equality. Such contacts would probably need to take place within a framework in which both people are working cooperatively on a common goal (e.g., a police team consisting of a male officer and a female officer) rather than working competitively against one another (e.g., two salespersons working in a store on the basis of commissions). Support for sexual equality in equal-status contact would also be more likely to increase if the contact is approved and supported in the formal and informal atmosphere. For example, support for sexual equality is not likely to increase in a man who has been told that he will have to work with a woman because the employer was forced to hire a woman for the job. The handling of such situations can lead to greater tolerance or less tolerance. Finally, equal-status contacts between men and women will probably lead to greater support for sexual equality if they get to know each other as human beings rather than simply as occupants of social roles.

In terms of support for freedom of expression, such support should be increased by contacts of the type suggested by Allport. Contact between two people of different beliefs can lead to greater support or less support by either person for the right of the other person to freedom of expression. First of all, such tolerance should be increased by equal-status contacts; contacts on an unequal level will probably just add to the resentment and distrust. Second, it helps if the two perceive common goals. Suppose an atheist and a fundamentalist Baptist meet. If the contact focuses on their differences, then their intolerance will probably increase. Suppose, however, that they have a genuine exchange of views and they find that they share certain humanitarian goals. Even though neither person changes religious beliefs, the perception of some common goals might lead to greater support for the right of the other to express religious or nonreligious beliefs. In many circumstances, of course, this will not happen. When two people of opposing beliefs encounter one another, the contact is often cool, formal, or superficial. If discussions of differences do occur, such discussions are more likely to resemble a contest (one person tries to defeat the other) rather than a genuine exchange in which two sides learn about each other's beliefs and evaluate them on their merits. Tolerance in equal-status contacts is also more likely to be increased if this type of contact is approved and encouraged. If the norms in a particular area encourage the expression and discussion of beliefs, then such contact is more likely to lead to greater tolerance. Finally, tolerance is more likely to increase if the two people of differing beliefs come to know each other as human beings rather than as sets of beliefs.

It appears, then, that Allport's conditions of contact can be generalized to indicate conditions under which direct experiences will lead to an increase or a decrease in tolerance—as either support for freedom of expression or as support for equality. However, two cautions need to be noted. First, such equal-status contacts are not usually the normal contacts; both the social structure and the propensity of people to avoid potentially unpleasant situations have a limiting effect on the number of equal-status contacts which take place. Second, the increased tolerance resulting from equal-status contacts will probably be very specific; e.g., a person who develops greater support for equality for women will not necessarily transfer that attitude to blacks.

CONCLUSION

The learning of tolerance has been examined from several different focal points. First, it is clear that education—in the sense of years of schooling—is strongly related to tolerance. Questions have been raised which indicate that some caution should be used in interpreting the education-tolerance relationship, but the relationship still remains. Further, it is clear that years of schooling is only a rough indicator of the educational processes which could be expected to contribute to political tolerance. There are other important factors involved, such as the student's degree of involvement, the type of teaching which takes place, the substance of the teaching, and the type of learning environment. Tolerance should be greatly increased in some schooling situations (e.g., the student's curiosity is stimulated, the student's perspective is widened, social diversity and conflict are regarded as legitimate); the increase in tolerance should be less dramatic in situations in which the student is simply going through routine motions in an uninterested way.

Second, it is clear that tolerance is related to certain personality characteristics. However, it is not clear whether this relationship is actually due to other factors such as education. My suggestion is that for most individuals the impact of personality characteristics will not be great enough to affect levels of tolerance substantially. For most individuals, the psychological traits which they possess will not be severe enough to account for intolerance; thus, other learning focal points will be more helpful in explaining their levels of tolerance or intolerance. For some people, however, personality traits will reflect deeper psychological problems; among these people, personality and tolerance might be strongly related. In such situations, intolerance might reflect a displacement of repressed hostility from oneself or one's parents onto socially accepted targets, such as minority groups or people who hold minority viewpoints. Intolerance might also result from personality traits (e.g., a low level of self-esteem) which impede social interaction and learning. In sum, personality traits probably play a relatively minor role in the development of attitudes relevant to tolerance for most of the population, but such traits might substantially affect the learning of tolerance for a minority of the population.

Third, social learning theory seems to account for the development of tolerance or intolerance among most people. People learn their attitudes through reinforcements in the social environment. Again, however, such learning can be affected by other factors which have been discussed. Education is an important part of the social environment and can provide the intellectual tools to see beyond one's immediate environment. Personality probably affects the learning of norms and the manner of adherence to such norms.

Fourth, cognitive development theory provides a framework to describe the capabilities and probabilities for an individual to learn tolerance. The intellectual capability and perspective of the individual expand from one stage of cognitive development to the next. Factors such as education, personality, and social learning have an effect on progression through these stages. Increased education, for example, can be expected to increase the speed of progression and the probability that one will achieve the highest stage of cognitive development. Personality problems might slow the progression or stop the process at some stage. It appears that many Americans cease cognitive development—at least with regard to norms concerning tolerance—at the conventional stage, in which their attitudes relevant to tolerance basically depend upon their perceptions of conventional social and legal norms. "True" tolerance, however, requires that people go beyond a simple acceptance of norms and base their views on a broader reasoning process. In sum, increased cognitive development appears to increase the probability that a person will adopt tolerant attitudes.

Finally, it is clear that tolerance or intolerance can be learned through direct experiences. Using Allport's concept of equal-status contacts, it has been suggested that direct experiences of a certain type will increase tolerance; contacts which do not meet these conditions, however, will simply reinforce existing attitudes.

All these different focal points concerning learning help to explain how tolerance or intolerance is learned. The learning of tolerance is not an easy matter. It involves restraining one's own impulses and the ability to accept the legitimacy of the rights of people who are different from oneself. Perhaps such difficulty involved in learning tolerance explains why so many Americans are intolerant in specific contexts. For many people, the learning process leading to tolerance is simply incomplete.

Tolerance and the Future

INTRODUCTION

Is American society headed toward greater tolerance or less tolerance? What are the hopeful signs? What are the danger signs? Can anything be done to increase tolerance in American society? In this chapter, I will speculate on such questions. To begin, some of the fundamental points made in earlier chapters will be reviewed. Having set the stage, I will comment on future prospects for changes in tolerance and make some suggestions as to what might be done in order to increase tolerance. It needs to be stipulated at the beginning, however, that future changes—if any—in levels of tolerance are not likely to be subject to deliberate control; such changes as might take place will very likely be due to events (e.g., world tensions) and trends (e.g., increases in education levels) which have little to do with any deliberate attempt to increase or decrease political tolerance.

TOLERANCE IN THE AMERICAN PAST

Tolerance in the United States has its theoretical roots in the liberal political theory of John Locke. This theory postulated that individuals are of great importance, that all men had certain natural rights (including freedom of expression), that all men are created equal, and that the basic function of government is to protect the rights of individuals. These basic ideas were incorporated into the American Declaration of Independence; the formulation of the U.S.

200

Constitution reflected a somewhat different version of liberalism, but it did incorporate—primarily in its amendments—many principles which are fundamental to a tolerant political system.

Tolerance has been defined in terms of support for freedom of expression and in terms of support for equality. Freedom of expression is covered by the First Amendment which concerns freedom of the press, freedom of speech, freedom of religion, the right to peaceable assembly, and the right to petition. In terms of equality, one might focus on the "equal protection of the laws" clause in the Fourteenth Amendment.

The scope of tolerance in American liberalism was broad, but the domain was limited; i.e., the rights provided by the American Constitution and its amendments provide a fairly good constitutional basis for a tolerant political system provided that these rights are extended to everyone and provided that such rights are adequately protected for everyone. However, these rights have not been extended to everyone and they have not been adequately protected. For example, it was not until the ratification of the Fourteenth Amendment that blacks had legal equality, and the lack of protection for such equality has made such equality on paper meaningless throughout most of American history since the ratification of the Fourteenth Amendment. Women still do not even have equality of rights on paper, and it appears that the Equal Rights Amendment might very well fail to be ratified.

Political institutions have not often been willing to defend the rights of unpopular persons or groups against the intense opposition of majority public attitudes. This applies to the Supreme Court as well as to other political institutions; throughout most of its history, the Supreme Court has avoided situations in which it might need to take an unpopular stand in favor of an individual or group which was strongly opposed by the general public. At the same time, however, political leaders as a group have been more committed to norms of tolerance than the general population has, and this has probably had an impact on levels of tolerance in society. In line with Dahl's (1961: 315) position, it appears that the average citizen leaves many affairs to political leaders to decide and—given that political leaders are usually more tolerant than the average citizen—political actions often reflect the higher level of tolerance of political leaders rather than the lower level of tolerance of the general public. Further, through their behavior, political leaders can demonstrate models of tolerance and thus educate the public. Thus, the tolerant norms of political leaders and institutions have helped to create a society which is more tolerant in action than we might expect on the basis of survey findings concerning tolerance in the general population. This process, however, works best when the general public is not greatly concerned about an issue or event. If the general public becomes intense in its views, the political leaders might support less tolerant norms or they might be replaced by new leaders who are much less tolerant.

In order for a tolerant society to exist, it would not be adequate to have tolerant political institutions and tolerant political leaders; the people who compose the society must be tolerant in their day-to-day attitudes and behaviors. In the history of the United States, Americans have demonstrated far less than complete tolerance for many groups because of their biological/physical characteristics (e.g., blacks), their social characteristics (e.g., ethnic groups), or their beliefs (e.g., atheists).

TOLERANCE IN THE AMERICAN PRESENT

Americans give strong support to abstract, general principles of tolerance, but it is amply clear that support for specific applications of such principles is much weaker. It has been demonstrated that Americans do not strongly support freedom of expression in situations in which they dislike the group or the viewpoint involved. Although Americans give strong support to the abstract concept of equality, they are not so supportive of specific applications of this concept for women, blacks, and others who are disliked or whose viewpoints are disliked.

It is not completely clear whether tolerance in general has increased in the United States during recent times. The Stouffer-related studies clearly indicate that tolerance toward certain groups (atheists, socialists, and Communists) has increased—perhaps because of the decline of the Cold War. However, the study by Sullivan et al. (1979) suggests that Americans may simply have switched the targets of intolerance; on the other hand, Abramson (1980) points out that Americans are more tolerant of their least liked group than they were of atheists and Communists in 1954. While the research by Sullivan et al. indicates that people are still very intolerant toward their least liked group, I would suggest that tolerance probably has increased if it is viewed in terms of a wide range of people or groups that might be tolerated instead of the least liked group or even several disliked groups. Nevertheless, it is quite clear that Americans can be very intolerant of people or viewpoints that they do not like. In the day-to-day lives of people, this might not present a conspicuous problem; i.e., there are not often dramatic situations these days in which the public directly denies freedom of expression to someone or denies equality to someone. However, the existence of the low levels of tolerance in the public to such a strong extent can prevent the problem from becoming conspicuous. For example, a person who holds unpopular views might not ever express those views publically because of fears of economic, social, or physical retaliation. In order for freedom of expression to exist or in order for equality to exist, people must be able to claim and use such rights without fear of reprisal. The low level of tolerance in the American public does not eliminate such fears of reprisal.

PROSPECTS FOR THE FUTURE

From my point of view, applied tolerance in the United States is not as high as it ought to be. The high support which Americans give for abstract, general principles of freedom of expression and equality needs to be translated into high support for specific applications of these principles. People who hold unpopular views—no matter what those views are—should be able to express their views without fear of reprisal. Support for equality needs to be raised to the point that equality in practice will be implemented. In comparison with most other nations in the world, the United States is a comparatively tolerant nation. Further, both support for freedom of expression and support for equality have increased over the last twenty or thirty years. Nevertheless, in comparison with its own expressed ideals, the United States has not yet become tolerant enough.

The extension of tolerance in the United States would provide several benefits. First, individuals would benefit by receiving equality or by being able to express freely their views. Second, the society as a whole should benefit from a freer flow of ideas and by freeing itself from the negative consequences of discrimination and inequality. Third, the nation would benefit in world affairs by eliminating a propoganda weapon used by unfriendly nations when they point out instances in which our ideals of free speech and equality are abandoned.

There are some possible dangers which could lead to less tolerance in the future. Basically, these dangers can be divided into two categories: crises situations and noncrisis trends. Crisis situations can bring out the best in people and they can also bring out the worst in people. One possible crisis which could reduce tolerance involves the energy situation. If the Arab nations shut off the flow of oil to the United States for an extended period of time, this would create a very grave crisis. In such times, people look for scapegoats. In view of the Arab-Israeli conflict, Jews would probably become scapegoats for many people, and anti-Semitism would increase. In times when people feel insecure, they tend to be intolerant generally. Economic problems could also lead to a crisis which could cause people to feel insecure. In times of economic crisis, people might turn to a strong leader who promises simple solutions, abandons restraint, and directs blame for the problems to certain groups in society. Gilmour and Lamb (1975: 157) provide a grim warning concerning the fragile nature of constitutionalism and its relation to the economy:

Attacked from without, we have a Maginot umbrella that could no doubt rain scorching destruction on the entire world. Attacked from within by economic dislocation and disorganization, we will most surely abandon our constitutional heritage in a matter of months or even weeks.

Foreign crises could also lead to the reduction of tolerance. If, for example, the Cold War between the United States and the U.S.S.R. intensifies again, then this could very well lead to a reduction in tolerance toward groups in the United States whose views are associated with the left wing of the political spectrum. The negative effects on tolerance of the Cold War were demonstrated best during the late 1940s and early 1950s. Fears concerning possible internal threats from Communist agents and sympathizers within the United States were very great, and some political figures during that time advanced their political careers by playing upon such fears. Senator Joseph McCarthy was the most prominent of those who engaged in "Red-baiting," and the early 1950s are often referred to as the "McCarthy Era." McCarthy's investigations and loose accusations of people he suspected of being Communist or sympathetic toward the Communists added to the climate of fear. No one was safe from the accusing finger. The rights of people were violated, people lost their jobs and reputations, academic freedom suffered, actors were blacklisted, and tolerance in general was at a low ebb. "Are you now or have you ever been a member of the Communist Party?" People could be ruined just by having McCarthy ask them this question. McCarthy's methods and loose accusations eventually resulted in an official censure from the Senate, one of the few times in history in which the U.S. Senate has taken such dramatic action against one of its own members. There is nothing, however, to prevent this type of pattern from occurring again.

In short, there are a number of different types of crisis situations which could lead to a reduction in tolerance; crisis situations probably very rarely, if ever, lead to an increase in tolerance. Further, it is clear that the potential is great for the occurrence of crisis situations in the domestic or international affairs of the United States.

Possible noncrisis trends in the United States could also lead to a less tolerant society. At present, for example, it appears that political trust and confidence in the American political system are relatively low among the population compared with earlier times. A deepening of such feelings could lead to support for a return to more traditional social and political values, including greater restrictions on freedom of expression and less support for equality. Two other trends pose possible dangers to the growth of tolerance. These two forces are sharply different in certain respects, yet they have joined forces to some extent. One is the apparent increase in the power of anticollectivist groups representing a more narrow, self-centered approach to economics and politics. The increase in the power of such groups taking a "conservative" (classical liberal) position on politics and economics represents an obstacle to efforts to achieve political and legal equality (as well as economic equality) for disadvantaged groups. The second trend is the apparent rise in the influence (or perceived influence—which can lead to a self-fulfilling prophecy) of groups with a restrictive collectivist viewpoint. Such groups usually associate themselves with fundamentalistic religious values. More important, they have begun to take a more active role in politics, and they have been perceived by many—whether accurately or not—to have been successful. The "targets" of such groups in elections are political leaders whose views include support for freedom of expression and support for equality. If such groups are successful in attempts to defeat tolerant candidates and leaders and in efforts to persuade many people to support their views, this will no doubt reduce the levels of tolerance in American society.

While there is ample reason to worry about tolerance in the future, there are also some hopeful signs. As already indicated, it does appear that tolerance in the United States has increased over the last twenty or thirty years. Perhaps this trend will continue. Stouffer (1955: 220) optimistically viewed the basis for the growth of tolerance earlier:

Great social, economic, and technological forces are working on the side of exposing ever larger proportions of our population to the idea that "people are different from me, with different systems of values, and they can be good people, too."

Stouffer (1955: 221) proposed that there were three forces which might lead to greater tolerance. First, increasing education was expected to lead to greater tolerance. Second, increased horizontal mobility—people moving about more instead of just staying in the same place all their lives—was expected to expose people to a greater diversity of people and ideas, and thus, increase their tolerance. Third, the growth of communications was expected to expose people to greater diversity and increase their tolerance. These types of trends still continue, and they could be expected to have a positive effect on the growth of tolerance.

WHAT MIGHT BE DONE?

If deliberate efforts were to be undertaken to increase tolerance, what types of things might be done? First of all, it needs to be stipulated that it seems unlikely that any deliberate efforts will be undertaken on a large scale to increase tolerance. It seems unlikely that people will perceive this as a problem that requires attention. Most people give very high support to the general, abstract slogans concerning freedom of expression and equality, and they are very likely to view such slogans as representative of reality rather than as ideals which have not been fully attained. Nevertheless, I will speculate on what might be done to increase tolerance. Despite the cautions implied by Sullivan et al. (1981), it appears that education is the key factor that could be deliberately used in order to increase tolerance. Before discussing this proposal, however, another factor over which control could be exerted needs to be discussed briefly.

In order to create a more tolerant society, the first task should be to complete the legislative agenda. This is primarily a problem for the question of equality rather than for freedom of expression, but the two overlap when the question concerns equal treatment for groups who hold unpopular views (e.g., atheists). Unjustified discrimination needs to be prohibited. First on this agenda would be the ratification of the Equal Rights Amendment to the Constitution which would outlaw discrimination on the basis of sex. Women constitute a majority of the population, but they still do not have equal status with men under the Constitution. Legislation is also needed to guarantee more fully that there will not be discrimination against unpopular groups, such as atheists, homosexuals, socialists, and so on. Would such legislation lead to greater tolerance in the American public? This legislation would certainly not guarantee that the levels of tolerance would increase, but it makes it more likely. Many people are at least partly influenced in their attitudes by what the law says. Outlawing unjustified discrimination should lead to at least some increase in tolerance. Further, based on the work of Allport (1954: 479), it could be expected that such legislation would increase the probability and frequency of equal status contacts; such equal status contacts, under the right conditions, should lead to greater tolerance. Looking at the matter from a different angle, when the laws or the courts do *not* prohibit discrimination against a group, it seems reasonable to conclude that this makes intolerance of that group more acceptable to people. For example, if the ERA is not ratified, it seems likely that many people will interpret this to mean that it is acceptable to discriminate against people on the basis of sex unless there is some specific law against it. When the courts uphold a school board for firing a homosexual teacher whose homosexuality has nothing to do with his or her teaching activities, this is a signal to society that intolerance of homosexuals is acceptable behavior. Thus, the first task in order to create a more tolerant society is to get rid of the legal vestiges which support unjustified discrimination.

In proposing that education is the key to produce greater political tolerance, let me first review several propositions made throughout the book. First, there is a clear connection between higher tolerance and higher education measured simply in terms of number of years of schooling. On the other hand, Sullivan *et al.* (1981) suggest that education has only an indirect effect on tolerance, that education helps to increase psychological security, and psychological security—which is affected by variables in addition to education—has the direct effect on tolerance. I am not proposing that merely increasing the number of years of schooling of individuals will automatically increase tolerance; on the contrary, I will propose that the nature of the education process with regard to tolerance needs to be altered. Nevertheless, it does appear that education viewed simply as the years of schooling completed increases the probability that the student will receive basic educational experiences which lead to greater cognitive development and, thus, to greater tolerance. Second, as implied above, greater cognitive development—which can be very highly influenced by schooling—leads to greater tolerance. Third, support for abstract, general principles of tolerance is taught in the schools, but support for specific applications of such principles is not ordinarily taught (Hess, 1968; Zellman and Sears, 1971; Zellman, 1975). Fourth, experimental research indicates that specific applications of principles of tolerance can be taught in the schools (Zellman and Sears, 1971). Fifth, I have suggested that many teachers are not prepared to teach specific applications of tolerance principles.

The basic proposal here is that a sustained, concentrated effort should be made in the schools to teach *specific applications* of principles of tolerance. There is no need to promote further teaching of *general principles*; given the high level of support for such general principles, further teaching of such slogans would be redundant and boring. In fact, if programs were undertaken to teach specific applications, the first problem to avoid is allowing such teaching to degenerate into further redundant teaching of abstract ideals. The goal should be to teach students to be able to apply the general principles in specific contexts. While not all possible contexts could be taken up, such teaching should include a wide variety of very specific situations.

If such teaching is to have an impact on students, then it should be made very interesting to them. Given the nature of the topic and the controversy surrounding specific applications of principles of tolerance, it should be very easy to make such teaching interesting. However, the salience of the teaching to the student could be increased further by inviting guests to the classes to present their positions. Such guests could represent both majority and minority viewpoints; they could appear separately or they could debate one another. This type of approach would expose students to conflict and diversity within society. By openly analyzing such conflict and by treating such conflict as legitimate in a democratic society, the student's acceptance of diversity should be increased and the student's level of tolerance should increase.

When should such teaching occur? While a little of this could be done in the early grades of school, cognitive development theory implies that it would not be very useful to attempt a concentrated effort on such teaching before the students have reached the requisite stage of cognitive development, probably around the age of twelve. On the other hand, social learning theory implies that we should not wait too long after this to begin such teaching; otherwise, the students will crystallize their values—values that are not very tolerant—and these values will remain in adulthood. A possible course of action, then, is to commence concentrated efforts on teaching applied tolerance in the sixth grade. Students might spend a year (one course) on citizenship training with a heavy emphasis on applied tolerance and the handling of conflict in society and then another year later, perhaps in the tenth grade. Elements or units concerning tolerance could also be incorporated into other classes during the other grades.

Aside from the danger that such teaching might simply degenerate into further redundant teaching of slogans, there are two other primary problems. First, when the topics become specific, they will be controversial, and this will probably create public pressure against such teaching. This is an extremely difficult problem: How do you teach tolerance to students when their parents are not tolerant enough to allow it? In many places, the idea of teaching applied tolerance would no doubt be doomed from the start. In some situations, however, teachers and administrators might be able to sell this idea to the public by appealing to the public's high support for general principles of tolerance.

The second problem, as already implied, is that many teachers might not be able to handle this type of teaching. In the first place, it is very unlikely that they have received any preparation for it. In the second place, while most teachers are likely to have a somewhat higher level of applied tolerance than the general public is, this level might not be high enough to enable the teacher to do an effective job. Thus, a possible solution is to have a mandatory, college-level course for all teachers which would cover both substance and teaching methods. Such a course should be designed to prepare teachers to teach applied tolerance to their students; for those who will not be involved in teaching such courses, the course would enable the teacher to supplement and support the efforts of those who do teach such courses.

As already indicated, it does not seem likely that any widespread effort will be undertaken to increase levels of tolerance in the American public. It appears, however, that any deliberate effort to increase tolerance would have to be along these suggested lines in order to have much impact.

CONCLUSION

The political philosophy of the United States is based to a large extent on a theory of human rights, human equality, and the role of the government. This theory has gradually expanded to include higher respect for human rights and a greater degree of equality. With regard to specific applications, however, neither the American political institutions nor the American public has taken the extensions of the political slogans to their logical conclusions. It is a mistake to view freedom of expression and equality as ideals; ideals, by implication, are rarely achieved in practice. Freedom of expression and equality should be viewed as goals which can be achieved. There is nothing to prevent them from being achieved if the American public is willing.

Description of 1977 NORC Survey and Wording of NORC Questions Not Given in Text

DESCRIPTION

With support from the National Science Foundation, the National Opinion Research Center (NORC) at the University of Chicago has conducted a General Social Survey of a national sample each year between 1972 and 1980 except for 1979. These surveys have been conducted as part of the National Data Program for the Social Sciences in order to provide survey data for a wide range of social scientists. In order to serve as a social indicator program, many questions were selected which had been used in previous national surveys, and these questions are asked periodically, although not in every General Social Survey.

Prior to 1977, the NORC samples were not full probability samples; a different kind of sampling, quota sampling, was used in certain stages of the sampling process, and this reduced the accuracy of such surveys. Beginning with the 1977 survey, full probability samples have been used by NORC. The 1977 NORC sample of 1530 persons represents a probability sample of English-speaking persons eighteen years of age or over in the continental United States.

In addition to the use of the 1977 NORC survey, information has been used from other NORC surveys in the 1972–1980 series. It needs to be kept in mind that the information from the surveys prior to 1977 is probably less accurate because the samples used were not full probability samples. The 1977 survey was selected for more extensive use in this book because it contained a greater number of questions relevant to tolerance.

In some cases, the exact wording of the NORC questions has been given in the text. The full wording of the other questions included in the analysis is given below. Also, it needs to be noted that the tolerance questions concerning atheists and Communists were first used in Stouffer's 1954 study. The questions concerning tolerance for socialists which were used by Stouffer in the same series of tolerance questions are also presented, although NORC did not include the socialist questions in its 1977 survey.

STOUFFER-NORC QUESTIONS
CONCERNING UNPOPULAR PERSONS

There are always some people whose ideas are considered bad or dangerous by other people. For instance, somebody who is against all churches and religion. [Used by Stouffer and NORC]

A If such a person wanted to make a speech in your community against churches and religion, should he be allowed to speak, or not?
B Should such a person be allowed to teach in a college or university, or not?
C If some people in your community suggested that a book he wrote against churches and religion should be taken out of your public library, would you favor removing this book, or not?

Or, consider a person who believes that blacks are genetically inferior. roads and all big industries. [Used by Stouffer only]

A If such a person wanted to make a speech in your community favoring government ownership of all the railroads and big industries, should he be allowed to speak, or not?
B Should such a person be allowed to teach in a college or university, or not?
C If some people in your community suggested a book he wrote favoring government ownership should be taken out of your public library, would you favor removing this book, or not?

Or, consider a person who believes that Blacks are genetically inferior. [Used by NORC only]

A If such a person wanted to make a speech in your community claiming that blacks are inferior, should he be allowed to speak, or not?
B Should such a person be allowed to teach in a college or university, or not?
C If some people in your community suggested that a book he wrote which said blacks are inferior should be taken out of your public library, would you favor removing this book, or not?

Now, I should like to ask you some questions about a man who admits he is a Communist. [Used by Stouffer and NORC]

A Suppose this admitted Communist wanted to make a speech in your community. Should he be allowed to speak, or not?
B Suppose he is teaching in a college. Should he be fired, or not?
C Suppose he wrote a book which is in your public library. Somebody in your community suggests that the book be removed from the library. Would you favor removing it, or not?

Consider a person who advocates doing away with elections and letting the military run the country. [Used by NORC only]

A If such a person wanted to make a speech in your community, should he be allowed to speak, or not?

B Should such a person be allowed to teach in a college or university, or not?

C Suppose he wrote a book advocating doing away with elections and letting the military run the country. Somebody in your community suggests that the book be removed from the public library. Would you favor removing it, or not?

And what about a man who admits that he is a homosexual? [Used by NORC only]

A Suppose this admitted homosexual wanted to make a speech in your community. Should he be allowed to speak, or not?

B Should such a person be allowed to teach in a college or university, or not?

C If some people in your community suggested that a book he wrote in favor of homosexuality should be taken out of your public library, would you favor removing this book, or not?

SEXUAL EQUALITY QUESTIONS

If your party nominated a woman for President, would you vote for her if she were qualified for the job?

Do you agree or disagree with this statement: Women should take care of running their homes and leave running the country up to men.

Do you understand what the Equal Rights Amendment means? Do you strongly favor, somewhat favor, somewhat oppose, or strongly oppose this amendment?

RACIAL EQUALITY QUESTIONS

Do you think there should be laws against marriages between blacks and whites?

Blacks shouldn't push themselves where they're not wanted. (*Agree–Disagree*)

White people have a right to keep blacks out of their neighborhoods if they want to, and blacks should respect that right. (*Agree–Disagree*)

BACKGROUND CHARACTERISTICS

Political Party Preference

Generally speaking, do you usually think of yourself as a Republican, Democrat, independent, or what? (*If Republican or Democrat*) Would you call yourself a strong (Democrat/Republican) or not a very strong (Democrat/Republican)? (*If independent*) Do you think of yourself as closer to the Republican or Democratic Party?

Liberalism and Conservatism

We hear a lot of talk these days about liberals and conservatives. I'm going to show you a seven-point scale on which the political views that people might hold are arranged from extremely liberal—point 1—to extremely conservative—point 7. Where would you place yourself on this scale?

Region at Age Sixteen

In what state or foreign country were you living when you were sixteen years old? [The states included in each region are given below.]

Northeast: Maine, Vermont, New Hampshire, Massachusetts, Connecticut, Rhode Island, New York, New Jersey, Pennsylvania
Midwest: Wisconsin, Illinois, Indiana, Michigan, Ohio, Minnesota, Iowa, Missouri, North Dakota, South Dakota, Nebraska, Kansas
South: Delaware, Maryland, West Virginia, Virginia, North Carolina, South Carolina, Georgia, Florida, Kentucky, Tennessee, Alabama, Mississippi, Arkansas, Oklahoma, Louisiana, Texas
West: Montana, Idaho, Wyoming, Nevada, Utah, Colorado, Arizona, New Mexico, Washington, Oregon, California

Religious Preference

What is your religious preference? Is it Protestant, Catholic, Jewish, some other religion, or no religion?

Protestant Denomination

[Asked of those who said Protestant in above question] What specific denomination is that, if any?

Strength of Religious Preference

Would you call yourself a strong (preference named above), or a not very strong (preference named above)?

Frequency of Church Attendance

How often do you attend religious services?

BIBLIOGRAPHY

Aberbach, Joel D., and Jack L. Walker. 1970. "Political Trust and Racial Ideology." *American Political Science Review*, 64 (December): 1119–1219.

———. 1973. *Race in the City*. Boston: Little, Brown & Company.

Abraham, Henry J. 1977. *Freedom and the Court, Third Edition*. New York: Oxford University Press.

Abramson, Paul R. 1980. "Comments on Sullivan, Piereson, and Marcus." *American Political Science Review*, 74 (September): 780–781.

Adorno, T. W., E. Frankel-Brunswik, D. J. Levinson, and R. N. Sanford. 1950. *The Authoritarian Personality*. New York: Harper & Row.

Allport, Gordon W. 1954. *The Nature of Prejudice*. Cambridge, Massachusetts: Addison-Wesley.

———, and Michael Ross. 1967. "Personal Religious Orientation and Prejudice." *Journal of Personality and Social Psychology*, 5 (April): 432–443.

Amundsen, Kirsten. 1977. *A New Look at the Silenced Majority: Women and American Democracy*. Englewood Cliffs, New Jersey: Prentice-Hall.

Blau, Francine D. 1976. "Women in the Labor Force: An Overview." Pp. 215–229 in Jerome H. Skolnick and Elliott Currie (Editors), *Crisis in American Institutions, Third Edition*. Boston: Little, Brown & Company.

Bogardus, E. 1959. *Social Distance*. Yellow Springs, Ohio: Antioch Press.

Boles, Janet K. 1979. *The Politics of the Equal Rights Amendment*. New York: Longman.

Brink, William, and Louis Harris. 1967. *Black and White*. New York: Simon & Schuster.

Brown, Roger. 1965. *Social Psychology*. New York: The Free Press.

Bullock, Charles S., III. 1976. "Interracial Contact and Student Prejudice." *Youth and Society*, 7 (March): 271–309.

Campbell, Angus. 1971. *White Attitudes toward Black People*. Ann Arbor, Michigan: Institute for Social Research, The University of Michigan.

Campbell, Bruce A. 1979. *The American Electorate*. New York: Holt, Rinehart & Winston.

Cantril, Hadley, 1951. *Public Opinion 1935–1946*. Princeton, New Jersey: Princeton University Press.

Chandler, Robert. 1972. *Public Opinion: Changing Attitudes on Contemporary Political and Social Issues*. New York: R. R. Bowker Company.

Christie, R., and M. Jahoda (Editors). 1954. *Studies in the Scope and Method of the Authoritarian Personality.* Glencoe, Illinois: The Free Press.

Corbett, Michael. 1978. "Tolerance, Religion, and Personality." Presented at the annual meeting of the Southern Political Science Association, Atlanta, Georgia.

———. 1980. "Education and Contextual Tolerance: Group-Relatedness and Consistency Reconsidered." *American Politics Quarterly,* 8 (July): 345–360.

———, E. Gene Frankland, and Dorothy Rudoni. 1977. "Sexism among College Students: Do Males and Females Differ?" *Youth and Society,* 9 (December): 171–190.

Crespi, Irving. 1971. "What Kinds of Attitude Measures Are Predictive of Behavior?" *Public Opinion Quarterly,* 35 (Fall): 327–334.

Cutler, Stephen J., and Robert L. Kaufman. 1975. "Cohort Changes in Political Attitudes: Tolerance of Ideological Nonconformity." *Public Opinion Quarterly,* 39 (Spring): 63–81.

Dahl, Robert A. 1956. *A Preface to Democratic Theory.* Chicago: University of Chicago Press.

———. 1957. "Decision-Making in a Democracy: The Supreme Court as a National Policy-Maker." *Journal of Public Law,* 6: 279–295.

———. 1961. *Who Governs?* New Haven: Yale University Press.

Davis, James A. 1975. "Communism, Conformity, Cohorts, and Categories: American Tolerance in 1954 and 1972–73." *American Journal of Sociology,* 81: 491–513.

De Boer, Connie. 1978. "The Polls: Attitudes toward Homosexuality." *Public Opinion Quarterly,* 42 (Summer): 265–276.

Dennis, Jack, Leon Lindberg, Donald McCrone, and Rodney Stiefbold. 1968. "Political Socialization to Democratic Orientations in Four Western Systems." *Comparative Political Studies,* 1 (April): 71–101.

Dworkin, Anthony Gary, and Rosalind J. Dworkin. 1976. *The Minority Report.* New York: Praeger.

Dye, Thomas R. 1971. *The Politics of Equality.* Indianapolis: Bobbs-Merrill.

———, and L. Harmon Zeigler. 1972. *The Few and the Many.* Belmont, California: Duxbury Press.

———, and L. Harmon Zeigler. 1978. *The Irony of Democracy, Fourth Edition.* North Scituate, Massachusetts: Duxbury Press.

Ebenstein, William. 1969. *Great Political Thinkers, Fourth Edition.* New York: Holt, Rinehart & Winston.

Edgerton, Henry. 1938. *Selected Essays in Constitutional Law.* Brooklyn: Foundation Press.

Ehrlich, Howard J. 1973. *The Social Psychology of Prejudice.* New York: John Wiley & Sons.

Emerson, Thomas I. 1966. *Toward a General Theory of the First Amendment.* New York: Random House.

Erikson, Robert S., Norman R. Luttbeg, and Kent L. Tedin. 1980. *American Public Opinion, Second Edition.* New York: John Wiley & Sons.

Erskine, Hazel. 1967. "The Polls: Demonstrations and Race Riots." *Public Opinion Quarterly,* 31 (Winter): 655–677.

Ferree, Myra Marx. 1974. "A Woman for President? Changing Responses: 1958–1972." *Public Opinion Quarterly,* 38 (Fall): 390–399.

Foner, Anne. 1974. "Age Stratification and Age Conflict in Political Life." *American Sociological Review,* 39: 187–196.

Free, Lloyd A., and Hadley Cantril. 1968. *The Political Beliefs of Americans.* New York: Simon & Schuster.

Freeman, Jo. 1976. "The Building of the Gilded Cage." Pp. 230–251 in Jerome H. Skolnick and Elliott Currie, *Crisis in American Institutions, Third Edition.* Boston: Little, Brown & Company.

Gallup, George H. 1972. *The Gallup Poll, Volume Three.* New York: Random House.

Gilmour, Robert S., and Robert B. Lamb. 1975. *Political Alienation in Contemporary America.* New York: St. Martin's Press.

Glock, Charles Y., and Rodney Stark. 1966. *Christian Beliefs and Anti-Semitism.* New York: Harper & Row.

Goldberg, Philip A. 1968. "Are Women Prejudiced against Other Women?" *Trans-Action,* April: 28–31.

———. 1974. "Prejudice toward Women: Some Personality Correlates." Pp. 55–66 in Florence Denmark (Editor), *Who Discriminates against Women?* Beverly Hills, California: Sage.

Gomez, Rudolph. 1974. "Mexican Americans: From Internal Colonialism to the Chicano Movement." Pp. 317–336 in Rudolph Gomez, Clement Cottingham, Jr., Russell Endo, and Kathleen Jackson (Editors), *The Social Reality of Ethnic America.* Lexington, Massachusetts: D. C. Heath.

Gorsuch, Richard L., and Daniel Aleshire. 1974. "Christian Faith and Ethnic Prejudice: A Review and Interpretation of Research." *Journal for the Scientific Study of Religion,* 13: 281–307.

Grabb, Edward G. 1979. "Working-Class Authoritarianism and Tolerance of Outgroups: A Reassessment." *Public Opinion Quarterly*, 43 (Spring): 36–47.

Greeley, Andrew M., and Paul B. Sheatsley. 1974. "Attitudes toward Racial Integration." Pp. 241–250 in Lee Rainwater (Editor), *Social Problems and Public Policy: Inequality and Justice*. Chicago: Aldine.

Gross, Steven Jay, and C. Michael Niman. 1975. "Attitude-Behavior Consistency: A Review." *Public Opinion Quarterly*, 39 (Fall): 358–368.

Hacker, Helen Mayer. 1974. "Women as a Minority Group: Twenty Years Later." Pp. 124–134 in Florence Denmark (Editor), *Who Discriminates against Women?* Beverly Hills, California: Sage.

Herson, Lawrence J. R., and C. Richard Hofstetter. 1975. "Tolerance, Consensus, and the Democratic Creed: A Contextual Exploration." *Journal of Politics*, 37 (November): 1007–1032.

Hess, Robert D. 1968. "Political Socialization in the Schools." *Harvard Educational Review*, 38 (Summer): 528–536.

Hole, Judith, and Ellen Levine. 1971. *Rebirth of Feminism*. Chicago: Quadrangle Books.

Horton, Roy E., Jr. 1963. "American Freedom and the Values of Youth." Pp. 18–60 in H. H. Remmers (Editor), *Anti-Democratic Attitudes in American Schools*. Evanston, Illinois: Northwestern University Press.

Hyman, Herbert H., and Charles R. Wright. 1979. *Education's Lasting Influence on Values*. Chicago: University of Chicago Press.

Jackman, Mary R. 1973. "Education and Prejudice or Education and Response Set?" *American Sociological Review*, 38: 327–339.

———. 1978. "General and Applied Tolerance: Does Education Increase Commitment to Racial Integration?" *American Journal of Political Science*, 22 (May): 302–324.

Jackman, Robert W. 1972. "Political Elites, Mass Publics, and Support for Democratic Principles." *Journal of Politics*, 34 (August): 753–773.

Jacobson, Marsha B. 1979. "A Rose by Any Other Name: Attitudes toward Feminism as a Function of Its Label." *Sex Roles*, 5 (June): 365–371.

Kilson, Martin. 1976. "Whither Integration." *Civil Rights Digest*, 8 (Summer): 20–29.

Kohlberg, Lawrence. 1969. "The Cognitive-Development Approach to Socialization." In D. Goslin (Editor), *Handbook of Socialization Theory and Research*. Chicago: Rand McNally.

———. 1971. "From Is to Ought." In T. Mischel (Editor), *Cognitive Development and Epistemology*. New York: Academic Press.

Kraditor, Aileen S. (Editor). 1969. *Up from the Pedestal*. Chicago: Quadrangle Books.

Krislov, Samuel. 1968. *The Supreme Court and Political Freedom*. New York: The Free Press.

Kuklinski, James H., and T. Wayne Parent. 1979. "Race and Big Government: An Exploration into the Sources of Racial Policy Attitudes and a Comment on Some of the SRC Race Items." Presented at the annual meeting of the American Political Science Association, Washington, D.C.

Lane, Robert E., and David O. Sears. 1964. *Public Opinion*. Englewood Cliffs, New Jersey: Prentice-Hall.

Langton, Kenneth P., and M. Kent Jennings. 1968. "Political Socialization and the High School Civics Curriculum in the United States." *American Political Science Review*, 62 (September): 852–867.

La Piere, R. T. 1934. "Attitudes vs. Actions." *Social Forces*, 13: 230–237.

Laurence, Joan E. 1970. "White Socialization: Black Reality." *Psychiatry*, 33 (May): 174–194.

Lawrence, David G. 1976. "Procedural Norms and Tolerance: A Reassessment." *American Political Science Review*, 70 (March): 80–100.

Lessard, Suzannah. 1970. "Gay Is Good for Us All." *The Washington Monthly*, December: 39–49.

Levitt, Eugene E., and Albert D. Klassen, Jr. 1974. "Public Attitudes toward Homosexuality: Part of the 1970 National Survey by the Institute for Sex Research." *Journal of Homosexuality*, 1 (Fall): 29–43.

Lipset, Seymour Martin. 1960. *Political Man*. Garden City, New York: Doubleday.

————, and Earl Raab. 1970. *The Politics of Unreason: Right-Wing Extremism in America*. New York: Harper & Row.

Lipsitz, Lewis. 1965. "Working-Class Authoritarianism: A Re-Evaluation." *American Sociological Review*, 24 (August): 521–528.

Lipsky, Michael. 1968. "Protest as a Political Resource." *American Political Science Review*, 62 (December): 1144–1158.

MacDonald, A. P., Jr. 1974. "Identification and Measurement of Multidimensional Attitudes toward Equality between the Sexes." *Journal of Homosexuality*, 1 (Winter): 165–182.

Maranell, Gary. 1967. "An Examination of Some Religious and Political Attitude Correlates of Bigotry." *Social Forces*, 46 (March): 356–362.

Marcuse, Herbert. 1969. "Repressive Tolerance." Pp. 81–123 in Robert

Paul Wolff, Barrington Moore, and Herbert Marcuse, *A Critique of Pure Tolerance*. Boston: Beacon Press.

Martin, James G., and Frank R. Westie. 1959. "The Tolerant Personality." *American Sociological Review*, 24 (August): 521–528.

Marx, Gary T. 1969. *Protest and Prejudice*. New York: Harper & Row.

Maslow, A. H. 1954. *Motivation and Personality*. New York: Harper & Row.

McClosky, Herbert. 1964. "Consensus and Ideology in American Politics." *American Political Science Review*, 58 (June): 361–382.

———, and John H. Schaar. 1965. "Psychological Dimensions of Anomy." *American Sociological Review*, 30 (February): 14–40.

Middleton, Russell. 1973. "Do Christian Beliefs Cause Anti-Semitism?" *American Sociological Review*, 38 (February): 33–52.

———. 1976. "Regional Differences in Prejudice." *American Sociological Review*, 41 (February): 94–117.

Mill, John Stuart. 1951. *Utilitarianism, Liberty, and Representative Government*. New York: E. P. Dutton and Company. Originally published in 1859.

Miller, S. M., and Frank Riessman. 1961. "Working-Class Authoritarianism: A Critique of Lipset." *British Journal of Sociology*, 12: 263–276.

Miller, Thomas W. 1974. "Male Attitudes toward Women's Rights as a Function of Their Level of Self-Esteem." Pp. 37–46 in Florence Denmark (Editor), *Who Discriminates against Women?* Beverly Hills, California: Sage.

Monroe, Alan D. 1975. *Public Opinion in America*. New York: Dodd, Mead & Company.

Monsma, Stephen V. 1971. "Potential Leaders and Democratic Values." *Public Opinion Quarterly*, 35 (Fall): 350–357.

Myrdal, Gunnar. 1944. *An American Dilemma*. New York: Harper.

Nunn, Clyde Z. 1973. "Support of Civil Liberties among College Students." *Social Problems*, 20: 300–310.

———, Harry J. Crockett, Jr., and J. Allen Williams, Jr. 1978. *Tolerance for Nonconformity*. San Francisco: Jossey-Bass.

Patterson, John W. 1979. "Moral Development and Political Thinking: The Case of Freedom of Speech." *Western Political Quarterly*, 32 (March): 7–20.

Patterson, Samuel C. 1968. "The Political Cultures of the American States." *Journal of Politics*, 30 (February): 187–209.

Pettigrew, Thomas F. 1971. *Racially Separate or Together?* New York: McGraw-Hill.

Piaget, Jean. 1965. *The Moral Judgment of the Child.* New York: The Free Press.

Piereson, James, John L. Sullivan, and George Marcus. 1980. "Political Tolerance: An Overview and Some New Findings." Pp. 157–178 in John C. Pierce and John L. Sullivan (Editors), *The Electorate Reconsidered.* Beverly Hills, California: Sage.

Plamenatz, John. 1963. *Man and Society, Volume One.* New York: McGraw-Hill.

Prothro, James W., and Charles M. Grigg. 1960. "Fundamental Principles of Democracy: Bases of Agreement and Disagreement." *Journal of Politics,* 22 (May): 276–294.

Quinley, Harold E., and Charles Y. Glock. 1979. *Anti-Semitism in America.* New York: The Free Press.

Remmers, H. H. (Editor). 1963. *Anti-Democratic Attitudes in American Schools.* Evanston, Illinois: Northwestern University Press.

Rist, Ray C. 1978. "Sorting Out the Issues: The Current Status of School Desegregation." *Civil Rights Digest,* 10 (Winter): 40–43.

Rivera, Julius. 1976. "Mexican Americans: The Conflict of Two Cultures." Pp. 165–189 in Anthony Gary Dworkin and Rosalind J. Dworkin, *The Minority Report.* New York: Praeger.

Rodgers, Harrell R., Jr., and Charles S. Bullock, III. 1974. "Political and Racial Attitudes: Black versus White." *Journal of Black Studies,* 4 (June): 463–485.

Rokeach, Milton. 1960. *The Open and Closed Mind.* New York: Basic Books.

Roof, Wade Clark. 1975. "Religious Orthodoxy and Minority Prejudice: Causal Relationship or Reflection of Localistic World View?" *American Journal of Sociology,* 80: 643–664.

Rustin, Bayard. 1965. "From Protest to Politics." *Commentary,* 39 (February): 25–31.

Schuman, Howard. 1972. "Attitudes vs. Actions versus Attitudes vs. Attitudes." *Public Opinion Quarterly,* 36 (Fall): 347–354.

Segall, Marshall H. 1976. *Human Behavior and Public Policy.* New York: Pergamon Press.

Selznick, Gertrude J., and Stephen Steinberg. 1969. *The Tenacity of Prejudice: Anti-Semitism in Contemporary America.* New York: Harper & Row.

Shingles, Richard D. 1979. "College as a Source of Black Alienation." *Journal of Black Studies*, 9 (March): 267–289.

———, and Donald J. Shoemaker. 1979. "A Developmental Thesis of Legal Cultures." *Law and Policy Quarterly*, 1 (October): 382–410.

———, and Colleen A. Walrath. 1981. "Class and Ideology in Advanced Industrial Society: A Re-Examination of *Transformations of the American Party System.*" Unpublished manuscript.

Sniderman, Paul M. 1975. *Personality and Democratic Politics*. Berkeley and Los Angeles: University of California Press.

Solotaroff, Theodore, and Marshall Sklare. 1966. "Introduction." Pp. 3–28 in Charles Herbert Stember and others, *Jews in the Mind of America*. New York: Basic Books.

Stark, Rodney, and Charles Y. Glock. 1969. "Prejudice and the Churches." Pp. 70–95 in Charles Y. Glock and Ellen Siegelman (Editors), *Prejudice, U.S.A.* New York: Praeger.

Stember, Charles Herbert. 1966. "Summary and Conclusions." Pp. 208–218 in Charles Herbert Stember and others, *Jews in the Mind of America*. New York: Basic Books.

Stouffer, Samuel. 1955. *Communism, Conformity, and Civil Liberties*. New York: Doubleday.

Sullivan, John L., James Piereson, and George E. Marcus. 1979. "An Alternative Conceptualization of Political Tolerance: Illusory Increases 1950s–1970s." *American Political Science Review*, 73 (September): 781–794.

———, George E. Marcus, Stanley Feldman, and James E. Piereson. 1981. "The Sources of Political Tolerance: A Multivariate Analysis." *American Political Science Review*, 75 (March): 92–106.

Tapp, June L., and Lawrence Kohlberg. 1971. "Developing Senses of Law and Legal Justice." *Journal of Social Issues*, 27: 65–91.

Tedin, Kent L. 1976. "Religious Preference and Pro/Anti Activism on the Equal Rights Amendment Issue." Presented at the annual meeting of the Southern Political Science Association, Atlanta, Georgia.

Thurow, Lester C. 1976. "The Economic Status of Minorities and Women." *Civil Rights Digest*, 8 (Winter-Spring): 3–9.

Tocqueville, Alexis de. 1966. *Democracy in America*. New York: Harper & Row. Originally published in 1835.

Welch, Susan. 1975. "Support among Women for the Issues of the Women's Movement." *Sociological Quarterly*, 16 (Spring): 216–227.

Westie, Frank R. 1965. "The American Dilemma: An Empirical Test." *American Sociological Review*, 30 (August): 527–538.

Whitt, Hugh P., and Hart M. Nelsen. 1975. "Residence, Moral Traditionalism, and Tolerance of Atheists." *Social Forces*, 54 (December): 328–340.

Williams, J. Allen, Jr., Clyde Z. Nunn, and Louis St. Peter. 1976. "Origins of Tolerance: Findings from a Replication of Stouffer's Communism, Conformity, and Civil Liberties." *Social Forces*, 55 (December): 394–408.

Wilson, W. Cody. 1975. "Belief in Freedom of Speech and Press." *Journal of Social Issues*, 31: 69–76.

Wilson, William Julius. 1978. *The Declining Significance of Race*. Chicago: University of Chicago Press.

Wolman, Benjamin B. 1974. "On Men Who Discriminate against Women." Pp. 47–54 in Florence Denmark (Editor), *Who Discriminates against Women?* Beverly Hills, California: Sage.

Zalkind, Sheldon S., Edward A. Gaugler, and Ronald M. Schwartz. 1975. "Civil Liberties Attitudes and Personality Measures: Some Exploratory Research." *Journal of Social Issues*, 31: 77–91.

Zellman, Gail L. 1975. "Antidemocratic Beliefs: A Survey and Some Explanations." *Journal of Social Issues*, 31: 31–53.

———, and David O. Sears. 1971. "Childhood Origins of Tolerance for Dissent." *Journal of Social Issues*, 27: 109–136.

Index